Active Learning:

Cooperation In The College Classroom

DATE DUE	

www.co-operation.org

Active Learning: Cooperation In The College Classroom, Interaction Book Company, 7208 Cornelia Drive, Edina, MN 55435, (612) 831-9500, FAX (612) 831-9332

This book is dedicated to the college professors who have taken our training in how to implement cooperative learning and have used it to create classrooms where students care about each other and about each other's learning.

ISBN: 0-939603-14-4

Active Learning: Cooperation In The College Classroom, Interaction Book Company, 7208 Cornelia Drive, Edina, MN 55435, (612) 831-9500, FAX (612) 831-9332

Table Of Contents

Active Learning: Cooperation In The College Classroom, Interaction Book Company, 7208 Cornelia Drive, Edina, MN 55435, (612) 831-9500, FAX (612) 831-9332

Preface

This book is about how college faculty can use cooperative learning to increase student achievement, create positive relationships among students, and promote healthy student psychological adjustment to college. It is about how you, the reader, can ensure that students in your courses actively create their knowledge rather than passively listening to yours. Your challenge is to inspire and motivate your students toward a common purpose of maximizing each other's learning.

This book contains (a) a set of practical strategies for structuring cooperative learning and (b) the conceptual framework needed to understand how to create a truly cooperative learning community in your classes and college. Gaining a high level of expertise in implementing cooperative learning is not easy. It takes training, perseverance, and support. Reading this book carefully and participating in the training that goes with these chapters provides a good start, but it may take a year or two of experience before structuring cooperative efforts becomes integrated and natural. Persisting until you can use cooperative procedures and strategies at a routine-use level will benefit your students in numerous ways. It is well worth your efforts.

It has taken us over 35 years to build the theory, research, and practical experience required to write this book. Our roots reach back through Morton Deutsch to Kurt Lewin. We wish to acknowledge our indebtedness to the work of both of these social psychologists. In the 1960s we began reviewing the research, conducting our initial research studies, and training teachers in the classroom use of cooperation. Since then our work has proliferated.

Faculty members from all over the world have taught us procedures for implementing cooperative learning and have field tested our ideas in their classrooms with considerable success. We have been in their classrooms and we have sometimes taught beside them. We appreciate their ideas and celebrate their successes. In addition, we have had many talented and productive graduate students who have conducted research studies that have made significant contributions to our understanding of cooperation. We feel privileged to have worked with them.

We wish to thank Linda M. Johnson for all of her hard work, help, and assistance in completing this book.

David W. Johnson
Roger T. Johnson
Karl A. Smith

iv

Active Learning: Cooperation In The College Classroom, Interaction Book Company, 7208 Cornelia Drive, Edina, MN 55435, (612) 831-9500, FAX (612) 831-9332

Chapter One:
College Teaching And Cooperative Learning

Introduction

Beginning in 1492 with the discovery of America, Spain acquired an empire that was one of the most vast and richest the world has ever known. The royal standard of Spain was proudly flown from California and Florida in the north to Chile in the south, in the Philippine Islands across the Pacific, and at scattered outposts along the coast of Africa. Never before had a country controlled such far-flung territories or gained such great wealth. Spain built such an empire through being the greatest naval power in the world.

In 1588 Spain decided to invade England, conquer it, and end its challenge to Spain's dominance of the seas. An armada of more than 130 ships sailed into the English Channel. A naval battle ensued, Spain suffered heavy casualties and retreated, and a storm came up and sank several more Spanish ships. Only about half of the great Armada returned home to Spain and the back of Spain's empire was broken. Amazingly, the English ships suffered almost no damage. The question is, "How did the English sink all those Spanish ships while suffering very little damage to their ships?"

A number of hypotheses have been advanced to answer this question. One hypothesis was that the armada ships were too large and slow. In fact, the largest and slowest ship in the battle was the Triumph, an English ship. A second hypothesis was that the Armada was too lightly armed. In fact, they did have one-third fewer cannons than the English, but all the cannons were of equivalent size and power and there were lots of them on the Spanish ships. A third hypothesis was that the armada ran out of ammunition. In fact, the research indicates that the Spanish had plenty of ammunition. The most interesting finding is that the Spanish cannons were fired on an average of one to two times a day during the battle.

Here is a sufficient explanation for the Spanish's remarkable failure to inflict serious damage on the English fleet. The Spanish simply did not fire their cannons, especially their heaviest cannons, often enough. Why? The answer appears to be that the Spanish had not planned to fire their cannon at sea. The cannons were to be used primarily for land artillery once the Spanish had landed in England.

Johnson, D. W., Johnson, R., & Smith, K. (1998). **Active Learning: Cooperation In The College Classroom**. Edina, MN: Interaction Book Company.

Figure 1.1 Circles Of Learning

Social Interdependence

Cooperative	Competitive	Individualistic

Research: Why Use Cooperative Learning

Effort To Achieve	Positive Relationships	Psychological Health

Five Basic Elements

Positive Inter-dependence	Individual Accountability	Promotive Interaction	Social Skills	Group Processing

Cooperative Learning

Formal Coop Learning	Informal Coop Learning	Coop Base Groups
Make Preinstructional Decisions	Conduct Introductory Focused Discussion	Opening Class Meeting To Check Homework, Ensure Members Understand Academic Material, Complete Routine Tasks Such As Attendance
Explain Task And Cooperative Structure	Conduct Intermittent Pair Discussions Every Ten Or Fifteen Minutes	Ending Class Meeting To Ensure Members Understand Academic Material, Homework Assignment
Monitor Learning Groups And Intervene To Improve Taskwork & Teamwork	Conduct Closure Focused Discussion	Members Help And Assist Each Other Learn In-Between Classes
Assess Student Learning And Process Group Effectiveness		Conduct Semester Or Year Long College Or Class Service Projects

Cooperative College

Teaching Teams	Site-Based Decision Making	Faculty Meetings

Constructive Conflict

Students		Faculty	
Academic Controversy	Negotiating, Mediating	Decision-Making Controversy	Negotiating, Mediating

Civic Values

Work For Mutual Benefit, Common Good	Equality Of All Members	Trusting, Caring Relationships	View Situations From All Perspectives	Unconditional Worth Of Self, Diverse Others

1 : 2

Johnson, D. W., Johnson, R., & Smith, K. (1998). **Active Learning: Cooperation In The College Classroom**. Edina, MN: Interaction Book Company.

Until that fateful day, naval battles consisted mostly of capturing enemy ships by maneuvering close, tying the two ships together, firing one round of grape-shot to clear the deck of the enemy ship, and then boarding and fighting it out hand-to-hand until the enemy ship was captured. The last thing you would want to do is blow a hole in the side of the enemy ship because if it sank while you were tied to it, it would take you down with it. The English changed the rules. Instead of tying their ships to Spanish ships, the English kept their distance and blew holes in the sides of Spanish ships, which then sank.

The Spanish did not know what to do. They could not adapt quickly enough to save themselves due to their highly specialized procedures and battle drills. They had no procedure for disciplined reloading on board ship: The cannons could not be withdrawn and run out, reloading crews were drawn from many different stations, cannons of different calibers and metrics were on the same ship which made it difficult to load the right cannon ball in the right cannon, and the Spanish crews were largely captured sailors pressed into service who spoke many different languages and could not understand each other. Given these problems, the Spanish could not respond to the English's change of paradigms of naval warfare.

The lesson to learn from the armada's failure is not to hang onto the past by trying to make do with slight modifications in the status quo when faced with a need to change paradigms. Paradigms have to change, and sometimes they have to change quickly.

Changing Nature Of College Teaching

Changing Paradigms Of College Teaching

A **paradigm** is a theory, perspective, or frame of reference that determines how you perceive, interpret, and understand the world. It is a **map** of certain aspects of the world. To deal with the world effectively, you need the right map. Suppose, for example, you wanted to find a specific location in central Minneapolis. If you were given a map of Seattle by mistake, you would be frustrated and your efforts would be futile. You might decide that the problem is your **behavior**. You could try harder, be more diligent, or double your speed. But your efforts would still be ineffective. You might decide that the problem is your **attitude**. You could think more positively. But you still would not find your destination. The fundamental problem has nothing to do with your behavior or your attitude. It has everything to do with having a wrong map. Your behavior and attitude only affect your outcomes when you have the right map.

Almost every significant breakthrough in the field of scientific endeavor is first a break with traditional old ways of thinking--with old paradigms (Kuhn, 1962). There are a number of classic examples. For Ptolemy, the great Egyptian astronomer, the earth was the center of the universe. But Copernicus created a paradigm shift (and a great deal of

1 : 3

Johnson, D. W., Johnson, R., & Smith, K. (1998). **Active Learning: Cooperation In The College Classroom**. Edina, MN: Interaction Book Company.

resistance and persecution as well) by placing the sun at the center. Suddenly, everything took on a different interpretation. Until the germ theory was developed, a high percentage of women and children died during childbirth, and no one could understand why. In military skirmishes, more men were dying from small wounds and diseases than from the major traumas on the front lines. No one knew what to do. But as soon as the germ theory was developed, dramatic medical improvement became possible due to the paradigm shift.

In college teaching a paradigm shift is taking place. Minor modifications in current teaching practices will not solve the current problems with college instruction. Teaching success in today's world requires a new approach to instruction.

History Of College Teaching

American higher education has moved through three distinct, yet overlapping, phases (Boyer, 1990). **First**, the colonial college focused on teaching students to build their character and prepare them for civic and religious leadership. Teaching was viewed as a sacred calling honored as fully as the ministry. Students were entrusted to faculty tutors responsible for their intellectual, moral, and spiritual development. Faculty were employed with the understanding that they would be educational mentors, both in the classroom and beyond.

The **second phase** focused on service to help the building of the nation. The mission of the university moved toward the practical serving of the democratic community. The service-oriented patriot was the ideal product. Professors were expected to (a) spread knowledge that would improve agriculture, manufacturing, and democracy, and (b) conduct applied research to help them do so.

The **third phase** began in the early 1900's and focused on the advancement of knowledge through research. Teaching and service began to be deemphasized. Creating new knowledge through conducting research to test theory was seen as fueling human progress. Faculty were hired to teach, but they were evaluated as published researchers. The highest status and most rewarded responsibility of the professor became conducting basic research and publishing results in reputable journals.

A **fourth phase** may be beginning where faculty have to be concerned about the success of the college as a business. Increasingly, (a) colleges see themselves as a business where departments must meet quality and productivity criteria in order to continue to exist (while traditional emphases on liberal arts and cutting edge research), (b) a college education is a necessity for an individual's economic advancement, and (c) a college education becomes more and more expensive as college spending increases, government financial support decreases, and colleges increase tuition to make up the difference. The result is a potential crisis where more and more people want to attend college and fewer and fewer people have enough money to do so. In addition, more and more attention

Johnson, D. W., Johnson, R., & Smith, K. (1998). **Active Learning: Cooperation In The College Classroom**. Edina, MN: Interaction Book Company.

may be placed on preparing students for specific careers and working effectively with other people. This fourth stage requires faculty to be assessed not only on the scholarship of discovery (creation of new knowledge), but also on the scholarship of teaching, application, service, and outreach (Boyer, 1990).

An essential aspect of the future of higher education is more effective teaching. In order to meet current challenges, faculty need to change from the old paradigm to the new paradigm of teaching.

Old Paradigm

> *Pardon him, Theodotus: he is a barbarian, and thinks that the customs of his tribe and island are the laws of nature.*
>
> G. B. Shaw, **Caesar and Cleopatra**

Like all organizations, colleges must adapt to changes in their environment or risk fading away like the dinosaurs. The dinosaurs presumably made good day-to-day adaptations to their environment. They probably made a pretty good choice of what leaves to eat from what trees, and selected the most desirable swamps in which to slosh. At a tactical level of decision, we have no reason to believe that these giant beasts were not reasonably competent. But when faced with major changes in the earth's climate and the resulting changes in plant and other animal life, the dinosaurs were unable to make the fundamental changes required to adapt to the new environmental conditions. Colleges may now be faced with new environmental conditions that require them to do what the dinosaurs could not. Colleges need to make fundamental changes in the ways students are instructed. The changes are known as the new paradigm of teaching.

Cooperative learning is part of a broader paradigm shift that is occurring in teaching. Essential elements of this paradigm shift are presented in Table 1.1 (Johnson, Johnson, & Holubec, 1992, 1998).

The **old paradigm of teaching** is based on John Locke's assumption that the untrained student mind is like a blank sheet of paper waiting for the instructor to write on it. Student minds are viewed as empty vessels into which instructors pour their wisdom. Because of these and other assumptions, instructors think of teaching in terms of these principal activities:

1 : 5

Johnson, D. W., Johnson, R., & Smith, K. (1998). **Active Learning: Cooperation In The College Classroom**. Edina, MN: Interaction Book Company.

Table 1.1: Comparison Of Old And New Paradigms Of Teaching

Factor	Old Paradigm Of Teaching	New Paradigm Of Teaching
Knowledge	Transferred From Faculty To Students	Jointly Constructed By Students And Faulty
Students	Passive Vessel To Be Filled By Faculty's Knowledge	Active Constructor, Discoverer, Transformer of Own Knowledge
Nature Of Learning	Learning Is Fundamentally Individual; Requires Extrinsic Motivation	Learning Is Fundamentally Social; Requires Supportive Environment/Community To Unleash Intrinsic Motivation
Faculty Purpose	Classify And Sort Students	Develop Students' Competencies And Talents
Relationships	Impersonal Relationships Among Students And Between Faculty And Students	Personal Transaction Among Students And Between Faculty And Students
Context	Competitive/Individualistic	Cooperative Learning In Classroom And Cooperative Teams Among Faculty
Assumption	Any Expert Can Teach	Teaching Is Complex And Requires Considerable Training

1. **Transferring knowledge from instructor to students.** The faculty's job is to give it; the student's job to is get it. Instructors transmit information that students are expected to memorize and then recall.

2. **Filling passive empty vessels with knowledge.** Students are passive recipients of knowledge. Instructors own the knowledge that students memorize and recall.

3. **Individuals learn and are motivated to do so by extrinsic rewards.** Faculty see failure to learn as the result of lack of individual motivation and try to increase motivation through offering rewards such as grades.

4. **Classifying and sorting students into categories.** Many American colleges have focused on (a) selecting only the most intelligent students for admission and then (b) inspecting continually to weed out defective students. Instructors classify and sort students into categories by norm-referenced grading and deciding who does and does not meet the requirements to be graduated. Faculty assume ability is fixed and is unaffected by student effort or the quality of the

Johnson, D. W., Johnson, R., & Smith, K. (1998). **Active Learning: Cooperation In The College Classroom**. Edina, MN: Interaction Book Company.

education provided by the college. Colleges are viewed as holding grounds for carefully selected students.

5. **Conducting education within a context of impersonal relationships among students and between instructors and students.** Based on the Taylor model of industrial organizations, students and instructors are perceived to be interchangeable and replaceable parts in the "education machine."

6. **Maintaining a competitive organizational structure** in which students work to outperform their classmates and instructors work to outperform their colleagues. Such uses of competition have their origins in the publication of Adam Smith's **The Wealth of Nations** in 1776 and Herbert Spencer argument in the 1860s that Darwin's survival-of-the-fittest concept of evolution could be transposed to human society. Despite their enthusiasm, Smith and Spencer were mistaken. When students interact within a competitive context communication is minimized, misleading and false information is often communicated, helping is minimized and viewed as cheating, and classmates and faculty tend to be disliked and distrusted. Competitive and individualistic learning situations isolate students and create negative relationships with classmates and faculty.

7. **Assuming that anyone with expertise in their field can teach without training to do so.** This is sometimes known as the content premise--if you have a Ph.D. in the field, you can teach.

The old paradigm is to transfer the instructor's knowledge to a passive student so instructors can classify and sort students in a norm-referenced, competitive way. The assumption was that if you have content expertise, you can teach. Many instructors consider the old paradigm the only alternative. Lecturing while requiring students to be passive, silent, isolated, and in competition with each other seems the only way to teach. The tradition of the old paradigm is carried forward by sheer momentum, while almost everyone persists in the hollow pretense that all is well. All is not well. Teaching is changing. The old paradigm of teaching is being dropped for a new paradigm.

Many faculty members consider the old paradigm the only alternative. They have no vision of what could be done instead. Lecturing while requiring students to be passive, silent, isolated, and in competition with each other seems the only way to teach. For such instructors it may be helpful to review Hans Christian Andersen's tale of **The Emperor's New Clothes**. An emperor invests substantial time and money in order to be well- dressed. One day two dishonest men arrive  at court. Pretending to be weavers, they claim that they are able to create garments so fine that they are not visible to people who are either unfit for the office that they hold, or stupid. The emperor's vanity and desire to test the competence of his staff leads him

Johnson, D. W., Johnson, R., & Smith, K. (1998). **Active Learning: Cooperation In The College Classroom**. Edina, MN: Interaction Book Company.

to be duped. The weavers are supplied with silk, gold thread, and money, all of which they keep for themselves while pretending to weave the emperor's new clothes.

When the weavers announce that the clothes are ready the emperor sends a succession of trusted ministers to see them. Not wanting to appear unfit for office or stupid, they all report that the new clothes are lovely. Finally, the emperor himself goes to see the clothes which were so heartily praised by his subordinates. Although he sees nothing, he proclaims, "Oh! The cloth is beautiful! I am delighted with the clothes!"

On the day of a great procession the emperor disrobes, dons his "new clothes," and marches through his kingdom, warmed only by the ooh's and ah's emitted by his subjects. Never before had any of the emperor's clothes caused so much excitement! Then, with an innocent persistence, a small child said, "But the emperor has nothing on at all!" The child was not yet constrained by the forces that silenced the adult crowd and caused them, despite the evidence of their senses, to validate their superior's false judgment.

This story is an example of events that all too often occur in colleges: **Not wanting to appear unfit or stupid, faculty members conform to the current consensus about instruction and are afraid to challenge the collective judgment of how best to teach.** The tradition of the old paradigm is carried forward by sheer momentum, while almost everyone persists in the hollow pretense that all is well.

All is not well. Students often do not learn what faculty think they are teaching. Student performance on exams or students' questions may indicate that they do not understand the material in the way or to the extent that faculty would like them to. Furthermore, students often ask boring questions, such as "What do I have to do to get an A?" or "Will it be on the final exam?" Students ask the latter question to determine if the material is important. What matters, of course, is not whether or not it will be on the exam but rather do professionals in practice use the concept or procedure regularly. Such problems wear professors down. There is a way to break out of the old paradigm of teaching and define in more creative ways what it means to be an instructor. The way is known as the new paradigm of teaching.

1 : 8

Johnson, D. W., Johnson, R., & Smith, K. (1998). **Active Learning: Cooperation In The College Classroom**. Edina, MN: Interaction Book Company.

New Paradigm Of Teaching

It is time for us to reaffirm that education--that is, teaching in all its forms--is the primary task of higher education.

Stanford University President Donald Kennedy

College teaching is changing. We are dropping the old paradigm of teaching and adopting a new paradigm based on theory and research that have clear applications to instruction. Educators now view teaching in terms of several principal activities.

First, knowledge is constructed, discovered, transformed, and extended by students. Faculty create the conditions within which students can construct meaning from the material studied by processing it through existing cognitive structures and then retaining it in long-term memory where it remains open to further processing and possible reconstruction.

Second, students actively construct their own knowledge. Learning is conceived of as something a learner does, not something that is done to a learner. The new view is that instead of passively accepting knowledge from the instructor or curriculum, students activate their existing cognitive structures or construct new ones to subsume the new input. College instruction is criticized for failing to involve students actively in the learning process and being focused on transmitting fixed bodies of information while ignoring (a) the preparation of students to engage in a continuing acquisition of knowledge and understanding and (b) the careful supervision of students reasoning about challenging problems (Association of American Colleges, 1985; Bok, 1986; Boyer, 1987; National Institute of Education, 1984; Task Group on General Education, 1988).

Despite the academic advantages of involving students, many instructors do not do so. Probably the most frequent strategy used is whole-class discussions. Many students refuse to participate, perhaps because they are so socialized into a "spectator" role. Barnes (1980) found in an observational study of instructor-student interaction that even when instructors attempted to solicit student participation through whole-class questioning, students responded only 50 percent of the time. Even when instructors manage to obtain student participation, a small minority of students tends to dominate. Karp and Yoels (1988) documented that in classes of less than 40 students, four to five students accounted for 75 percent of all interactions and, in classes with more than 40 students, two to three students accounted for over half of the exchanges. Stones (1970) surveyed over 1,000 college students and found that 60 percent stated that a large number of classmates listening would deter them from asking questions, even if the instructor encouraged them to do so.

Third, learning is a social enterprise in which students need to interact with the instructor and classmates. Education is a social process that cannot occur except

Johnson, D. W., Johnson, R., & Smith, K. (1998). **Active Learning: Cooperation In The College Classroom.** Edina, MN: Interaction Book Company.

through interpersonal interaction (real or implied). The interpersonal interaction in which students construct their knowledge is enhanced by a supportive environment and the development of a learning community. Caring relationships in which students are committed to their own and each other's learning and development unleashes intrinsic motivation to learn (Johnson & Johnson, 1989). Caring and committed relationships provide meaning and purpose to learning. Both academic and personal social support contribute to achievement and productivity, physical health, psychological health, and constructive management of stress (Johnson & Johnson, 1989a). The more difficult and complex the learning, the harder students have to struggle to achieve, the more social support students need. There is a general rule of instruction: **The more pressure placed on students to achieve and the more difficult the material to be learned, the more important it is to provide social support within the learning situation.** Challenge and social support must be balanced if students are to cope successfully with the stress inherent in learning situations.

Fourth, faculty effort is aimed at developing students' competencies and talents.
Student effort should be inspired and colleges must "add value" by cultivating talent. James Duderstadt, President of the University of Michigan, noted that colleges and universities have focussed on selection processes in the recruitment of students and faculty and have given little or no attention to developing human potential (Sheahan & White, 1990). Astin (1985) has challenged the four traditional models of excellence in higher education--reputation, content, resources, outcome--and advocated a talent-development model in which the development of student and faculty talent is primary. Within colleges and universities, a "cultivate and develop" philosophy must replace a "select and weed out" philosophy. Instead of classifying and sorting students into categories that are considered more or less permanent, colleges develop student competencies and talents that are considered dynamic and always susceptible to change.

The implications of the difference between the old and new paradigms may be seen in the history of the IQ test (Davison, 1991). When Benet built his IQ test, he conceived of a measure that would facilitate student development through the promotion of effort. Just as children matured physically, Benet was convinced that children matured mentally. He wanted to be able to show students through IQ scores that they are smarter this year than they were last year. Each year a student's IQ score would increase, and the instructor could say, "*If you work hard and learn a great deal, next year you will have an even higher IQ.*" What Terman at Stanford University did to the IQ was to reverse the emphasis from effort and development to classifying and sorting students. By dividing IQ by chronological age, Terman created a situation in which IQ does not change. Thus, a instructor says to a student, "*No matter how hard you work, no matter how much you learn, your IQ will stay the same. You will never get smarter.*" In the new paradigm, with its emphasis on student development, it is important for students to associate effort with achievement and intelligence. Colleges add value by developing students' potential and transforming students into more knowledgeable and committed individuals. Student performance is monitored and when students falter (a) help and support is provided and

Johnson, D. W., Johnson, R., & Smith, K. (1998). **Active Learning: Cooperation In The College Classroom**. Edina, MN: Interaction Book Company.

(b) the educational practices are examined and modified to prevent such a failure occurring again in the future. Faculty assume student effort and educational practices can be improved. Colleges want students to go to bed each night celebrating the fact that they are smarter today than they were yesterday.

Fifth, education is a personal transaction among students and between the faculty and students as they work together. It is not enough for faculty and students to interact. The interactions must be personal. Learning is a personal but social process that results when individuals cooperate to construct shared understandings and knowledge. Faculty must be able to build positive relationships with students and to create the conditions within which students build caring and committed relationships with each other. The college then becomes a learning community of committed scholars.

Within the new paradigm, faculty recognize that (a) long-term, hard, persistent efforts to achieve come from the heart, not the head, and (b) the fastest way to reach a student's heart is through personal relationships (Johnson & Johnson, 1989b). Students work together to construct their knowledge and as they succeed in doing so, they become committed to and care about each other's learning and each other as people. Caring about how much a person achieves and caring about him or her as a person go hand-in-hand (Johnson & Johnson, 1989a). In challenging learning situations, it is acts of caring and support that draw students together and move them forward. What sustains students' efforts is the knowledge that classmates care about, and are depending on, their progress. Love of learning and love of each other are what inspire students to commit more and more energy to their studies.

Sixth, all of the above best take place within a cooperative context. Classmates and faculty need to be viewed as collaborators rather than as obstacles to students' own academic and personal success. Faculty, therefore, structure learning situations so that students work together cooperatively to maximize each other's achievement. Ideally, administrators would in turn create a cooperative, team-based organizational structure within which faculty work together to ensure each other's success. There is considerable data indicating that higher achievement, more positive relationships, and better psychological adjustment result from cooperative than from competitive or individualistic learning (Johnson & Johnson, 1989a). That data are reviewed in Appendix A.

Ensuring that students are active in class usually requires the use of cooperative learning groups. It takes two or more people interacting within a cooperative context to think creatively in divergent ways so that **new** ideas, solutions and procedures are generated and conceptual frameworks are constructed (i.e., process gain) (Johnson & Johnson, 1989a). McKeachie and his associates (1986, 1988) have recently reviewed the research on methods of college teaching and found that students were more likely to acquire critical thinking skills and meta-cognitive learning strategies such as self-monitoring and learning-how-to-learn skills from discussions with groupmates. Bligh (1972) reviewed close to 100 studies of college teaching that were conducted over 50 years. He found that students who participated in active discussions of their ideas with classmates had fewer irrelevant or distracting thoughts and spent more time synthesizing and integrating concepts than students who listened to lectures. Bligh concluded that during discussion students tended to be more attentive, active, and thoughtful than during lectures. Kulik and Kulik (1979) concluded from a review of research on college teaching that student discussion groups were more effective than lectures in promoting students' problem-solving abilities. Smith (1977, 1980) conducted an observation study of college classes in a variety of academic subjects and found student-student interaction to be related to critical thinking outcomes and study habits characterized by more active thinking and less rote memorization.

What these studies all demonstrate is that a cooperative context is required for knowledge to be jointly constructed by active students who seek to develop their competencies and talents within personal relationships with classmates and faculty. In a competitive or individualistic context, such active and constructive learning processes cannot take place.

Seventh, teaching is assumed to be a complex application of theory and research that requires considerable instructor training and continuous refinement of skills and procedures. Becoming a good instructor takes at least one lifetime of continuous effort to improve.

Implementing The New Paradigm: Cooperative Learning

The implementation of the new paradigm of teaching in college classes begins with the use cooperative learning. Expertise in using cooperative learning begins with understanding the answers to the following questions:

1. What is cooperative learning and what are the differences among cooperative, competitive, and individualistic efforts?

2. Why use cooperative learning? What are the expected outcomes resulting from cooperative efforts?

3. What are the basic elements of cooperative learning that make it work?

4. How do you structure positive interdependence into cooperative lessons?

5. How do you teach students the interpersonal and small group skills they need to work together effectively?

Johnson, D. W., Johnson, R., & Smith, K. (1998). **Active Learning: Cooperation In The College Classroom**. Edina, MN: Interaction Book Company.

6. How do you structure group processing to ensure cooperative groups continuously improve their effectiveness?

7. How do you assess the quality and quantity of students' work in cooperative groups?

8. How do you structure cooperation among faculty and staff to ensure that cooperative efforts are institutionalized throughout college life?

Definitions Exercise

Given below are three concepts and three definitions taken from Deutsch (1962) and Johnson and Johnson (1989). Match the correct definition with the correct concept. Find a partner and (a) compare answers and (b) explain your reasoning for each answer.

_____	1. Competitive Efforts	a. Exists when there is positive interdependence among students' goal attainments; students perceive that they can reach their goals if and only if the other students in the group also reach their goals.
_____	2. Individualistic Efforts	b. Exists when there is negative interdependence among goal achievements; students perceive that they can obtain their goals if and only if the other students in the class fail to obtain their goals.
_____	3. Cooperative Efforts	c. Exists when there is no interdependence among goal achievements; students perceive that the achievement of their goals is unrelated to what other students do.

1 : 13

Johnson, D. W., Johnson, R., & Smith, K. (1998). **Active Learning: Cooperation In The College Classroom**. Edina, MN: Interaction Book Company.

Learning Together Or Alone

Two are better than one, because they have a good reward for toil. For if they fall, one will lift up his fellow; but woe to him who is alone when he falls and has not another to lift him up...And though a man might prevail against one who is alone, two will withstand him. A threefold cord is not quickly broken.

Ecclesiastics 4:9-12

Instructors may structure lessons so that students:

1. Work together in small groups, ensuring that all members complete the assignment.

2. Engage in a win-lose struggle to see who is best in completing the assignment.

3. Work independently to complete the assignment.

Students' learning goals may be structured to promote cooperative, competitive, or individualistic efforts. In every classroom, instructional activities are aimed at accomplishing goals and are conducted under a goal structure. A **learning goal** is a desired future state of demonstrating competence or mastery in the subject area being studied. The **goal structure** specifies the ways in which students will interact with each other and the instructor during the instructional session. Each goal structure has its place (Johnson & Johnson, 1989, 1994). In the ideal classroom, all students would learn how to work cooperatively with others, compete for fun and enjoyment, and work autonomously on their own. The instructor decides which goal structure to implement within each lesson. The most important goal structure, and the one that should be used the majority of the time in learning situations, is cooperation.

Cooperation is working together to accomplish shared goals. Within cooperative situations, individuals seek outcomes that are beneficial to themselves and beneficial to all other group members. **Cooperative learning** is the instructional use of small groups so that students work together to maximize their own and each other's learning. It may be contrasted with **competitive** (students work against each other to achieve an academic goal such as a grade of "A" that only one or a few students can attain) and **individualistic** (students work by themselves to accomplish learning goals unrelated to those of the other students) learning. In cooperative and individualistic learning, you evaluate student efforts on a criteria-referenced basis while in competitive learning you grade students on a norm-referenced basis. While there are limitations on when and where you may use competitive and individualistic learning appropriately, you may structure any learning task in any subject area with any curriculum cooperatively.

Johnson, D. W., Johnson, R., & Smith, K. (1998). **Active Learning: Cooperation In The College Classroom**. Edina, MN: Interaction Book Company.

What Is It?

Given below are twelve statements. Form a pair and agree on whether each statement reflects a cooperative, competitive, or individualistic situation. Place each statement in the appropriate column in the table given below.

Statements

1. Strive for everyone's success.
2. Strive to be better than others.
3. Strive for own success only.
4. What benefits self does not affect others.
5. Joint success is celebrated.
6. What benefits self benefits others.
7. Only own success is celebrated.
8. Motivated to help and assist others.
9. What benefits self deprives/hurts others.
10. Motivated only to maximize own productivity.
11. Own success and other's failure is celebrated.
12. Motivated to ensure that no one else does better than oneself.

Cooperative	Competitive	Individualistic

Why Use Cooperative Learning?

The conviction to use cooperative learning flows from knowing the research. Since the first research study was published in 1898, there have been over 600 experimental and over 100 correlational studies conducted on cooperative, competitive, and individualistic efforts (see Johnson & Johnson, 1989 for a complete review of these studies). The multiple outcomes studied can be classified into three major categories (see Figure 1.3): efforts to achieve, positive relationships, and psychological health. From the research,

Johnson, D. W., Johnson, R., & Smith, K. (1998). **Active Learning: Cooperation In The College Classroom**. Edina, MN: Interaction Book Company.

we know that cooperation, compared with competitive and individualistic efforts, typically results in:

1. **Greater Efforts To Achieve:** This includes higher achievement and greater productivity by all students (high-, medium-, and low-achievers), long-term retention, intrinsic motivation, achievement motivation, time-on-task, higher-level reasoning, and critical thinking.

2. **More Positive Relationships Among Students:** This includes esprit-de-corps, caring and committed relationships, personal and academic social support, valuing of diversity, and cohesion.

3. **Greater Psychological Health:** This includes general psychological adjustment, ego-strength, social development, social competencies, self-esteem, self-identity, and ability to cope with adversity and stress.

The powerful effects of cooperation on so many important outcomes separates it from other instructional methods and makes it one of your most important instructional tools.

Types Of Cooperative Learning Groups

These problems are endemic to all institutions of education, regardless of level. Children sit for 12 years in classrooms where the implicit goal is to listen to the teacher and memorize the information in order to regurgitate it on a test. Little or no attention is paid to the learning process, even though much research exists documenting that real understanding is a case of active restructuring on the part of the learner. Restructuring occurs through engagement in problem posing as well as problem solving, inference making and investigation, resolving of contradictions, and reflecting. These processes all mandate far more active learners, as well as a different model of education than the one subscribed to at present by most institutions. Rather than being powerless and dependent on the institution, learners need to be empowered to think and learn for themselves. Thus, learning needs to be conceived of as something a learner does, not something that is done to a learner.

Catherine Fosnot (1989)

There are three types of cooperative learning groups. **Formal cooperative learning** groups last from one class period to several weeks. You may structure any academic assignment or course requirement for formal cooperative learning. Formal cooperative learning groups ensure that students are actively involved in the intellectual work of organizing material, explaining it, summarizing it, and integrating it into existing conceptual structures. They are the heart of using cooperative learning. **Informal cooperative learning** groups are ad-hoc groups that last from a few minutes to one class period. You use them during direct teaching (lectures, demonstrations, films, videos) to

1 : 16

Johnson, D. W., Johnson, R., & Smith, K. (1998). **Active Learning: Cooperation In The College Classroom**. Edina, MN: Interaction Book Company.

focus student attention on the material they are to learn, set a mood conducive to learning, help set expectations as to what the lesson will cover, ensure that students cognitively process the material you are teaching, and provide closure to an instructional session. **Cooperative base groups** are long-term (lasting for at least a year), heterogeneous groups with stable membership whose primary purpose is for members to give each other the support, help, encouragement, and assistance each needs to progress academically. Base groups provide students with long-term, committed relationships.

For each of the three types of cooperative learning there are **cooperative learning scripts.** Scripts are standard cooperative procedures for (a) conducting generic, repetitive lessons (such as writing reports or giving presentations) and (b) managing classroom routines (such as checking homework and reviewing a test). Once planned and conducted several times, scripted repetitive cooperative lessons and classroom routines become automatic activities in the classroom.

When you use formal, informal, and cooperative base groups repeatedly, you will gain a routine-level of expertise in doing so. **Expertise** is reflected in your proficiency, adroitness, competence, and skill in doing something. Expertise in structuring cooperative efforts is reflected in your being able to:

1. Take any lesson in any subject area with any age student and structure it cooperatively.

2. Use cooperative learning (at a routine-use level) 60 to 80 percent of the time.

3. Describe precisely what you are doing and why in order to (a) communicate to others the nature and advantages of cooperative learning and (b) teach colleagues how to implement cooperative learning.

4. Apply the principles of cooperation to other settings, such as colleagial relationships and faculty meetings.

You usually gain such expertise through a progressive-refinement procedure of (a) teaching a cooperative lesson, (b) assessing how well it went, (c) reflecting on how cooperation could have been better structured, and then (d) teaching an improved cooperative lesson, (b) assessing how well it went, and so forth. You thus gain experience in an incremental step-by-step manner. The **routine-use level of instructor expertise** is the ability to structure cooperative learning situations automatically without conscious thought or planning. You can then use cooperative learning with fidelity for the rest of your teaching career.

The coordinated use of all three types of cooperative learning groups provides a structure to courses. A typical class period, for example, may start with a base group meeting, move to a short lecture utilizing informal cooperative learning groups, give an

Johnson, D. W., Johnson, R., & Smith, K. (1998). **Active Learning: Cooperation In The College Classroom**. Edina, MN: Interaction Book Company.

assignment that is completed in formal cooperative learning groups, and end with a base group meeting. In Chapters 2, 3, and 4 the three types of cooperative learning groups are explained in detail and practical suggestions given as to how they may be used. In Chapter 6 the integrated use of the three will be discussed.

Types Of Cooperative Learning

Form a pair. In the spaces below, write out the definition of each type of cooperative learning in your own words.

Formal	Informal	Base Groups

What Kind Of Group Am I Using?

There are many kinds of groups that can be used in the classroom. Cooperative learning groups are just one of them. There is nothing magical about working in a group. Cooperative learning groups facilitate student learning and increase the quality of life in the classroom. Other types of learning groups hinder student learning and create disharmony and dissatisfaction with classroom life. When you use instructional groups, you have to ask yourself, "*What type of group am I using?*"

1. **Pseudo-Learning Group:** In this type of group, the sum of the whole is less than the potential of the individual members. Students are assigned to work together but believe they will be evaluated by being ranked from the highest to the lowest performer. They see each other as rivals who must be defeated. Students would achieve more if they were working alone.

2. **Traditional Classroom Learning Group:** In this type of group, the sum of the whole is more than the potential of some members. Students are told to work together but assignments are structured so that very little joint work is required. Students

Johnson, D. W., Johnson, R., & Smith, K. (1998). **Active Learning: Cooperation In The College Classroom**. Edina, MN: Interaction Book Company.

believe that they will be evaluated and rewarded as individuals, not as group members.

3. **Cooperative Learning Group:** This type of group is more than a sum of its parts and all students perform higher academically than they would if they worked alone. Students are assigned to work together and they believe that their success depends on the efforts of all group members.

4. **High-Performance Cooperative Learning Group:** This is a group that meets all the criteria for being a cooperative learning group and outperforms all reasonable expectations, given its membership.

Types Of Groups

Demonstrate your understanding of the different types of groups by matching the definitions with the appropriate group. Check your answers with your partner and explain why you believe your answers to be correct.

Type Of Group	Definition
_____ Pseudo Group	a. A group in which students work together to accomplish shared goals. Students perceive they can reach their learning goals if and only if the other group members also reach their goals.
_____ Traditional Learning Group	b. A group whose members have been assigned to work together but they have no interest in doing so. The structure promotes competition at close quarters.
_____ Cooperative Learning Group	d. A group that meets all the criteria for being a cooperative group and outperforms all reasonable expectations, given its membership.
_____ High- Performance Cooperative Learning Group	c. A group whose members agree to work together, but see little benefit from doing so. The structure promotes individualistic work with talking.

Johnson, D. W., Johnson, R., & Smith, K. (1998). **Active Learning: Cooperation In The College Classroom**. Edina, MN: Interaction Book Company.

What Makes Cooperation Work

Together we stand, divided we fall.

Watchword Of The American Revolution

On July 15, 1982, Don Bennett, a Seattle businessman, was the first amputee ever to climb Mount Rainier (reported in Kouzes & Posner, 1987). He climbed 14,410 feet on one leg and two crutches. It took him five days. When asked to state the most important lesson he learned from doing so, without hesitation he said, "*You can't do it alone.*"

What did he mean? During one very difficult trek across an ice field in Don Bennett's hop to the top of Mount Rainier, his daughter stayed by his side for four hours and with each new hop told him, "*You can do it, Dad. You're the best dad in the world. You can do it, Dad.*" There was no way Bennett would quit hopping to the top with his daughter yelling words of love and encouragement in his ear. The encouragement of his daughter kept him going, strengthening his commitment to make it to the top. The classroom is similar. With members of their cooperative group cheering them on, students amaze themselves and their instructors with what they can achieve.

To structure lessons so students do in fact work cooperatively with each other, you must understand the basic elements that make cooperation work. Mastering the basic elements of cooperation allows you to:

1. Take your existing lessons, curricula, and courses and structure them cooperatively.

2. Tailor cooperative learning lessons to your unique instructional needs, circumstances, curricula, subject areas, and students.

3. Diagnose the problems some students may have in working together and intervene to increase the effectiveness of the student learning groups.

For cooperation to work well, you explicitly have to structure five essential elements in each lesson. **The first and most important element is positive interdependence.** You must give a clear task and a group goal so students believe they "*sink or swim together.*" **Positive interdependence** exists when group members perceive that they are linked with each other in a way that one cannot succeed unless everyone succeeds. If one fails, all fail. Group members realize, therefore, that each person's efforts benefit not only him- or herself, but all other group members as well. Positive interdependence creates a commitment to other people's success as well as one's own and is the heart of cooperative learning. If there is no positive interdependence, there is no cooperation.

Johnson, D. W., Johnson, R., & Smith, K. (1998). **Active Learning: Cooperation In The College Classroom.** Edina, MN: Interaction Book Company.

Why Power Of Cooperation Is Ignored

Directions: Consider the five sources of resistance to using cooperative learning given above. Rate yourself from "1" to "5" on each source.

1----------------2----------------3-------------4--------------5

Low	Middle	High
Not A Concern Of Mine	Somewhat A Concern	Consistently And Strongly A Concern

	The Causes Of The Missed Opportunities To Capitalize On The Power Of Groups
	1. **Belief that isolated work is the natural order of the world**. Such myopic focus blinds educators to the realization that no one person could have built a cathedral, achieved America's independence from England, or created a supercomputer.
	2. **Resistance to taking responsibility for others**. Many educators do not easily (a) take responsibility for the performance of colleagues or (b) let colleagues assume responsibility for their work. The same educators may resist letting students take responsibility for each other's learning.
	3. **Confusion about what makes groups work**. Many educators may not know the difference between cooperative learning groups and traditional groupwork.
	4. **Fear that they cannot use groups effectively to enhance learning and improve teaching**. Not all groups work. Most adults have had personal experiences with very ineffective and inefficient committees, task forces, and clubs and know firsthand how bad groups can be. When many educators weigh the potential power of learning groups against the possibility of failure, they choose to play it safe and stick with the status quo of isolated work.
	5. **Concern about time and effort required to change**. Using cooperative learning requires educators to apply what is known about effective groups in a disciplined way. Learning how to do so and engaging in such disciplined action may seem daunting.

The second essential element of cooperative learning is individual and group accountability. The group must be accountable for achieving its goals. Each member must be accountable for contributing his or her share of the work (which ensures that no

Johnson, D. W., Johnson, R., & Smith, K. (1998). **Active Learning: Cooperation In The College Classroom**. Edina, MN: Interaction Book Company.

© Johnson, Johnson, & Smith

one can "hitch-hike" on the work of others). The group has to be clear about its goals and be able to measure (a) its progress in achieving them and (b) the individual efforts of each of its members. **Individual accountability** exists when the performance of each individual student is assessed and the results are given back to the group and the individual in order to ascertain who needs more assistance, support, and encouragement in completing the assignment. The purpose of cooperative learning groups is to make each member a stronger individual in his or her right. Students learn together so that they can subsequently perform higher as individuals.

The third essential component of cooperative learning is promotive interaction, preferably face-to-face. Students need to do real work together while promoting each other's success. **Promotive interaction** occurs when members share resources and help, support, encourage, and praise each other's efforts to learn. Cooperative learning groups are both an academic support system (every student has someone who is committed to helping him or her learn) and a personal support system (every student has someone who is committed to him or her as a person). There are important cognitive activities and interpersonal dynamics that can only occur when students promote each other's learning. This includes orally explaining how to solve problems, discussing the nature of the concepts being learned, teaching one's knowledge to classmates, and connecting present with past learning. It is through promoting each other's learning face-to-face that members become personally committed to each other as well as to their mutual goals.

The fourth essential element of cooperative learning is teaching students the required interpersonal and small group skills. In cooperative learning groups students are required to learn academic subject matter (taskwork) and also to learn the interpersonal and small group skills required to function as part of a group (teamwork). Cooperative learning is inherently more complex than competitive or individualistic learning because students have to engage simultaneously in taskwork and teamwork. Group members must know how to provide effective leadership, decision-making, trust-building, communication, and conflict-management, and be motivated to use the prerequisite skills. You have to teach teamwork skills just as purposefully and precisely as you do academic skills. Since cooperation and conflict are inherently related (see Johnson & Johnson, 1995a, 1995b), the procedures and skills for managing conflicts constructively are especially important for the long-term success of learning groups. Procedures and strategies for teaching students social skills may be found in Johnson (1991, 1997), Johnson and F. Johnson (1997), and Johnson and R. Johnson (1998).

The fifth essential component of cooperative learning is group processing. Group processing exists when group members discuss how well they are achieving their goals and maintaining effective working relationships. Groups need to describe what member actions are helpful and unhelpful and make decisions about what behaviors to continue or change. Continuous improvement of the process of learning results from the careful analysis of how members are working together and determining how group effectiveness can be enhanced.

Johnson, D. W., Johnson, R., & Smith, K. (1998). **Active Learning: Cooperation In The College Classroom**. Edina, MN: Interaction Book Company.

Using the power of groups to maximize each student's learning requires faculty (and administrators) to apply the basics of how groups work with discipline and diligence. While the power of cooperative learning is obvious to many faculty, the discipline needed to use cooperative learning effectively is not. The basic elements that make cooperation work cannot be taken for granted or treated lightly. They must be carefully and precisely structured into every learning group. **Your use of cooperative learning becomes effective through disciplined action.** The five basic elements are not just characteristics of good cooperative learning groups, they are a discipline that you have to rigorously apply (much like a diet has to be adhered to) to produce the conditions for effective cooperative action.

Understanding Cooperative Learning			
Types Of Groups	**Cooperative Groups**	**Essential Elements**	**Outcomes**
Pseudo Groups	Formal Cooperative Learning	Positive Interdependence	Effort To Achieve
Traditional Groups	Informal Cooperative Learning	Individual Accountability	Positive Relationships
Cooperative Groups	Cooperative Base Groups	Promotive Interaction	Psychological Health
High-Performing Cooperative Groups		Interpersonal And Small Group Skills	
		Group Processing	

Managing Conflicts Constructively

Cooperation and conflict go hand-in-hand (Johnson, 1970). The more group members care about achieving the group's goals, and the more they care about each other, the more likely they are to have conflicts with each other. How conflict is managed largely determines how successful cooperative efforts tend to be. In order to ensure that conflicts are managed constructively, students must be taught two procedures and sets of skills.

Johnson, D. W., Johnson, R., & Smith, K. (1998). **Active Learning: Cooperation In The College Classroom**. Edina, MN: Interaction Book Company.

First, students must be taught the procedures and skills needed to manage the academic/intellectual conflicts inherent in learning groups (Johnson & Johnson, 1995b). Intellectual challenge is created by structuring academic controversies. Students are placed in cooperative groups of four, divided into two pairs, and each pair is given either the "pro" or "con" position on an issue being studied. Students then research and prepare their position, present the base case possible for their position, refute the opposing position, try to see the issue from both sides, and create a synthesis that incorporates the best reasoning from both sides. Such "intellectual disputed passages" create higher level reasoning, and higher achievement, and greater long-term retention.

Extraordinary Achievement

Sandy Koufax was one of the greatest pitchers in the history of baseball. Although he was naturally talented, he was also unusually well trained and disciplined. He was perhaps the only major-league pitcher whose fastball could be heard to hum. Opposing batters, instead of talking and joking around in the dugout, would sit quietly and listen for Koufax's fastball to hum. When it was their turn to bat, they were already intimidated. There was, however, a simple way for Koufax's genius to have been negated. By making the first author of this book his catcher. To be great, a pitcher needs an outstanding catcher (his great partner was Johnny Roseboro). David is such an unskilled catcher that Koufax would have had to throw the ball much slower in order for David to catch it. This would have deprived Koufax of his greatest weapon. Placing Roger and Edythe at key defensive positions in the infield or outfield, furthermore, would have seriously affected Koufax's success. Sandy Koufax was not a great pitcher on his own. Only as part of a team could Koufax achieve greatness. In baseball and in the classroom it takes a cooperative effort. Extraordinary achievement comes from a cooperative group, not from the individualistic or competitive efforts of an isolated individual.

Second, students must be taught the procedures and skills needed to negotiate constructive resolutions to their conflicts and mediate classmates' conflicts (Johnson & Johnson, 1995a). Students are trained to be peacemakers in a two-step process. The **first** step is to train students to negotiate constructive resolutions to their conflicts of interests. When two students want the same book or want to use the computer at the same time, for example, they must negotiate an agreement that is acceptable to both. Once students know how to negotiate, the **second** step is to train students to be mediators. A peer mediation program is then implemented where students take the conflicts they cannot negotiate successfully to a mediator who helps then do so.

1 : 24

Johnson, D. W., Johnson, R., & Smith, K. (1998). **Active Learning: Cooperation In The College Classroom**. Edina, MN: Interaction Book Company.

The combination of knowing how to manage intellectual disagreements and how to negotiate/mediate conflicts among students' wants, needs, and goals ensures that the power of cooperative efforts will be maximized. The productivity of groups increases dramatically when members are skilled in how to manage conflicts constructively.

Table 1.2 Conflict Resolution Procedures

Academic Controversy	Peacemaker Program	
	Problem-Solving Negotiations	Peer Mediation
Research And Prepare Positions	State What You Want	End Hostilities
Present And Advocate Position	State How You Feel	Ensure Commitment To Mediation Process
Open Discussion: Advocate, Refute, Rebut	State Your Reasons For Wanting And Feeling As You Do	Facilitate Problem-Solving Negotiations
Reverse Perspectives: Present Opposing Position	Reverse Perspectives: Summarize Opposing Position	Formalize Contract
Reach Consensus On Best Reasoned Judgment: Synthesize	Create Three Optional Agreements That Maximize Joint Outcomes	
	Choose One And Formalize Agreement	

The Cooperative College

W. Edwards Deming, J. Juran, and other founders of the quality movement have stated that more than 85 percent of the behavior of members of an organization is directly attributable to the organization's structure, not the nature of the individuals involved. Your classes are no exception. If competitive or individualistic learning dominates your classes, your students will behave accordingly, regardless of whether you have temporarily put them in cooperative groups. If cooperative learning dominates your classes, your students will behave accordingly and a true learning community will result.

The issue of cooperation among students is part of a larger issue of the organizational structure of college (Johnson & Johnson, 1994). For decades colleges have functioned as "*mass production*" organizations that divided work into component parts (first grade,

Johnson, D. W., Johnson, R., & Smith, K. (1998). **Active Learning: Cooperation In The College Classroom**. Edina, MN: Interaction Book Company.

second grade; English, social studies, science) to be performed by instructors who are isolated from their colleagues and work alone, in their own room, with their own set of students, and with their own set of curriculum materials. Students can be assigned to any instructor because students are considered to be interchangeable parts in the education machine. By using cooperative learning the majority of the time you are changing the basic organizational structure of your classes to a team-based, high-performance one. In other words, cooperation is more than an instructional procedure. It is a basic shift in organizational structure that will affect all aspects of college life.

In a **cooperative college**, students work primarily in cooperative learning groups, faculty work in cooperative teams, and administrators work in cooperative teams (Johnson & Johnson, 1994). The organizational structure of the classroom and college are then congruent. Each level of cooperative teams supports and enhances the other levels.

A cooperative college structure begins in the classroom with the use of cooperative learning the majority of the time (Johnson & Johnson, 1994). Work teams are the heart of the team-based organizational structure and cooperative learning groups are the primary work team. Cooperative learning is used to increase student achievement, create more positive relationships among students, and generally improve students' psychological well-being. Having instructors advocate cooperation to their students, furthermore, changes their own attitudes toward working collaboratively with colleagues.

The second level in creating a cooperative college is to form colleagial teaching teams, task forces, and ad hoc decision-making groups within the college (Johnson & Johnson, 1994). Instructor teams are just as effective as student teams. The use of cooperation to structure faculty and staff work involves (a) colleagial teaching teams, (b) college-based decision making, and (c) faculty meetings. Just as the heart of the classroom is cooperative learning, the heart of the college is the colleagial teaching team. **Colleagial teaching teams** are small cooperative groups (two to five instructors) whose purpose is to increase instructors' instructional expertise and success (Johnson & Johnson, 1994).

A college-based decision-making procedure is implemented through the use of two types of cooperative teams (Johnson & Johnson, 1994). A **task force** considers a college problem and proposes a solution to the faculty as a whole. The faculty is then divided into **ad hoc decision-making groups** and considers whether to accept or modify the proposal. The decisions made by the ad hoc groups are summarized, and the entire faculty then decides on the action to be taken to solve the problem.

The third level in creating a cooperative college is to implement administrative cooperative teams within the district (Johnson & Johnson, 1994). Administrators are organized into colleagial teams to increase their administrative expertise as well as task forces and ad hoc decision making groups.

1 : 26

Johnson, D. W., Johnson, R., & Smith, K. (1998). **Active Learning: Cooperation In The College Classroom.** Edina, MN: Interaction Book Company.

Willi Unsoeld, a mountain climber and philosopher, gave this advice *"as the secret to survival"* to all those who set off to climb a mountain: *"Take care of each other, share your energies with the group, no one must feel alone, cut off, for that is when you do not make it."* The same may be said for everyone entering a college.

Year	Training And Application
One	Instructors (and administrators) are organized into colleagial teaching teams that meet weekly and are trained in the fundamentals of cooperative learning. The instructors become an inhouse demonstration project for other instructors to view and then emulate.
Two	Instructors are trained in the integrated use of (a) formal, informal, and base groups, (b) cooperative, competitive, and individualistic learning, as well as the teaching of advanced social skills. Administrators receive six days of training on the cooperative college.
Three	Instructors are trained in how to (a) create academic conflicts to intellectually challenge students, and (b) use a peer mediation program to manage classroom and college discipline problems. The "superstar" instructors receive leadership training on how to (a) conduct the training on cooperative learning, (b) give inclassroom help and support to the instructors being trained, and (c) organize colleagial teaching teams. The leaders are then given responsibility for conducting the training in their district.
Four	Continued functioning of colleagial support groups supported by the instructors trained to be leaders.

Gaining Expertise In Cooperative Learning

Civic Values

Some historians claim that the decline and fall of Rome was set in motion by corruption from within rather than by conquest from without. Rome fell, it can be argued, because Romans lost their civic virtue. **Civic virtue** exists when individuals meet both the letter and spirit of their public obligations. For a community to exist and be sustained, members must share common goals and values aimed at increasing the quality of life within the community. No one should be surprised that in a community where competitive and individualistic values are taught, people will behave in accordance with such values. When that happens in a society, for example, people may stop obeying the law. Running stoplights may become a common occurrence as the individualist thinks it

Johnson, D. W., Johnson, R., & Smith, K. (1998). **Active Learning: Cooperation In The College Classroom**. Edina, MN: Interaction Book Company.

is rational to do so, as he or she will arrive at the destination sooner. If someone is killed, it will be a pedestrian, not the driver. But each of us is at some time a pedestrian. Community cannot be maintained unless members value others and the community as a whole, as well as themselves.

College and classroom management requires that all members of the college community adopt a set of civic values (Johnson & Johnson, 1996b, in press). To create the common culture that defines a community, there must be common goals and shared values that help define appropriate behavior. A learning community cannot exist in colleges dominated by (a) competition where students are taught to value striving for their personal success at the expense of others or (b) individualistic efforts where students value only their own self-interests. Rather, students need to internalize values underlying cooperation and integrative negotiations, such as commitment to the common good and to the well being of other members, a sense of responsibility to contribute one's fair share of the work, respect for the efforts of others and for them as people, behaving with integrity, caring for other members, compassion when other members are in need, and appreciation of diversity. Such civic values both underlie and are promoted by the cooperation and constructive conflict resolution that take place in the college.

Nature Of This Book And How To Use It

This is not a book you can read with detachment. It is written to involve you with its contents. By reading this book you will not only be able to learn the theoretical and empirical knowledge now available on cooperative learning, but you will also learn to apply this knowledge in practical ways within your classroom and college. Often in the past, practitioners concerned with cooperative learning did not pay attention to the research literature, and cooperation researchers neglected to specify how their findings could be applied. Thus, the knowledge about effective use of cooperation was often divided. In this book we directly apply existing theory and research to the learning and application of effective cooperative learning procedures and skills. In other words, this book combines theory, research, and practical application to the classroom. In using this book, diagnose your present knowledge and skills, actively participate in the exercises, reflect on your experiences, read the chapters carefully, discuss the relevant theory and research provided, and integrate the information and experiences into your teaching repertoire. In doing so, you will bridge the gap between theory and practice. You should then plan how to continue your skill- and knowledge-building activities after you have finished this book. Most important of all, you should systematically plan how to implement the material covered in each chapter into your classroom.

1 : 28

Johnson, D. W., Johnson, R., & Smith, K. (1998). **Active Learning: Cooperation In The College Classroom**. Edina, MN: Interaction Book Company.

Summary

In college teaching a paradigm shift is taking place. Minor modifications in current teaching practices will not solve the current problems with college instruction. Teaching success in today's world requires a new approach to instruction. In planning the new approach, it may be helpful to review the history of college teaching in America. There have been four general definitions of the faculty's role in American colleges. In colonial America, the emphasis was on teaching. In the latter half of the 19th-Century, the emphasis was on practical service to promote America's economic and political strength. In the early 20th-Century, faculty were given the challenge of basic research. In more recent years, faculty have become more concerned about the success of the college as a business. It is time for the pendulum to swing back to include an emphasis on teaching and service as well as research. In doing so, teaching and service must be matched to the modern world. Teaching in the old way harder and faster with more bells and whistles will not do. The "select and weed out" approach to teaching must be replaced with the "cultivate and develop" approach. Colleges must refocus on teaching in order to develop student potential and talents. College faculty must "add value" through their teaching. The new paradigm of teaching may only be operationalized and implemented through the use of cooperative learning procedures.

In this chapter we have seen that there are three types of social interdependence: competitive, individualistic, and cooperative, Of the three, cooperation tends to promote the highest achievement, most positive relationships, and greatest psychological health. In order to harness the power of cooperation, however, it is necessary to know what makes it work and apply those elements with discipline and diligence. Like Sandy Koufax, natural talent is not enough to make a great instructor. Being well trained in how to use cooperative learning and unusually well disciplined in structuring the five basic elements in every lesson are also necessary. The five essential components are positive interdependence, individual accountability, promotive interaction, social skills, and group processing. From structuring these five elements into lessons, instructors can create formal cooperative learning lessons, informal cooperative learning lessons, and cooperative base groups. Repetitive lessons and procedures may be turned into cooperative scripts. The use of cooperative learning takes place within an organizational context. If the organizational context emphasizes mass production of educated students, it works against the use of cooperative learning. If the organizational context is a team-based, high-performance structure, then it encourages and supports the use of cooperative learning. In a high-performance college, the five basic elements of cooperation are used to structure teaching teams, faculty meetings, and site-based decision making. Finally, the long-term success of cooperative efforts depends on members having frequent conflicts that are managed constructively.

1 : 29

Johnson, D. W., Johnson, R., & Smith, K. (1998). **Active Learning: Cooperation In The College Classroom**. Edina, MN: Interaction Book Company.

The next chapter focuses on the instructor's role in using formal cooperative learning. This provides the foundation for using all types of cooperative learning.

Final Note

Reorganizing a college is like reorganizing a graveyard.

Warren Bennis

The recent Carnegie Foundation study of student life revealed growing social separations and divisions on campus, increased acts of incivility, and a deepening concern that the spirit of community has diminished. In response, colleges and universities from coast to coast are searching for ways to affirm diversity while strengthening the loyalties on campuses. Issues like the quality of campus life for students, however, are not considered by the old paradigm. The work of the faculty needs to be defined in ways that enrich, rather than restrict, the quality of campus life. Cooperative learning provides a procedure for doing so. In choosing between the old and new paradigms of teaching, faculty may wish to remember how to broil a frog.

If you place a frog in a pot of boiling water, it will immediately jump out with little damage to itself. But if you place a frog in a pot of cold water, and slowly raise the temperature, the frog seems to adapt well to the new conditions, and stays in the pot until the water reaches 212 degrees Fahrenheit - boiling - and then the frog quickly dies. The frog does not have the sensors needed to detect the gradual rise in water temperature. Colleges and universities may be in danger of making the same mistake. They may make incremental changes to their dynamic environment until they suddenly realize that there has been a fundamental change and they are obsolete and out of date.

Johnson, D. W., Johnson, R., & Smith, K. (1998). **Active Learning: Cooperation In The College Classroom**. Edina, MN: Interaction Book Company.

Cooperative Learning Contract

Write down your major learnings from reading this chapter and participating in training session one. Then write down how you plan to implement each learning. Share what you learned and your implementation plans with your base group. Listen carefully to their major learnings and implementation plans. You may modify your own plans on the basis of what you have learned from your groupmates. Volunteer one thing you can do to help each groupmate with his or her implementation plans. Utilize the help groupmates offer to you. Sign each member's plans to seal the contract.

Major Learnings	Implementation Plans

Date: _____ Participant's Signature: _____

Signatures Of Group Members: _____

_____

Johnson, D. W., Johnson, R., & Smith, K. (1998). **Active Learning: Cooperation In The College Classroom**. Edina, MN: Interaction Book Company.

Cooperative Learning Progress Report

Name: _____ School: _____

Subject Area: _____ Grade: _____

Date	Lesson	Successes	Problems

Describe Critical Or Interesting Incidents:

1 : 32

Johnson, D. W., Johnson, R., & Smith, K. (1998). **Active Learning: Cooperation In The College Classroom**. Edina, MN: Interaction Book Company.

Cooperative Learning Log Sheet

Name: _____ School: _____

Subject Area: _____ Grade: _____

Week	Lessons Planned, Taught	Social Skills Included	Planned With	Observed By	Given Away To
1					
2					
3					
4					
5					
6					
7					
8					
9					
10					
11					
12					
13					
14					
15					
Group					
Total					

Johnson, D. W., Johnson, R., & Smith, K. (1998). **Active Learning: Cooperation In The College Classroom**. Edina, MN: Interaction Book Company.

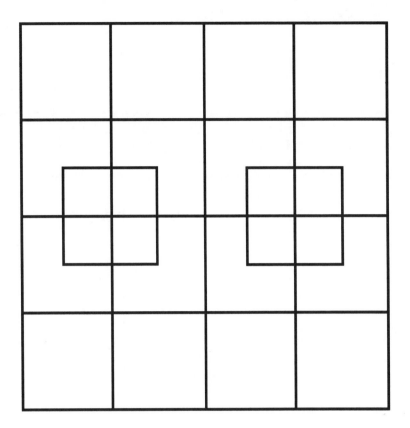

How Do I Feel?

What Did I Notice?

Johnson, D. W., Johnson, R., & Smith, K. (1998). **Active Learning: Cooperation In The College Classroom**. Edina, MN: Interaction Book Company.

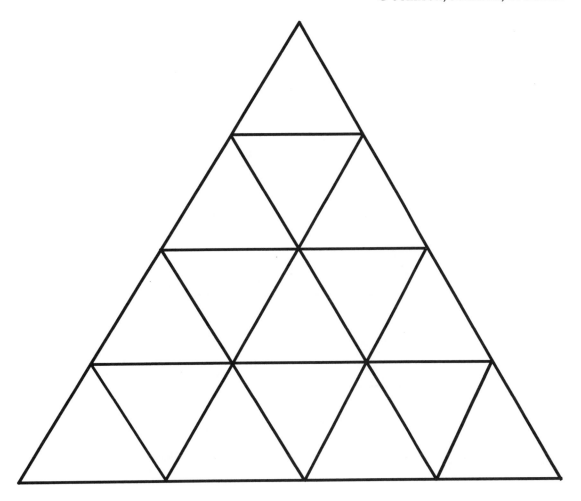

How Do I Feel?

What Did I Notice?

Johnson, D. W., Johnson, R., & Smith, K. (1998). **Active Learning: Cooperation In The College Classroom**. Edina, MN: Interaction Book Company.

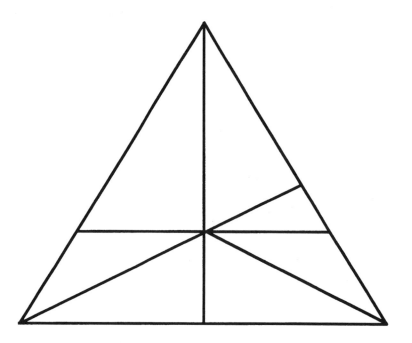

How Do I Feel?

What Did I Notice?

1 : 36

Johnson, D. W., Johnson, R., & Smith, K. (1998). **Active Learning: Cooperation In The College Classroom**. Edina, MN: Interaction Book Company.

Definitions

A **learning goal** is a desired future state of competence or mastery in the subject area being studied. A **goal structure** specifies the type of interdependence among individuals as they strive to accomplish their goals. Interdependence may be positive (cooperation), negative (competition), or none (individualistic efforts).

Cooperation: We Sink Or Swim Together

Individuals work together to achieve shared goals (maximize own and others' learning).

    Work in small, often heterogeneous groups
    Strive for all group members' success
    What benefits self benefits others
    Joint success is celebrated
    Rewards are viewed as unlimited
    Evaluated by comparing performance to preset criteria

Competition: I Swim, You Sink; I Sink, You Swim

Individuals work against each other to achieve a goal only one or a few can attain.

    Work alone
    Strive to be better than classmates
    What benefits self deprives others
    Own success and others' failure is celebrated
    Rewards are limited
    Graded on a curve or ranked from "best" to "worst"

Individualistic: We Are Each In This Alone

Individuals work by themselves to achieve goals unrelated to others' goals.

    Work alone
    Strive for own success
    What benefits self does not affect others
    Own success is celebrated
    Rewards are viewed as unlimited
    Evaluated by comparing performance to preset criteria

Johnson, D. W., Johnson, R., & Smith, K. (1998). **Active Learning: Cooperation In The College Classroom**. Edina, MN: Interaction Book Company.

BASIC ELEMENTS OF COOPERATIVE TEAMS

Positive Interdependence

Team members perceive that they need each other in order to complete the group's task ("sink or swim together"). Instructors may structure positive interdependence by establishing **mutual goals** (maximize own and each other's productivity), **joint rewards** (if all group members achieve above the criteria, each will receive bonus points), **shared resources** (members have different expertise), and **assigned roles** (summarizer, encourager of participation, elaborator).

Individual Accountability

Assessing the quality and quantity of each member's contributions and giving the results to the group and the individual.

Face-to-Face Promotive Interaction

Team members promote each other's productivity by helping, sharing, and encouraging efforts to produce. Members explain, discuss, and teach what they know to teammates. Instructors structure teams so that members sit knee-to-knee and talk through each aspect of the tasks they are working to complete.

Interpersonal And Small Group Skills

Groups cannot function effectively if members do not have and use the needed social skills. Instructors emphasize these skills as purposefully and precisely as job-performance skills. Collaborative skills include instructorship, decision-making, trust-building, communication, and conflict-management skills.

Group Processing

Groups need specific time to discuss how well they are achieving their goals and maintaining effective working relationships among members. Instructors structure group processing by assigning such tasks as (a) list at least three member actions that helped the group be successful and (b) list one action that could be added to make the group even more successful tomorrow. Instructors also monitor the groups and give feedback on how well the groups are working together.

Johnson, D. W., Johnson, R., & Smith, K. (1998). **Active Learning: Cooperation In The College Classroom**. Edina, MN: Interaction Book Company.

Basic Elements Of Cooperation

Task: Learn the five basic elements of a well-structured cooperative lesson so that you never forget them for as long as you live. For each element:
1. Read the paragraph defining it.
2. Restate its definition in your own words and write it down.
3. Rate from 1-to-10 the extent to which your group experienced the element while you completed the previous cooperative task.
4. Write down at least two things your instructor did to ensure that the element was structured into the previous cooperative task.

Cooperative: Ensure that all members complete the assignment by coming to agreement on the answers and ensuring that everyone can explain each answer. To assist in doing so, each member takes one of the following roles: Reader, Recorder, Checker.

Expected Criteria For Success: Everyone must be able to name and explain the basic elements.

Individual Accountability: One member from your group will be randomly chosen to name and explain the basic elements.

Expected Behaviors: Active participating, checking, encouraging, and elaborating by all members.

Intergroup Cooperation: Whenever it is helpful, check procedures, answers, and strategies with another group.

Your Definition	Rating	Ways It Was Structured

Johnson, D. W., Johnson, R., & Smith, K. (1998). **Active Learning: Cooperation In The College Classroom**. Edina, MN: Interaction Book Company.

Cooperative Learning Lesson Scripts

During the training sessions you will participate in a number of cooperative lessons. These lessons are generic in that they can be used daily (or at least several times a week). The cooperative lesson scripts modeled in this training may be used repeatedly with any curriculum in any subject area. They are content free. Your **tasks** are to:

1. Attend to the script of the activities as well as the content.

2. For each cooperative learning script complete the chart given below.

3. Plan how to use each cooperative learning script in your classes. Translate each script to make it useable with your students, curricula, and circumstances.

4. Use each cooperative lesson script and adapt and fine-tune it until it produces the results you wish.

WHAT I LIKE ABOUT THE SCRIPT	WHAT TO WATCH OUT FOR	WHERE AND WHEN I WILL USE IT

1 : 40

Johnson, D. W., Johnson, R., & Smith, K. (1998). **Active Learning: Cooperation In The College Classroom**. Edina, MN: Interaction Book Company.

CHAPTER TWO:
FORMAL COOPERATIVE LEARNING

Sisyphus And The Old Paradigm

And I saw Sisyphus at his endless task, raising his prodigious stone, with both his hands. With hands and feet he tried to roll it up to the top of the hill, but always, just before he could roll it over onto the other side, its weight would be too much for him, and the pitiless stone would come thundering down again onto the plain. Then he would begin trying to push it uphill again, as the sweat ran off him and steam rose after him.

Homer (Oddyessy, Book 11)

Repetitive but futile efforts were personified by the ancient Greeks in the person of Sisyphus. Sisyphus was the legendary king of Corinth who was punished in Hades by having to roll a stone uphill eternally. As he neared the top of the hill, the stone always slipped from his grasp, and he had to start again. It is easy to feel that way while teaching in the old paradigm. The old paradigm of teaching assumes that the way we impart knowledge is to pour it into students' heads. Telling students what we know while students are bored and uninterested feels like Sisyphus rolling a boulder up a hill.

The next step was to break the knowledge being taught into small parts and take it up the hill a few parts at a time. This did not seem to increase the intellectual interest or involvement of students. If anything, it may have made the class even more boring. At that point we had to ask, *"Who is doing the hard intellectual work of conceptualizing, organizing, elaborating, presenting, summarizing, synthesizing, and reconceptualizing?"* If the answer is, *"The instructor,"* you know that everything is backwards. It is the students who are supposed to be doing the hard intellectual work in their courses. At that point we had to ask, *"Who is having the most fun?"* The answer may be, "No one." But if the answer is, *"The instructor,"* you know that everything is backwards. It is the students who are supposed to be enjoying the class.

We may not obtain the results we want with our teaching until we directly involved students in the learning process through cooperative learning groups. Instead of our rolling the rock up the hill only to have it slip from our grasp when we analyze the results of midterms and finals, we structure cooperative learning in our courses so that all students help to roll the boulder up the hill. When everyone, students as well as faculty, work together to roll the rock up the hill, then it does not slip from our grasp--it stays!

Johnson, D. W., Johnson, R., & Smith, K. (1998). **Active Learning: Cooperation In The College Classroom**. Edina, MN: Interaction Book Company. (612) 831-9500; FAX (612) 831-9332.

Formal Cooperative Learning Groups

Howard Eaton, an English professor at Douglas College in Vancouver, British Columbia introduces his course, **Argumentative Writing for College Students,** by stating to the students, *"You have paid for an opportunity to learn something, not a service. This is not a prison and it is not social entertainment of the useless and unemployable. This is work. Your tuition only pays for 15 percent of the cost for this course. Taxpayers fund the other 85 percent. You have, therefore, a social obligation that translates into two responsibilities:*

1. You are responsible for your own learning. It is up to you to learn something useful and interesting from this course.

*2. You are **equally** responsible for the learning of your groupmates. It is up to you to ensure that they learn something useful and interesting from this course."*

This introduction prepares students to do much of their work in formal cooperative learning groups. **Formal cooperative learning groups** last from a class session to several weeks. You may structure any academic assignment or course requirement for formal cooperative learning. It is the heart of using cooperative learning.

Instructor's Role: Being "A Guide On The Side"

At age 55, after his defeat by Woodrow Wilson for President of the United States, Teddy Roosevelt took a journey to South America. The Brazilian Government suggested he lead an expedition to explore a vast, unmapped river deep in the jungle. Known as the River of Doubt, it was believed to be a tributary to the Amazon.

2 : 2

Johnson, D. W., Johnson, R., & Smith, K. (1998). **Active Learning: Cooperation In The College Classroom.** Edina, MN: Interaction Book Company. (612) 831-9500; FAX (612) 831-9332.

Roosevelt accepted instantly. *"We will go down the unknown river,"* he declared, and the Brazilian government organized an expedition for the trip. *"I had to go,"* he said later, *"it was my last chance to be a boy."* Roosevelt, with his son Kermit and a party of eighteen, headed into the jungle. *"On February 27, 1914, shortly after midday, we started down the River of Doubt into the unknown,"* Roosevelt wrote. The journey was an ordeal. Hostile Indians harassed them. Five canoes were shattered and had to be rebuilt. Their food ran short and valuable equipment was lost. One man drowned when his canoe capsized. Another went berserk and killed a member of the expedition and then disappeared into the wilderness. Roosevelt, ill with fever, badly injured his leg when he tried to keep two capsized canoes from being smashed against rocks. Unable to walk, he had to be carried. Lying in a tent with an infected leg and a temperature of 105, he requested to be left behind. Ignoring such pleas, Kermit brought his father to safety with the help of the other members of the expedition. Teddy Roosevelt barely survived, but he and his companions accomplished their mission. The party mapped the 1000 mile River of Doubt and collected priceless specimens for the Museum of Natural History. The river was renamed in his honor, **Rio Theodore**.

An expedition such as Roosevelt's consists of four phases:

1. Making a series of pre-journey decisions about the number of people needed, the materials and equipment required, and the route to be taken.

2. Briefing all participants on the goals and objectives of the journey, emphasizing that members' survival depends on the joint efforts of all, and specifying the behaviors expected of members of the expedition.

3. Making the journey, carefully mapping the area traveled, and collecting the targeted specimens.

4. Reporting your findings to interested parties, reflecting on what went right and wrong with fellow members, and writing your memoirs.

Conducting a cooperative lesson is done in the same way. You, the instructor, make a number of preinstructional decisions, explain to students the instructional task and the cooperative nature of the lesson, conduct the lesson, and evaluate and process the results. More specifically, instructors:

1. **Make Preinstructional Decisions:** In every lesson you (a) formulate objectives, (b) decide on the size of groups, (c) choose a method for assigning students to groups, (d) decide which roles to assign group members, (e) arrange the room, and (f) arrange the materials students need to complete the assignment.

2. **Explain the Task and Cooperative Structure:** In every lesson you (a) explain the academic assignment to students, (b) explain the criteria for success, (c)

Johnson, D. W., Johnson, R., & Smith, K. (1998). **Active Learning: Cooperation In The College Classroom**. Edina, MN: Interaction Book Company. (612) 831-9500; FAX (612) 831-9332.

structure positive interdependence, (d) explain the individual accountability, and (e) explain the behaviors you expect to see during the lesson.

3. **Monitor and Intervene:** While you (a) conduct the lesson, you (b) monitor each learning group and (c) intervene when needed to improve taskwork and teamwork, and (d) bring closure to the lesson.

4. **Evaluate and Process:** You (a) assess and evaluate the quality and quantity of student achievement, (b) ensure students carefully process the effectiveness of their learning groups, (c) have students make a plan for improvement, and (d) have students celebrate the hard work of group members.

In each class session instructors must make the choice of being "a sage on the stage" or "a guide on the side." In doing so they might remember that **the challenge in teaching is not covering the material for the students, it's uncovering the material with the students.**

 # Preinstructional Decisions

Specifying the Instructional Objectives

The Roman philosopher Seneca once said, "*When you do not know to which port you are sailing, no wind is favorable*." The same may be said for teaching. To plan for a lesson you must know what the lesson is aimed at accomplishing. You need to specify **academic objectives** (based on a conceptual or task analysis) and **social skills objectives** that detail what interpersonal and small group skills you wish to emphasize during the lesson. You choose social skills by:

1. Monitoring the learning groups and diagnosing the specific skills needed to solve the problems students are having in working with each other.

2. Asking students to identify social skills that would improve their teamwork.

3. Keeping a list of social skills you teach to every class. The next one on the list becomes the skill emphasized in today's lesson.

4. Analyzing what social skills are required to complete the assignment.

The most sophisticated way to determine the social skills students need to complete a lesson is through creating a flow chart. A **Flow Chart** is a simple yet powerful visual tool to display all the steps in a process. Creating a flow chart involves six steps.

Johnson, D. W., Johnson, R., & Smith, K. (1998). **Active Learning: Cooperation In The College Classroom**. Edina, MN: Interaction Book Company. (612) 831-9500; FAX (612) 831-9332.

1. Define the boundaries of the learning process by specifying (a) the beginning and end and (b) the inputs and the outputs.

2. Identify all the steps the process actually follows (the key steps, who is involved, and who does what, when).

4. Observe what the group actually does.

3. Draw the steps in sequence.

5. Compare actual performance with the flow chart.

6. Either revise the flow chart or plan how to increase the quality of group members' engagement in each step.

Deciding on the Size of the Group

There is a folk saying about snowflakes. Each snowflake is so fragile and small. But when they stick together, it is amazing what they can do. The same is true for people. When we work together, there is no limit to human ingenuity and potential. For students to work together, they must be assigned to groups. To assign students to groups, you must decide (a) how large a group should be, (b) how students should be assigned to a group, (c) how long the groups will exist, and (d) what combination of groups will be used in the lesson.

While cooperative learning groups typically range in size from two to four, **the basic rule of thumb is**: "*The smaller the better*." There is, however, no ideal size for a cooperative learning group. A common mistake is to have students work in groups of four, five, and six members before the students have the skills to do so competently. In selecting the size of a cooperative learning group, remember this advice:

> **Group Size Depends On "Team"**
>
> **T** = Time Limits
>
> **E** = Students' Experience In Working In Groups
>
> **A** = Students' Age
>
> **M** = Materials And Equipment Available

1. **With the addition of each group member, the resources to help the group succeed increase.** As the size of the learning group increases, so does (a) the range of abilities, expertise, skills, (b) the number of minds available for acquiring and processing information, and (c) the diversity of viewpoints.

2 : 5

Johnson, D. W., Johnson, R., & Smith, K. (1998). **Active Learning: Cooperation In The College Classroom**. Edina, MN: Interaction Book Company. (612) 831-9500; FAX (612) 831-9332.

2. **The shorter the period of time available, the smaller the learning group should be.** If there is only a brief period of time available for the lesson, then smaller groups such as pairs will be more effective because they take less time to get organized, they operate faster, and there is more "air time" per member.

3. **The smaller the group, the more difficult it is for students to hide and not contribute their share of the work.** Small groups increase the visibility of students' efforts and thereby make them more accountable.

4. **The larger the group, the more skillful group members must be.** In a pair, students have to manage two interactions. In a group of three, there are six interactions to manage. In a group of four, there are twelve interactions to manage. As the size of the group increases, the interpersonal and small group skills required to manage the interactions among group members become far more complex and sophisticated.

THE GROUP SIZE WHEEL

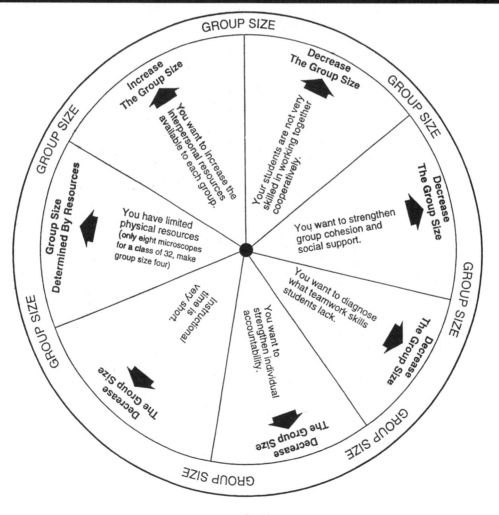

2 : 6

Johnson, D. W., Johnson, R., & Smith, K. (1998). **Active Learning: Cooperation In The College Classroom**. Edina, MN: Interaction Book Company. (612) 831-9500; FAX (612) 831-9332.

5. **The larger the group, the less the interaction among members.** What results is less group cohesion, fewer friendships, and less personal support.

6. **The materials available or the specific nature of the task may dictate a group size.** When you have ten computers and thirty students, you may wish to assign students to groups of three. When the task is practice tennis, group size of two seems natural.

7. **The smaller the group, the easier it is to identify any difficulties students have in working together.** Problems in leadership, unresolved conflicts among group members, issues over power and control, tendencies such as sitting back and waiting for others to do the work, and other problems students have in working together are more visible and apparent when groups are small. Groups need to be small enough to ensure all students are actively involved and participating equally.

Assigning Students to Groups

Sic parvis magna (Great things have small beginnings).

Sir Francis Drake's Motto

There is no ideal group membership. What determines a group's productivity is not who its members are, but rather how well the members work together. There may be times when you may use cooperative learning groups that are homogeneous in ability to teach specific skills or to achieve certain instructional objectives. Generally, however, there are advantages to heterogeneous groups in which students come from diverse backgrounds and have different abilities, experiences, and interests:

1. Students are exposed to a variety of ideas, multiple perspectives, and different problem-solving methods.

2. Students generate more cognitive disequilibrium, which stimulates learning, creativity, and cognitive and social development.

3. Students engage in more elaborative thinking, give and receive more explanations, and engage in more frequent perspective-taking in discussing material, all of which increase the depth of understanding, the quality of reasoning, and the accuracy of long-term retention.

To make groups heterogeneous, you assign students to groups using a random or stratified random procedure. Instructor selected groups can be either homogeneous or heterogeneous. When students select their own groups they usually form homogeneous ones. Each of these methods is explained below.

Johnson, D. W., Johnson, R., & Smith, K. (1998). **Active Learning: Cooperation In The College Classroom**. Edina, MN: Interaction Book Company. (612) 831-9500; FAX (612) 831-9332.

Random Assignment

The easiest and most effective way to assign students to group is randomly. You divide the number of students in your class by the size of the group desired. If you wish to have groups of three and you have thirty students in your class, you divide thirty by three. You have students number off by the result (e.g., ten). Students with the same number find each other (all one's get together, all two's get together, and so forth). David's favorite variation is to have students count off in a different language (e.g., English, Spanish, French, Hungarian) each time they are assigned to groups.

Literature Characters	Geographical Areas
Give students cards with the names of characters in the literature they recently have read. Ask them to group with characters from the same story, play, or poem. Examples are Romeo and Juliet; Captain Hook, Peter Pan and Wendy; and Hansel, Gretel, Witch, and Step-Mother.	List a number of countries or states and have students group themselves according to most preferred to visit. Variations include grouping according to least preferred to visit, similar in terms of climate, similar in geological features, having the same exports, and so forth.
Math Method	**States and Capitols**
There are endless variations to the math method of assigning students to groups. The basic structure is to give each student a math problem and ask them to (a) solve their problem, (b) find the classmates whose problems have the same answer, and (c) form a group. This may vary from simple addition in the first grade to complex equations in high school classes. Thus, to form a group of three, you may distribute the following three equations throughout the class $(3 + 3 = \_)$, $(4 + 2 = \_)$, $(5 + 1 = \_)$.	To assign students to groups of two or four, divide the number of students in the class by two (30 divided by 2 = 15). Pick a geographic area of the U.S. and write out on cards the names of 15 states. Then on another set of cards write out the names of their capitol cities. Shuffle the cards and pass them out to students. Then have the students find the classmate who has the matching state or capitol. To form groups of four, have two adjacent states and their capitols combine.

Stratified Random Assignment

A related procedure is stratified random assignment. This is the same as random assignment except that you choose one (or two) characteristics of students (such as reading level, learning style, task-orientation, or personal interest) and make sure that one

Johnson, D. W., Johnson, R., & Smith, K. (1998). **Active Learning: Cooperation In The College Classroom.** Edina, MN: Interaction Book Company. (612) 831-9500; FAX (612) 831-9332.

or more students in each group have that characteristic. To assign students to learning groups randomly, stratifying for achievement level, use the following procedure.

1. Rank order students from highest to lowest in terms of a pretest on the unit, a recent past test, past grades, or your best guess as a instructor.

2. Select the first group by choosing the highest student, the lowest student, and the two middle achievers. Assign them to the group unless they are all of one sex, they do not reflect the ethnic composition of the class, they are worst enemies, or they are best friends. If any of these is true, move up or down one student from the middle to readjust. (You may modify the procedure to assign students to groups of three or two members.)

3. Select the remaining groups by repeating the above procedure with the reduced list. If there are students left over, make one or two groups of three members.

There is a danger in assigning students to groups on the basis of certain characteristics. If you form groups so that there is a white male, a white female, a black male, and a black female in every group, for example, you are giving the class a clear message that gender and ethnicity are important factors to you as a instructor. Making these categories salient may cue students' stereotypes and prejudices. **The general rule is: If you assign students to groups based on categories, make them unique categories needed to complete the group task** (such as summarizer, creative thinker, time keeper, and library expert). As a instructor, you tell students, "*In your groups there is a creative thinker, a person who is good at keeping track of time, someone who knows how to use the library, and someone who is good at summarizing all the ideas suggested in the group. To complete this assignment, you will need the resources of each member.*" By emphasizing the personal abilities and talents of students rather than their social categories, you focus students on the person, not the social group.

Preferences

Have students write their favorite sport to participate in on a slip of paper. Then have them find groupmates who like to participate in the same sport. Variations include favorite food, celebrity, skill, car, president, animal, vegetable, fairy tale character, and so forth.

Instructor Selected Groups

You, the instructor, can decide who is going to work with whom. You can ensure that nonachievement-oriented students are a minority in each group or that students who trigger disruptive behavior in each other are not together. **One of our favorite methods is creating support groups for each isolated student.** You ask students to list three

2 : 9

Johnson, D. W., Johnson, R., & Smith, K. (1998). **Active Learning: Cooperation In The College Classroom**. Edina, MN: Interaction Book Company. (612) 831-9500; FAX (612) 831-9332.

classmates with whom they would like to work. From their lists, you tally for each student the number of times classmates chose the student. You can then identify the classroom isolates (students who are not chosen by any of their classmates). These are the "at-risk" students who need your help. You take the most socially isolated student and assign two of the most skillful, popular, supportive, and caring students in the class to work with him or her. Then you take the second most isolated student and do the same. In this way you optimize the likelihood that the isolated students will become involved in the learning activities and build positive relationships with classmates. You want to ensure that in your classes, no student is left out, rejected, or believes that he or she does not belong.

Self-Selected Groups

The least recommended procedure is to have students select their own groups. Student-selected groups often are homogeneous with high-achieving students working with other high-achieving students, white students working with other white students, minority students working with other minority students, and males working with other males. Often there is more off-task behavior in student-selected than in instructor-selected groups. A useful modification of the "select your own group" method is to have students list whom they would like to work with and then place them in a learning group with one person they choose and one or two or more students that the instructor selects.

Length Of Group Life

A common concern is, "*How long should cooperative learning groups stay together?*" The type of cooperative learning group you use determines one answer to this question. Base groups last for at least one and ideally for several years. Informal cooperative learning groups last for only a few minutes or at most one class period. For formal cooperative learning groups there is no formula or simple answer to this question. Groups usually stay together to complete a task, unit, or chapter. During a course every student should work with every other classmate. Groups should stay together long enough to be successful. Breaking up groups that are having trouble functioning effectively is often counterproductive; students do not have the opportunity to learn the skills they need to resolve problems in collaborating with each other.

Using Combinations Of Cooperative Learning Groups

In many lessons you will want to use a combination of formal and informal cooperative learning groups as well as base groups. You will use more than one size group in any one lesson. You will need ways to assign students to new groups quickly. You will need procedures for making transitions among groups, moving students from pairs to fours to pairs to threes and so forth. It sometimes helps to have timed drills on how fast students can move from a formal cooperative learning group to an informal pair and then back to their formal group.

Johnson, D. W., Johnson, R., & Smith, K. (1998). **Active Learning: Cooperation In The College Classroom**. Edina, MN: Interaction Book Company. (612) 831-9500; FAX (612) 831-9332.

Assigning Roles to Ensure Interdependence

In planning the lesson, you think through what are the actions that need to occur to maximize student learning. **Roles** prescribe what other group members expect from a student (and therefore what the student is obligated to do) and what that person has a right to expect from other group members who have complementary roles. There is a progression for using roles to structure cooperative efforts:

1. Do not assign roles to let students get used to working together.

2. Assign only very simple roles to students such as forming roles or the roles of reader, recorder, and encourager of participation. Rotate the roles so that each group member plays each one several times.

3. Add to the rotation a new role that is slightly more sophisticated, such as checker-for-understanding. You assign the functioning roles at this point.

IDENTIFYING THE VARIOUS TYPES OF ROLES

Form a pair. For each type of skill there are two examples of the roles that may be assigned to ensure students work together effectively. In column one, write the letters of the two roles that teach the skill.

	SKILLS	ROLES
	Forming Skills	a. Encouraging everyone to participate
		b. Use quiet voices
	Functioning Skills	c. Relating new learning to previous learning
		d. Criticizing ideas, not people
	Formulating Skills	e. Stay with your group
		f. Changing mind only if logically persuaded
	Fermenting Skills	g. Explaining step-by-step one's reasoning
		h. Giving one's ideas and conclusions

Johnson, D. W., Johnson, R., & Smith, K. (1998). **Active Learning: Cooperation In The College Classroom**. Edina, MN: Interaction Book Company. (612) 831-9500; FAX (612) 831-9332.

4. Over time add formulating and fermenting roles that do not occur naturally in the group, such as elaborator. Students typically do not relate what they are learning to what they already know until you specifically train them to do so.

First, roles can be sequenced so that more and more complex and difficult roles are assigned to students each week, month, and year. Initially, students may need to be assigned roles that help them form the group. Second, roles may be assigned that help the group function well in achieving learning goals and maintaining good working relationships among members. Third, roles may be assigned that help students formulate what they are learning and create conceptual frameworks. Finally, roles may be assigned that help students ferment each other's thinking. It is at this point that cognitive and social roles merge. The social skills represented by the roles should be taught like a spiral curriculum with a more complex version of the skill taught every year.

Solving And Preventing Problems In Working Together

At times there are students who refuse to participate in a cooperative group or who do not understand how to help the group succeed. You can solve and prevent such problems when you give each group member a specific role to play in the group. Assigning appropriate roles may be used to:

1. Reduce problems such as one or more members' making no contribution to the group or one member dominating the group.

2. Ensure that vital group skills are enacted in the group and that group members learn targeted skills.

3. Create interdependence among group members. You structure **role interdependence** by assigning members complementary, interconnected roles.

Arranging the Room

The design and arrangement of classroom space and furniture communicates what is appropriate behavior and what learning activities will take place. Desks in a row communicate a different message and expectation than desks grouped in small circles. Spatial design also defines the circulation patterns in the classroom. **Circulation** is the flow of movement into, out of, and within the classroom. It is movement through space. You determine what students see, when they see it, and with whom students interact by the way you design your classroom.

No single classroom arrangement will meet the requirements of all lessons. Reference points and well-defined boundaries of work spaces are needed to move students from rows to triads to pairs to fours to rows. Color, form, and lighting (a) focus students'

Johnson, D. W., Johnson, R., & Smith, K. (1998). **Active Learning: Cooperation In The College Classroom.** Edina, MN: Interaction Book Company. (612) 831-9500; FAX (612) 831-9332.

visual attention on points of emphasis in the classroom (the learning group, you, instructional materials) and (b) define the territorial boundaries of workspaces. You define boundaries by:

1. **Using labels and signs** that designate areas.

2. **Using colors** to attract visual attention and define group and individual spaces as well as different storage areas and resource centers.

IMPORTANCE OF CLASSROOM DESIGN

Form a pair. Rank order the following outcomes of classroom design from most important ("1") to least important ("9").

	Students' academic achievement. The way in which interior space is designed influences the amount of time students spend on task and other variables affecting achievement.
	Students' visual and auditory focus. The way in which interior space is designed creates overall visual order, focuses visual attention, and controls acoustics.
	Students' participation in learning groups and activities. Classroom design influences the patterns of student (and instructor) participation in instructional activities, the emergence of leadership in learning groups, and the patterns of communication among students and between students and instructors.
	Opportunities for social contact and friendships among students.
	Learning climate. The design of interior space affects students and instructors' feelings (such as comfort, enjoyment, well-being, anger, depression) and general morale. Good spatial definition helps students feel secure by delineating structured learning areas.
	Classroom management. Spatial definition prevents discipline problems by defining how and where students work, how to interact with others, and how to move through the classroom.
	Students ease of access to each other, instructors, learning materials.
	Students ability to make quick transitions from one grouping to another.
	Instructors movement from group to group to monitor student interaction carefully during the lesson.

Johnson, D. W., Johnson, R., & Smith, K. (1998). **Active Learning: Cooperation In The College Classroom**. Edina, MN: Interaction Book Company. (612) 831-9500; FAX (612) 831-9332.

3. **Taping lines** on the floor or wall to define the different work areas.

4. **Using mobiles and forms** (such as arrows) taped on the wall or hanging from the ceiling to direct attention. You can designate work areas by hanging mobiles from the ceiling.

5. **Using lighting** to define specific work areas. Directed light (illuminating part of the room while leaving other areas dim) intensifies and directs students' attention. Brightly lit areas can draw people toward the areas and suggest activity. More dimly lit areas surrounding the lighted ones become area boundaries. As the activity in the classroom changes, the lighting could also change.

6. **Moving furniture** to define work and resource areas. Even tall plants, when placed in pots with wheels, can be moved to provide spatial boundaries.

You can use many of these same procedures to control the level of noise in the classroom.

Planning the Instructional Materials

The types of task students are required to complete determine what materials are needed for the lesson. You, the instructor, decide how materials are to be arranged and distributed among group members to maximize their participation and achievement. Usually, you will wish to distribute materials to communicate that the assignment is to be a joint (not an individual) effort. You create:

1. **Materials interdependence** by giving each group only one copy of the materials. The students will then have to work together in order to be successful. This is especially effective the first few times the group meets. After students are accustomed to working cooperatively, instructors can give a copy of the materials to each student.

2. **Information interdependence** by arranging materials like a jigsaw puzzle so that each student has part of the materials needed to complete the assignment. Each group member can receive different resource materials to be synthesized. Such procedures require that every member participate for the group to be successful.

3. **Interdependence from outside enemies** by structuring materials into an intergroup tournament format and having groups compete to see who has learned the most. Such a procedure was introduced by DeVries and Edwards (1973). In the Teams-Games-Tournament format, students are divided into heterogeneous cooperative learning teams to prepare members for a tournament in which they compete with the other teams. During the intergroup competition the students individually compete against members of about the same ability level from other

Johnson, D. W., Johnson, R., & Smith, K. (1998). **Active Learning: Cooperation In The College Classroom**. Edina, MN: Interaction Book Company. (612) 831-9500; FAX (612) 831-9332.

teams. The team whose members do the best in the competition is pronounced the winner by the instructor.

EXPLAINING THE TASK: FLOW CHART

1. Explain the assignment. The assignment needs to be a clear, measurable task.

2. Explain lesson objectives to ensure transfer and retention. Objectives may be stated as outcomes--*"At the end of this lesson you will be able to explain the causes of the French and Indian War."*

4. Explain the procedures students are to follow in completing the assignment.

3. Explain the concepts, principles, and strategies students need to use during the lesson and relate them to students' past experience and learning.

5. Require a visible product that each student signs. This keeps students on task and helps ensure they will behave responsibly.

6. Ask class members specific questions to check their understanding of the assignment.

7. Ask students to answer in pairs or triads the questions the lesson will focus on to (a) establish expectations about what the lesson will cover and (b) organize in advance what they know about the topic.

Johnson, D. W., Johnson, R., & Smith, K. (1998). **Active Learning: Cooperation In The College Classroom**. Edina, MN: Interaction Book Company. (612) 831-9500; FAX (612) 831-9332.

 Structuring Task & Cooperative Structure

Explaining the Academic Task

At this point you have planned your lesson by making the preinstructional decisions and preparations. The next step is to face your class and inform them of (a) what to do to complete the assignment and (b) how to do it. The steps are explained on the flow chart on the previous page.

Explaining Criteria for Success

Grade	Percent Correct
A	95 – 100
B	85 – 94
C	75 – 84
D	65 – 74
F	Less Than 64

While explaining to students the academic task they are to complete, you need to communicate the level of performance you expect of students. Cooperative learning requires criterion-based evaluation. **Criterion-referenced or categorical judgments** are made by adopting a fixed set of standards and judging the achievement of each student against these standards. A common version of criterion-referenced grading involves assigning letter grades on the basis of the percentage of test items answered correctly. Or you might say, *"The group is not finished until every member has demonstrated mastery."* Sometimes improvement (doing better this week than one did last week) may be set as the criterion of excellence. To promote intergroup cooperation, you may also set criteria for the whole class to reach. *"If we as a class can score over 520 words correct on our vocabulary test, each student will receive two bonus points."*

Structuring Positive Interdependence

Positive goal interdependence exists when a mutually/joint goal is established so that individuals perceive they can attain their goals if and only if their groupmates attain their goals (see Johnson & Johnson, 1992b, 1992c). Members know that they cannot succeed unless all other members of their group succeed. Positive interdependence is the heart of cooperative learning. Without positive interdependence, cooperation does not exist. Students must believe that they are in a "sink or swim together" learning situation.

First, you structure positive goal interdependence. Every cooperative lesson begins with positive goal interdependence. To ensure that students think "**We, not me**" you (the instructor) say to students, *"You have three responsibilities. You are responsible for learning the assigned material. You are responsible for making sure that all other members of your group learn the assigned material. And you are responsible for making sure that all other class members successfully learn the assigned material."*

Johnson, D. W., Johnson, R., & Smith, K. (1998). **Active Learning: Cooperation In The College Classroom**. Edina, MN: Interaction Book Company. (612) 831-9500; FAX (612) 831-9332.

Second, you supplement positive goal interdependence with other types of positive interdependence (such as reward, role, resource, or identity). Positive reward interdependence, for example, may be structured through providing group rewards--*"If all members of your group score above 90 percent on the test, each of you will receive five bonus points."* Usually, the more ways positive interdependence is structured in a lesson, the better.

Positive interdependence creates peer encouragement and support for learning. Such positive peer pressure influences underachieving students to become academically involved. Members of cooperative learning groups should give two interrelated messages, *"Do your work--we're counting on you!"* and *"How can I help you to do better?"*

Structuring Individual Accountability

In cooperative groups, everyone has to do his or her fair share of the work. **An underlying purpose of cooperative learning is to make each group member a stronger individual in his or her own right.** This is accomplished by holding all members accountable to learn the assigned material and help other group members learn. You do this by:

1. Assessing the performance of each individual member.

2. Giving the results back to the individual and the group to compare to preset criteria. The feedback enables members to (a) recognize and celebrate efforts to learn and contributions to groupmates' learning, (b) provide immediate remediation and any needed assistance or encouragement, and (c) reassign responsibilities to avoid any redundant efforts by members.

Individual accountability results in group members knowing they cannot "hitch-hike" on the work of others, loaf, or get a free ride. **Ways of ensuring individual accountability** include keeping group size small, giving an individual test to each student, giving random individual oral examinations, observing and recording the frequency with which each member contributes to the group's work, having students teach what they know to someone else, and having students use what they have learned on different problems.

Structuring Intergroup Cooperation

You can extend the positive outcomes resulting from cooperative learning throughout a whole class by structuring intergroup cooperation. You establish class goals as well as group and individual goals. When a group finishes its work, you encourage members to find other groups (a) who are not finished and help them understand how to complete the assignment successfully or (b) who are finished and compare answers and strategies.

Johnson, D. W., Johnson, R., & Smith, K. (1998). **Active Learning: Cooperation In The College Classroom**. Edina, MN: Interaction Book Company. (612) 831-9500; FAX (612) 831-9332.

Specifying Desired Behaviors

When you use cooperative learning you must teach students the small group and interpersonal skills they need to work effectively with each other. In cooperative learning groups, students must learn both academic subject matter (**taskwork**) and the interpersonal and small group skills required to work as part of a group (**teamwork**). Cooperative learning is inherently more complex than competitive or individualistic learning because students have to simultaneously engage in taskwork and teamwork. If students do not learn the teamwork skills, then they cannot complete the taskwork. The greater the members' teamwork skills, the higher will be the quality and quantity of their learning. **You define the needed teamwork skills operationally by specifying the behaviors that are appropriate and desirable within learning groups**. How to do so is discussed at length in Chapter Five.

Three rules-of-thumb in specifying desired behaviors are as follows. **Be specific.** Operationally define each social skill through the use of a "T-Chart" (see Chapter 5). **Start small.** Do not overload your students with more social skills than they can learn at one time. One or two behaviors to emphasize for a few lessons is enough. Students need to know what behavior is appropriate and desirable within a cooperative learning group, but they should not be subjected to information overload. **Emphasize overlearning.** Having students practice skills once or twice is not enough. Keep emphasizing a skill until the students have integrated it into their behavioral repertoires and do it automatically and habitually.

The Cooperative Lesson

During the lesson students work together to complete the assignment. Their actions can be loosely or highly prescribed by explicit scripts (Johnson & Johnson, 1994). At the highest level of implementation you (the instructor) learn an **expert system** consisting of the five basic elements and the instructor's role and use it to create lessons uniquely tailored for your students, curriculum, needs, and teaching circumstances. Expertise in using cooperative learning is based on a conceptual, metacognitive understanding of its nature.

Besides implementing an expert system, there are other ways to implement cooperative lessons. **Group investigation** (Sharan & Hertz-Lazarowitz, 1980), in which students form cooperative groups according to common interests in a topic. All group members help plan how to research their topic. Then they divide the work. Each group member carries out his or her part of the investigation. The group synthesizes its work and presents these findings to the class.

Johnson, D. W., Johnson, R., & Smith, K. (1998). **Active Learning: Cooperation In The College Classroom**. Edina, MN: Interaction Book Company. (612) 831-9500; FAX (612) 831-9332.

You may use highly structured scripts, structures, and curriculum packages that are implemented in a prescribed lockstep manner. Dansereau (1985) and his colleagues have developed a number of **cooperative scripts** that structure student interaction as they work together. Kagan (1988) has identified a number of **cooperative learning structures**--ways of organizing the interaction of students by prescribing student behavior step-by-step to complete the assignment. **Cooperative curriculum packages** include Teams-Games-Tournament (TGT), a combination of ingroup cooperation, intergroup competition, and instructional games (DeVries & Edwards, 1974). Students then meet in cooperative learning teams of four or five members (a mixture of high, medium, and low achievers) to complete a set of worksheets on the lesson. Students then play academic games as representatives of their teams. Who competes with whom is modified each week to ensure that students compete with classmates who achieve at a similar level. The highest scoring teams are publicly recognized in a weekly class newsletter. Grades are given on the basis of individual performance. **Student Team Learning** (STAD) (Slavin, 1980) is a modification of TGT that has students take a weekly quiz instead of playing an academic game. **Team-Assisted-Individualization** (TAI) is a highly individualized math curriculum for grades 3 to 6 in which students work individualistically to complete math assignments using self-instructional (programmed learning) curriculum materials (Slavin, 1985). **Cooperative Integrated Reading And Composition** (CIRC) consists of a set of curriculum materials to supplement basal readers and ensure that cooperative learning is applied to reading, writing, spelling, and language mechanics (Stevens, Madden, Slavin, & Farnish, 1987).

During the lesson students work together to complete the assignment. Using cooperative learning effectively is an art based on engineering lessons so that they include the five basic elements. There are, however, standard procedures that can be used over and over again that provide a pattern and flow to classroom life. A class session, for example, can include the following cooperative procedures:

1. Checking homework.

2. Engaging in discussions.

3. Taking notes.

4. Reading assigned material (Read and Explain Pairs, Reading Comprehension Triads, Jigsaw).

5. Drilling and reviewing.

6. Writing compositions.

7. Resolving intellectual conflicts.

8. Conducting projects.

2 : 19

Johnson, D. W., Johnson, R., & Smith, K. (1998). **Active Learning: Cooperation In The College Classroom**. Edina, MN: Interaction Book Company. (612) 831-9500; FAX (612) 831-9332.

CHECKING HOMEWORK

Task: Students are to bring their completed homework to class and understand how to do it correctly.

Cooperative: Students meet in their cooperative base groups that are heterogeneous in terms of math and reading ability to ensure that all group members understand how to complete all parts of the assignment correctly.

Procedure:

1. At the beginning of class students meet in cooperative base groups.

2. One member of each group, **the runner**, goes to the instructor's desk, picks up the group's folder, and hands out any materials in the folder to the appropriate members.

3. The group reviews the assignment step-by-step to determine how much of the assignment each member completed and how well each member understands how to complete the material covered. Two roles are utilized: **Explainer** (explains step-by-step how the homework is correctly completed) and **accuracy checker** (verifies that the explanation is accurate, encourages, and provides coaching if needed). The role of explainer is rotated so that each member takes turns explaining step-by-step how a portion of the homework is correctly completed. The other members are accuracy checkers. The base groups concentrate on clarifying the parts of the assignment that one or more members do not understand.

4. At the end of the review the runner records how much of the assignment each member completed, places members' homework in the group's folder, and returns the folder to the instructor's desk.

Expected Criteria For Success: All group members understand how to complete each part of the assignment correctly.

Individual Accountability: Regular examinations and daily randomly selecting group members to explain how to solve randomly selected problems from the homework.

Alternative Of Directed Homework Review: Students are assigned to pairs. Instructor randomly picks questions from the homework assignment. One student explains step-by-step the correct answer. The other student listens, checks for accuracy, and prompts the explainer if he or she does not know the answer. Roles are switched for each question.

Johnson, D. W., Johnson, R., & Smith, K. (1998). **Active Learning: Cooperation In The College Classroom**. Edina, MN: Interaction Book Company. (612) 831-9500; FAX (612) 831-9332.

TURN TO YOUR NEIGHBOR SUMMARIES

A common practice in most classrooms is to hold a "whole-class discussion." You choose one student or a student volunteers to answer a question or provide a summary of what the lesson has covered so far. The student doing the explaining has an opportunity to clarify and extend what he or she knows through being actively involved in the learning process. The rest of the class is passive. You (the instructor) may ensure that all students are actively learning (and no one is passive) by requiring all students to explain their answers or to summarize simultaneously through the formulate, share, listen, and create procedure.

1. The task for students is to explain their answers and reasoning to a classmate and practice the skill of explaining. The cooperative goal is to create a joint answer that both members agree to and can explain.

2. **Students formulate an answer to a question** that requires them to summarize what the lesson has covered so far.

3. Students turn to a neighbor (classmate class by) and share their answers and reasoning.

4. **Students listen carefully to their partner's explanation**. They should take notes, nod their head, smile, and encourage their partner to explain the answer and reasoning in detail.

5. **The pair creates a new answer that is superior to their initial formulations** through the processes of association, building on each other's thoughts, and synthesizing.

6. The instructor monitors the pairs and assists students in following the procedure. To ensure individual accountability, you may wish to ask randomly selected students to explain the joint answer they created with their partner.

FORMULATE, SHARE, LISTEN, CREATE

Johnson, D. W., Johnson, R., & Smith, K. (1998). **Active Learning: Cooperation In The College Classroom**. Edina, MN: Interaction Book Company. (612) 831-9500; FAX (612) 831-9332.

READ AND EXPLAIN PAIRS

Whenever you give material to students to read, students may read it more effectively in cooperative pairs than individually.

1. Assign students to pairs (one high reader and one low reader in each pair. Tell students what specific pages you wish them to read. The **expected criterion for success** is that both members are able to explain the meaning of the assigned material correctly.

2. The **task** is to learn the material being read by establishing the meaning of each paragraph and integrating the meaning of the paragraphs. The cooperative goal is for both members to agree on the meaning of each paragraph, formulate a joint summary, and be able to explain its meaning to the instructor.

3. The **procedure** the student pairs follow is:

   a. Read all the headings to get an overview.

   b. Both students silently read the first paragraph. Student A is initially the **summarizer** and Student Be is the **accuracy checker**. Students rotate the roles after each paragraph.

   c. The **summarizer** summarizes in his or her own words the content of the paragraph to his or her partner.

   d. The **accuracy checker** listens carefully, corrects any misstatements, and adds anything left out. Then he or she tells how the material relates to something they already know.

   e. The students move on to the next paragraph, switch roles, and repeat the procedure. They continue until they have read all the assignment. They summarize and agree on the overall meaning of the assigned material.

4. During the lesson you (the instructor) systematically (a) monitor each reading pair and assist students in following the procedure, (b) ensure **individual accountability** by randomly asking students to summarize what they have read so far, and (c) remind students that there is **intergroup cooperation** (whenever it is helpful they may check procedures, answers, and strategies with another group or compare answers with those of another group if they finish early).

Johnson, D. W., Johnson, R., & Smith, K. (1998). **Active Learning: Cooperation In The College Classroom**. Edina, MN: Interaction Book Company. (612) 831-9500; FAX (612) 831-9332.

READING COMPREHENSION TRIADS

Tasks:

1. Read the (poem, chapter, story, handout) and answer the questions.
2. Practice the skill of checking.

Cooperative:

1. One set of answers from the group, everyone has to agree, everyone has to be able to explain each answer.
2. If all members score 90 percent or better on the test, each member will receive 5 bonus points.
3. To facilitate the group's work, each member is assigned a role: Reader, recorder, checker.

Expected Criteria For Success: Everyone must be able to answer each question correctly.

Individual Accountability:

1. One member from your group will be randomly chosen to explain the group's answers.
2. A test will be given on the assigned reading that each member takes individually.
3. Each group member will be required to explain the group's answers to a member of another group.

Expected Behaviors: Active participating, checking, encouraging, and elaborating by all members.

Intergroup Cooperation: Whenever it is helpful, check procedures, answers, and strategies with another group. When you are finished, compare your answers with those of another group and discuss.

Johnson, D. W., Johnson, R., & Smith, K. (1998). **Active Learning: Cooperation In The College Classroom**. Edina, MN: Interaction Book Company. (612) 831-9500; FAX (612) 831-9332.

JIGSAW PROCEDURE

Whenever there is material you wish to present to a class or you wish students to read, the jigsaw method is an alternative to lecture and individual reading. You assign students to cooperative groups, give all groups the same topic, and take the material and divide it into parts like a jigsaw puzzle so that each student has part of the materials needed to complete the assignment. You give each member one unique section of the topic to learn and then teach to the other members of the group. Members study the topic and teach their part to the rest of the group. The group synthesizes the presentations of the members into the whole picture. In studying the life of Sojourner Truth (a black abolitionist and women's rights activist), for example, you give one student material on Truth's childhood, another material on her middle life, and another material on the final years of her life. Group members, therefore, cannot learn her total life unless all members teach their parts. In a jigsaw each student then has to participate actively in order for his or her group to be successful. The **task** for students is to learn all the assigned material. The **cooperative goal** is for each member to ensure that everyone in their group learn all the assigned material. The **Jigsaw Procedure** is as follows:

1. **Cooperative Groups:** Assign students to cooperative groups (you usually use groups of three, but you may jigsaw materials for groups of any size). Distribute a set of materials to each group so that each group gets one part of the materials. The set needs to be divisible into the number of members of the group. Number each part (Part 1, Part 2, Part 3).

2. **Preparation Pairs:** Ask students to form a preparation pair with a member of another group who has the same part they do (a pair of Part 1's, a pair of Part 2's, a pair of Part 3's). Students have two tasks:

   a. Learning and becoming an expert on their part of the lesson materials.

   b. Planning how to teach their part of the material to the other members of their groups.

   Students are to read their part of the material together, using the pair reading procedure of (a) both students silently read each paragraph (or "chunk"), (b) one student summarizes its meaning while the other student checks the summary for accuracy, and (c) the students reverse roles after each paragraph. In doing so pair members should list the

Johnson, D. W., Johnson, R., & Smith, K. (1998). **Active Learning: Cooperation In The College Classroom**. Edina, MN: Interaction Book Company. (612) 831-9500; FAX (612) 831-9332.

major points they wish to teach, list practical advice related to major points, prepare a visual aid to help them teach the content, and prepare procedures to make the other members of their group active, not passive, learners. The **cooperative goal** is to create one teaching plan for the two members that both members are able to teach. Both members need their individual copy of the plan.

3. **Practice Pairs:** Ask students to form a practice pair with a member of another group who has the same part they do but who was in a different preparation pair. The **tasks** are for the members to practice teaching their part of the assigned material, listen carefully the their partner's practice, and incorporate the best ideas from the other's presentation into their own. The **cooperative goal** is to ensure that both members are practiced and ready to teach.

4. **Cooperative Groups:** Students return to their cooperative groups. Their tasks are to:

    a. Teach their area of expertise to the other group members.

    b. Learn the material being taught by the other members.

    The **cooperative goal** is to ensure that members master all parts of the assigned material.

5. **Monitoring:** While the pairs and the cooperative groups work, you systematically move from group to group and assist students in following the procedures.

6. **Evaluation:** Assess students' degree of mastery of all the material by giving a test on all the material that students take individually. You may wish to give members of groups whose members all score 90 percent or above five bonus points.

2 : 25

Johnson, D. W., Johnson, R., & Smith, K. (1998). **Active Learning: Cooperation In The College Classroom**. Edina, MN: Interaction Book Company. (612) 831-9500; FAX (612) 831-9332.

DRILL-REVIEW PAIRS

There are times during a lesson that you may wish to have students review what they have previously learned and drill on certain procedures to ensure that they are overlearned. When you do so, cooperative learning is indispensable.

Task: Correctly solve the problems or engage in the procedures.

Cooperative: The mutual goal is to ensure that both pair members understand the strategies and procedures required to solve the problems correctly. The instructor assigns two roles: *Explainer* (explains step-by-step how to solve the problem) and *accuracy checker* (verifies that the explanation is accurate, encourages, and provides coaching if needed). Students rotate the two roles after each problem.

Individual Accountability: The instructor randomly chooses one member to explain how to solve a randomly selected problem.

Procedure: The instructor assigns (a) students to pairs and (b) assigns each pair to a foursome. The instructor then implements the following procedure:

1. Person A reads the problem and explains step-by-step the procedures and strategies required to solve it. Person B checks the accuracy of the solution and provides encouragement and coaching.

2. Person B solves the second problem, describing step-by-step the procedures and strategies required to solve it. Person A checks the accuracy of the solution and provides encouragement and coaching.

3. When the pair completes the problems, members check their answers with another pair. If they do not agree, they resolve the problem until there is consensus about the answer. If they do agree, they thank each other and continue work in their pairs.

4. The procedure continues until all problems are completed.

Johnson, D. W., Johnson, R., & Smith, K. (1998). **Active Learning: Cooperation In The College Classroom.** Edina, MN: Interaction Book Company. (612) 831-9500; FAX (612) 831-9332.

COOPERATIVE WRITING AND EDITING PAIRS

When your lesson includes students writing an essay, report, poem, story, or review of what they have read, you should use cooperative writing and editing pairs.

Tasks: Write a composition and edit other students' compositions.

Criteria For Success: A well-written composition by each student. Depending on the instructional objectives, the compositions may be evaluated for grammar, punctuation, organization, content, or other criteria set by the instructor.

Cooperative Goal: All group members must verify that each member's composition is perfect according to the criteria set by the instructor. Students receive an individual score on the quality of their compositions. You can also give a group score based on the total number of errors made by the pair (the number of errors in their composition plus the number of errors in their partner's composition).

Individual Accountability: Each student writes his or her own composition.

Procedure:

1. The instructor assigns students to pairs with at least one good reader in each pair.

2. Student A describes to Student B what he or she is planning to write. Student B listens carefully, probes with a set of questions, and outlines Student A's composition. The written outline is given to Student A.

3. This procedure is reversed with Student B describing what he or she is going to write and Student A listening and completing an outline of Student B's composition, which is then given to Student B.

4. The students research individualistically the material they need to write their compositions, keeping an eye out for material useful to their partner.

5. The two students work together to write the first paragraph of each composition. This ensures that both have a clear start on their compositions.

Johnson, D. W., Johnson, R., & Smith, K. (1998). **Active Learning: Cooperation In The College Classroom**. Edina, MN: Interaction Book Company. (612) 831-9500; FAX (612) 831-9332.

6. The students write their compositions individualistically.

7. When completed, the students proofread each other's compositions, making corrections in capitalization, punctuation, spelling, language usage, topic sentence usage, and other aspects of writing specified by the instructor. Students also give each other suggestions for revision.

8. The students revise their compositions, making all of the suggested revisions.

9. The two students then reread each other's compositions and sign their names (indicating that they guarantee that no errors exist in the composition).

While the students work, the instructor monitors the pairs, intervening where appropriate to help students master the needed writing and cooperative skills. When students complete their compositions, students discuss how effectively they worked together (listing the specific actions they engaged in to help each other), plan what behaviors they are going to emphasize in the next writing pair, and thank each other for the help and assistance received.

COOPERATIVE NOTE-TAKING PAIRS

The notes students take during a lesson are important in understanding what a student learns, both during the lesson and during reviews of the lesson. Most students, however, take notes very incompletely because of low working memory capacities, the information processing load required, and lack of skills in note taking. Students can benefit from learning how to take better notes and how to review notes more effectively.

1. You assign students to note-taking pairs. The **task** is to focus on increasing the quantity and quality of the notes taken during a lesson. The **cooperative goal** is for both students to generate a comprehensive set of accurate notes that will enable them to learn and review the material covered in the lesson.

2. Every ten minutes or so, you stop the lesson and have students hare their notes. Student A summarizes his or her notes to Student B. Student Be summarizes his or her notes to Student A. Each pair member must take something from their partner's notes to improve his or her own notes.

Johnson, D. W., Johnson, R., & Smith, K. (1998). **Active Learning: Cooperation In The College Classroom**. Edina, MN: Interaction Book Company. (612) 831-9500; FAX (612) 831-9332.

ACADEMIC CONTROVERSIES

Creating intellectual conflict (**controversy**) to improve academic learning is one of the most powerful and important instructional tools (Johnson & Johnson, 1995c). Academic controversies require a cooperative context and are actually an advanced form of cooperative learning. The basic format for structuring academic controversies is as follows.

1. Choose a topic that has content manageable by the students and on which at least two well-documented positions (pro and con) can be prepared. Organize the instructional materials into pro and con packets. Students need to know what their position is and where to find relevant information so they can build the rationale underlying the pro or con position on the issue.

2. Assign students to groups of four. Divide each group into two pairs. Assign pro and con positions to the pairs. A good reader or researcher should be in each pair.

3. Assign each pair the **tasks** of (a) learning its position and the supporting arguments and information, (b) researching all information relevant to its position (giving the opposing pair any information found supporting the opposing position), (c) preparing a series of persuasive arguments to support its position, and (d) preparing a persuasive presentation to be given to the opposing pair. Give students the following instructions:

   "Plan with your partner how to advocate your position effectively. Read the materials supporting your position. Find more information in the library reference books to support your position. Plan a persuasive presentation. Make sure you and your partner master the information supporting your assigned position and present it in a persuasive and complete way so that the other group members will comprehend and learn the information."

4. Highlight the **cooperative goals** of reaching a consensus on the issue, mastering all the information relevant to both sides of the issue (measure by a test taken individually), and writing a quality group report on which all members will be evaluated. Note that each group member will receive five bonus points if all members score 90 percent or better on the test covering both sides of the issue.

Johnson, D. W., Johnson, R., & Smith, K. (1998). **Active Learning: Cooperation In The College Classroom**. Edina, MN: Interaction Book Company. (612) 831-9500; FAX (612) 831-9332.

5. Having each pair present its position to the other. Presentations should involve more than one media and persuasively advocate the "best case" for the position. There is no arguing during this time. Students should listen carefully to the opposing position and take notes. You tell students:

"As a pair, present your position forcefully and persuasively. Listen carefully and learn the opposing position. Take notes, and clarify anything you do not understand."

6. Having students openly discuss the issue by freely exchanging their information and ideas. For higher-level reasoning and critical thinking to occur, it is necessary to probe and push each other's conclusions. Students ask for data to support each other's statements, clarify rationales, and show why their position is a rational one. Students evaluate critically the opposing position and its rationale, defend their own positions, and compare the strengths and weaknesses of the two positions. Students refute the claims being made by the opposing pair, and rebut the attacks on their own position. Students are to follow the specific rules for constructive controversy. Students should also take careful notes on and thoroughly learn the opposing position. Sometimes a *"time-out"* period needs to be provided so that pairs can caucus and prepare new arguments. Instructors encourage more spirited arguing, take sides when a pair is in trouble, play devil's advocate, ask one group to observe another group engaging in a spirited argument, and generally stir up the discussions.

"Argue forcefully and persuasively for your position, presenting as many facts as you can to support your point of view. Listen critically to the opposing pair's position, asking them for the facts that support their viewpoint, and then present counter-arguments. Remember this is a complex issue, and you need to know both sides to write a good report."

7. Have the pairs reverse perspectives and positions by presenting the opposing position as sincerely and forcefully as they can. It helps to have the pairs change chairs. They can use their own notes, but may not see the materials developed by the opposing pair. Students' instructions are:

"Working as a pair, present the opposing pair's position as if you were they. Be as sincere and forceful as you can. Add any new facts you know. Elaborate their position by relating it to other information you have previously learned."

8. Have the group members drop their advocacy and reach a decision by consensus. Then they:

Johnson, D. W., Johnson, R., & Smith, K. (1998). **Active Learning: Cooperation In The College Classroom**. Edina, MN: Interaction Book Company. (612) 831-9500; FAX (612) 831-9332.

a. Write a group report that includes their joint position and the supporting evidence and rationale. Often the resulting position is a third perspective or synthesis that is more rational than the two assigned. All group members sign the report indicating that they agree with it, can explain its content, and consider it ready to be evaluated.

b. Take a test on both positions individually. If all group members score above the preset criteria of excellence (90 percent), each receives five bonus points.

JOINT PROJECT

Task: Complete a project.

Cooperative: Each group completes one project. Members sign the project to indicate that they have contributed their share of the work, agree with the content, and can present/explain it. When a variety of materials are used (such as scissors, paper, glue, markers), assign each team member a responsibility for one of the materials. If appropriate, assign each group member a specific role.

Criteria For Success: A completed project that each group member can explain/present.

Individual Accountability:

1. Each group member may be given different color pens, markers, or pencils.

2. Each group member presents the group project to a member of another group.

3. Each student takes a test individually on the content covered by the project.

Expected Social Skills: Presenting ideas, eliciting ideas, and organizing work.

Intergroup Cooperation: Whenever it is helpful, check procedures, information, and progress with other groups.

2 : 31

Johnson, D. W., Johnson, R., & Smith, K. (1998). **Active Learning: Cooperation In The College Classroom**. Edina, MN: Interaction Book Company. (612) 831-9500; FAX (612) 831-9332.

Monitoring And Intervening

The only thing that endures over time is the law of the farm: I must prepare the ground, put in the seed, cultivate it, water it, then gradually nurture growth and development to full maturity...there is no quick fix.

Stephen Covey

Once the students begin working in cooperative learning groups, the instructor's role is to monitor students' interaction and intervene to help students learn and interact more skillfully.

Monitoring Students' Behavior

Your job begins in earnest when the cooperative learning groups start working. Resist that urge to get a cup of coffee or to grade papers. You observe the interaction among group members to assess students' (a) academic progress and (b) appropriate use of interpersonal and small group skills. Monitoring is covered in depth in Chapter Six.

Observations can be formal (with an observation schedule on which frequencies are tallied) or anecdotal (informal descriptions of students' statements and actions). Based on your observations, you can then intervene to improve students' academic learning and/or interpersonal and small group skills. Remember, **students respect what we inspect**. To **monitor** means to check continuously. **Monitoring has four stages:**

1. **Preparing for observing** the learning groups by deciding who will be the observers, what observation forms to use, and training the observers.

2. **Observing** to assess the quality of cooperative efforts in the learning groups.

3. **Intervening when it is necessary** to improve a group's taskwork or teamwork.

4. **Having students assess the quality of their own individual participation** in the learning groups to encourage self-monitoring, having groups assess the level of their effectiveness, and having both individuals and groups set growth goals.

In monitoring cooperative learning groups, there are a number of guidelines for instructors to follow.

1. Plan a route through the classroom and the length of time spent observing each group so that all groups are observed during a lesson.

Johnson, D. W., Johnson, R., & Smith, K. (1998). **Active Learning: Cooperation In The College Classroom**. Edina, MN: Interaction Book Company. (612) 831-9500; FAX (612) 831-9332.

2. Use a formal observation sheet to count the number of times they observe appropriate behaviors being used by students. The more concrete the data, the more useful it is to you (the instructor) and to students.

3. Initially, do not try to count too many different behaviors. At first you may wish simply to keep track of who talks. Your observations should focus on positive behaviors.

4. Supplement and extend the frequency data with notes on specific student actions. Especially useful are descriptions of skillful interchanges that can be shared with students later and with parents in conferences or telephone conversations.

5. Train and utilize student observers. Student observers can obtain more complete data on each group's functioning and may learn important lessons about appropriate and inappropriate behavior. We can remember one first grade instructor who had a student who talked all the time (even to himself while working alone). He tended to dominate any group he was in. When she introduced student observers to the class, she made him an observer. One important rule for observers was not to interfere in the task but to gather data without talking. He was gathering data on who talks and he did a good job, noticing that one student had done quite a bit of talking in the group whereas another had talked very little. The next day when he was a group member, and there was another observer, he was seen starting to talk, clamping his hand over his mouth and glancing at the observer. He knew what was being observed and he didn't want to be the only one with marks. The instructor said he may have listened for the first time in the year. So the observer often benefits in learning about group skills.

6. Allocate sufficient time at the end of each group session for discussion of the data gathered by the observers.

Providing Task Assistance

Cooperative learning groups provide instructors with a "window" into students' minds. Through working cooperatively students make hidden thinking processes overt and subject to observation and commentary. From carefully listening to students explain to each other what they are learning, instructors can determine what students do and do not understand. Consequently, you may will wish to intervene to clarify instructions, review important procedures and strategies for completing the assignment, answer questions, and teach both task skills as necessary. In discussing the concepts and information to be learned, you should make specific statements, such as *"Yes, that is one way to find the main idea of a paragraph,"* not *"Yes, that is right."* The more specific statement reinforces the desired learning and promotes positive transfer by helping the students associate a term with their learning. Metacognitive thought may be encouraged

Johnson, D. W., Johnson, R., & Smith, K. (1998). **Active Learning: Cooperation In The College Classroom**. Edina, MN: Interaction Book Company. (612) 831-9500; FAX (612) 831-9332.

by asking students (a) *"What are you doing?"* (b) *"Why are you doing it?"* and (c) *"How will it help you?"*

Intervening to Teach Social Skills

Cooperative learning groups provide instructors with a picture of students' social skills. The social skills required for productive group work are discussed in detail in Chapter Five. They, along with activities that may be used in teaching them, are covered in even more depth in Johnson and F. Johnson (1997) and Johnson (1991, 1997). While monitoring the learning groups, you may intervene to suggest more effective procedures for working together or reinforce particularly effective and skillful behaviors. Choosing when to intervene is part of the art of teaching. In intervening, ask group members to:

1. Set aside their task.		2. Listen to your statement of the problem.
4. Decide which solution they are going to try first.		3. Create three possible solutions.

In one third grade class, the instructor noticed when distributing papers that one student was sitting back from the other three group members. A moment later the instructor glanced over and only three students were sitting where four were a moment before. As she watched, the three students came marching over to her and complained that Johnny was under the table and wouldn't come out. *"Make him come out!"* they insisted (the instructor's role: police officer, judge, and executioner). The instructor told them that Johnny was a member of their group and asked what they had tried to solve their problem. *"Tried?"* the puzzled reply. *"Yes, have you asked him to come out?"* the instructor suggested. The group marched back and the instructor continued distributing papers to groups. A moment later the instructor glanced over to their table and saw no heads above the table (which is one way to solve the problem). After a few more minutes, four heads came struggling out from under the table and the group (including Johnny) went back to work with great energy. We don't know what happened under that table, but whatever it was, it was effective. What makes this story even more interesting is that the group received a 100 percent on the paper and later, when the instructor was standing by Johnny's desk, she noticed he had the paper clutched in his hand. The group had given Johnny the paper and he was taking it home. He confided to the instructor that this was the first time he could ever remember earning a 100 on anything in school. (If that was your record, you might slip under a few tables yourself.)

Johnson, D. W., Johnson, R., & Smith, K. (1998). **Active Learning: Cooperation In The College Classroom**. Edina, MN: Interaction Book Company. (612) 831-9500; FAX (612) 831-9332.

Evaluating Learning And Processing Interaction

Providing Closure to the Lesson

You provide closure to lessons by having students summarize the major points in the lesson, recall ideas, and identify final questions for the instructor (see Johnson, Johnson, & Holubec, 1992). At the end of the lesson students should be able to summarize what they have learned and to understand where they will use it in future lessons.

Assessing the Quality and Quantity of Learning

The quality and quantity of student learning should be regularly assessed and occasionally evaluated using a criterion-referenced system (see **Meaningful and Manageable Assessment Through Cooperative Learning** [Johnson & Johnson, 1996]). Cooperative learning, furthermore, provides an arena in which **performance-based assessment** (requiring students to demonstrate what they can do with what they know by performing a procedure or skill), **authentic assessment** (requiring students to demonstrate the desired procedure or skill in a "real life" context), and **total quality learning** (continuous improvement of the process of students helping teammates learn) can take place. A wide variety of assessment formats may be used and students may be directly involved in assessing each other's level of learning and then providing immediate remediation to ensure all group members' learning is maximized.

Form a pair. Rank order each of the following columns from most important to you ("1") to least important to you.

What Is Assessed	Procedures	Ways CL Helps
_____ Academic Learning	_____ Goal Setting	_____ Additional Sources Of Labor
_____ Reasoning Strategies	_____ Testing	_____ More Modalities In Assessment
_____ Skills, Competencies	_____ Compositions	_____ More Diverse Outcomes
_____ Attitudes	_____ Presentations	_____ More Sources Of Information
_____ Work Habits	_____ Projects	_____ Reduction Of Bias
	_____ Portfolios	_____ Development Of Rubrics
	_____ Logs, Journals	_____ Implement Improvement Plan

2 : 35

Johnson, D. W., Johnson, R., & Smith, K. (1998). **Active Learning: Cooperation In The College Classroom**. Edina, MN: Interaction Book Company. (612) 831-9500; FAX (612) 831-9332.

Processing How Well the Group Functioned

When students have completed the assignment, or at the end of each class session, students describe what member actions were helpful (and unhelpful) in completing the group's work and make decisions about what behaviors to continue or change. This is discussed in detail in Chapter Six. Group processing occurs at two levels--in each learning group and in the class as a whole. In **small group processing,** in each group members discuss how effectively they worked together and what could be improved. In **whole-class processing** instructors give the class feedback and have students share incidents that occurred in their groups. There are four parts to processing:

1. **Feedback:** You ensure that each student and each group and the class receives (and gives) feedback on the effectiveness of taskwork and teamwork. Feedback given to students should be descriptive and specific, not evaluative and general (see Johnson, 1997).

2. **Reflection:** You ensure that students analyze and reflect on the feedback they receive. You avoid questions that can be answered "yes" or "no." Instead of saying, *"Did everyone help each other learn?"* you should ask, *"How frequently did each member (a) explain how to solve a problem and (b) correct or clarify other member's explanations?*

3. **Improvement Goals:** You help individuals and groups set goals for improving the quality of their work.

4. **Celebration:** You encourage the celebration of members' hard work and the group's success.

Summary And Conclusions

At this point you know what cooperative learning is and how it is different from competitive and individualistic learning. You know that there are three types of cooperative learning groups--formal cooperative learning groups, informal cooperative learning groups, and cooperative base groups. You know that the essence of cooperative learning is positive interdependence where students recognize that "*we are in this together, sink or swim.*" Other essential components include individual accountability (where every student is accountable for both learning the assigned material and helping other group members learn), face-to-face interaction among students within which students promote each other's success, students appropriately using interpersonal and group skills, and students processing how effectively their learning group has functioned. These five essential components of cooperation form the conceptual basis for constructing cooperative procedures. You know that the research supports the

Johnson, D. W., Johnson, R., & Smith, K. (1998). **Active Learning: Cooperation In The College Classroom**. Edina, MN: Interaction Book Company. (612) 831-9500; FAX (612) 831-9332.

proposition that cooperation results in greater effort to achieve, more positive interpersonal relationships, and greater psychological health and self-esteem than do competitive or individualistic efforts. You know the instructor's role in implementing formal cooperative learning. Any assignment in any subject area may be structured cooperatively. In using formal cooperative learning, the instructor decides on the objectives of the lesson, makes a number of preinstructional decisions about the size of the group and the materials required to conduct the lesson, explains to students the task and the cooperative goalstructure, monitors the groups as they work, intervenes when it is necessary, and then evaluates.

One of the things we have been told many times by instructors who have mastered the use of cooperative learning is, *"Don't say it is easy!"* We know it's not. It can take years to become an expert. There is a lot of pressure to teach like everyone else, to have students learn alone, and not to let students look at each other's papers. Students will not be accustomed to working together and are likely to have a competitive orientation. You may wish to start small by using cooperative learning for one topic or in one class until you feel comfortable, and then expand into other topics or classes. **Implementing formal cooperative learning in your classroom is not easy, but it is worth the effort.** The next chapter will focus on informal cooperative learning.

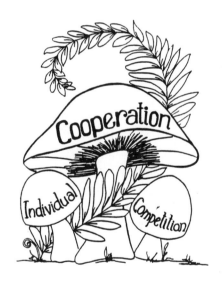

Johnson, D. W., Johnson, R., & Smith, K. (1998). **Active Learning: Cooperation In The College Classroom**. Edina, MN: Interaction Book Company. (612) 831-9500; FAX (612) 831-9332.

CHAPTER TWO QUIZ SHOW

Here Are The Answers, What Are The Questions

Given below are a set of answers. Work cooperatively in pairs to determine the question for each answer. Come to agreement as to which question should be paired with each answer and write the letter in the block.

ANSWERS

_____ 1. Two or three.
_____ 2. Start small and build.
_____ 3. Knee-to-knee, eye-to-eye.
_____ 4. Maximize heterogeneity.
_____ 5. Random, instructor assigned.
_____ 6. Group learning goal, jigsaw, roles, one book, bonus points.
_____ 7. Random checking, tests, homework completed, jigsaw, roles.
_____ 8. "Everyone participate, listen with care, check everyone's learning."
_____ 9. Provide task assistance and encourage cooperative skills.
_____ 10. Observation sheet.
_____ 11. Turn problems back to the group to solve.
_____ 12. Name 3 things members did well and 1 thing they could improve.

QUESTIONS

1. What is a way to formally observe the groups?
2. What is usually the best group composition?
3. What is the first strategy for solving group problems?
4. What are ways to structure positive interdependence?
5. What are some group expected behaviors?
6. What is the best group size?
7. How should students be seated?
8. What are questions to help groups process their interactions?
9. What does the instructor do while the groups are working?
10. How should students be assigned to groups?
11. What are ways to structure individual accountability?
12. How should you start using cooperative learning?

Johnson, D. W., Johnson, R., & Smith, K. (1998). **Active Learning: Cooperation In The College Classroom.** Edina, MN: Interaction Book Company. (612) 831-9500; FAX (612) 831-9332.

The Instructor's Role in Cooperative Learning

Make Pre-Instructional Decisions

Specify Academic and Social Skills Objectives: Every lesson has both (a) academic and (b) interpersonal and small group skills objectives.

Decide on Group Size: Learning groups should be small (groups of two or three members, four at the most).

Decide on Group Composition (Assign Students to Groups): Assign students to groups randomly or select groups yourself. Usually you will wish to maximize the heterogeneity in each group.

Assign Roles: Structure student-student interaction by assigning roles such as Reader, Recorder, Encourager of Participation and Checker for Understanding.

Arrange the Room: Group members should be "knee to knee and eye to eye" but arranged so they all can see the instructor at the front of the room.

Plan Materials: Arrange materials to give a "sink or swim together" message. Give only one paper to the group or give each member part of the material to be learned.

Explain Task And Cooperative Structure

Explain the Academic Task: Explain the task, the objectives of the lesson, the concepts and principles students need to know to complete the assignment, and the procedures they are to follow.

Explain the Criteria for Success: Student work should be evaluated on a criteria-referenced basis. Make clear your criteria for evaluating students' work.

Structure Positive Interdependence: Students must believe they "sink or swim together." Always establish mutual goals (students are responsible for their own learning and the learning of all other group members). Supplement, goal interdependence with celebration/reward, resource, role, and identity interdependence.

Structure Intergroup Cooperation: Have groups check with and help other groups. Extend the benefits of cooperation to the whole class.

Johnson, D. W., Johnson, R., & Smith, K. (1998). **Active Learning: Cooperation In The College Classroom.** Edina, MN: Interaction Book Company. (612) 831-9500; FAX (612) 831-9332.

Structure Individual Accountability: Each student must feel responsible for doing his or her share of the work and helping the other group members. Ways to ensure accountability are frequent oral quizzes of group members picked at random, individual tests, and assigning a member the role of Checker for Understanding.

Specify Expected Behaviors: The more specific you are about the behaviors you want to see in the groups, the more likely students will do them. Social skills may be classified as **forming** (staying with the group, using quiet voices), **functioning** (contributing, encouraging others to participate), **formulating** (summarizing, elaborating), and **fermenting** (criticizing ideas, asking for justification). Regularly teach the interpersonal and small group skills you wish to see used in the learning groups.

Monitor and Intervene

Arrange Face-to-Face Promotive Interaction: Conduct the lesson in ways that ensure that students promote each other's success face-to-face.

Monitor Students' Behavior: This is the fun part! While students are working, you circulate to see whether they understand the assignment and the material, give immediate feedback and reinforcement, and praise good use of group skills. Collect observation data on each group and student.

Intervene to Improve Taskwork and Teamwork: Provide **taskwork assistance** (clarify, reteach) if students do not understand the assignment. Provide **teamwork assistance** if students are having difficulties in working together productively.

Assess and Process

Evaluate Student Learning: Assess and evaluate the quality and quantity of student learning. Involve students in the assessment process.

Process Group Functioning: Ensure each student receives feedback, analyzes the data on group functioning, sets an improvement goal, and participates in a team celebration. Have groups routinely list three things they did well in working together and one thing they will do better tomorrow. Summarize as a whole class. Have groups celebrate their success and hard work.

Johnson, D. W., Johnson, R., & Smith, K. (1998). **Active Learning: Cooperation In The College Classroom.** Edina, MN: Interaction Book Company. (612) 831-9500; FAX (612) 831-9332.

COOPERATIVE LESSON PLANNING FORM

Subject Area: _____ Date: _____

Lesson: _____

Making Preinstructional Decisions

Academic Objectives: _____

Social Skills Objectives: _____

Group Size: _____ Method Of Assigning Students: _____

Roles: _____

Room Arrangement: _____

Materials: _____

    ◊ One Copy Per Group   ◊ One Copy Per Person

    ◊ Jigsaw   ◊ Tournament

    ◊ Other: _____

Explaining Task And Cooperative Goal Structure

1. Task: _____

    _____

2. Criteria For Success: _____

    _____

3. Positive Interdependence: _____

    _____

4. Individual Accountability: _____

5. Intergroup Cooperation: _____

6. Expected Behaviors: _____

    _____

2 : 41

Johnson, D. W., Johnson, R., & Smith, K. (1998). **Active Learning: Cooperation In The College Classroom**. Edina, MN: Interaction Book Company. (612) 831-9500; FAX (612) 831-9332.

Monitoring And Intervening

1. Observation Procedure: _____ Formal _____ Informal

2. Observation By: _____ Instructor _____ Students _____ Visitors

3. Intervening For Task Assistance: _____

   _____

4. Intervening For Teamwork Assistance: _____

   _____

5. Other: _____

Assessing And Processing

1. Assessment Of Members' Individual Learning: _____

   _____

2. Assessment Of Group Productivity: _____

   _____

3. Small Group Processing: _____

   _____

4. Whole Class Processing: _____

   _____

5. Charts And Graphs Used: _____

   _____

6. Positive Feedback To Each Student: _____

   _____

7. Goal Setting For Improvement: _____

   _____

8. Celebration: _____

9. Other: _____

2 : 42

Johnson, D. W., Johnson, R., & Smith, K. (1998). **Active Learning: Cooperation In The College Classroom**. Edina, MN: Interaction Book Company. (612) 831-9500; FAX (612) 831-9332.

CL LESSON PLANNING SHORT FORM

Subject Area: _____ Date: _____

Lesson: _____

Objectives: _____Academic _____Social Skills

Group Size: _____ Method Of Assigning Students: _____

Roles: _____ Materials: _____

Academic Task:	**Criteria For Success:**

Positive Interdependence:	**Individual Accountability:**	**Expected Behaviors:**

Montoring: _____ Instructor _____ Students _____ Visitors

Behaviors Observed: _____

Assessment Of Learning: _____

Small Group Processing:	**Goal Setting:**	**Whole Class Processing:**

Celebration: _____

Other: _____

Johnson, D. W., Johnson, R., & Smith, K. (1998). **Active Learning: Cooperation In The College Classroom**. Edina, MN: Interaction Book Company. (612) 831-9500; FAX (612) 831-9332.

GUIDED PRACTICE IN STRUCTURING COOPERATIVE LEARNING

An important aspect of mastering cooperative learning is actually using it. A instructor may need to structure and teach 20 to 30 lessons cooperatively before gaining a rudimentary competence in doing so. During this training you will practice structuring several lessons cooperatively.

Task: Take the lesson you have just planned. Practice presenting the task and the positive interdependence components of the lesson.

Cooperative: Working in a pair, role play teaching the task and positive interdependence components of the lesson. Present the lesson as if the other person were your class. Use the following procedure:

1. Present your lesson:

    a. The **task** is...

    b. On this task I want you to work **cooperatively**. That means...

2. Listen carefully while your partner presents his or her lesson.

3. Help each other make the task and positive interdependence statements even more effective. After a cooperative goal, what other methods of positive interdependence could be added? How could the statements be more precise and specific next time?

Expected Criteria For Success: Both persons able to present the task and positive interdependence components of a cooperative lesson.

Individual Accountability: One member from your group will be randomly chosen to present his or her task and positive interdependence statements.

Expected Behaviors: Presenting, listening, processing, and encouraging.

Intergroup Cooperation: Whenever it is helpful, check your task and positive interdependence statements with another group.

Johnson, D. W., Johnson, R., & Smith, K. (1998). **Active Learning: Cooperation In The College Classroom.** Edina, MN: Interaction Book Company. (612) 831-9500; FAX (612) 831-9332.

CHAPTER THREE:

INFORMAL COOPERATIVE LEARNING

The Lure Of Lecturing

No logic or wisdom or will-power could prevail to stop the sailors. Buffeted by the hardships of life at sea, the voices came out of the mist to the ancient Greek sailors like a mystical, ethereal love song with tempting and seductive promises of ecstasy and delight. The voices and the song were irresistible. The mariners helplessly turned their ships to follow the Sirens' call with scarcely a second thought. Lured to their destruction, the sailors crashed their ships on the waiting rocks and drowned in the tossing waves, struggling with their last breath to reach the source of that beckoning song.

Centuries later, the Sirens still call. Professors seem drawn to lecturing, crashing their teaching on the rocks due to the seductive and tempting attractions of explicating knowledge to an adoring audience and teaching as they were taught. The old paradigm has an irresistible call to many faculty. The new paradigm may seem idealistic but undoable. Cooperative learning provides an alternative to the "empty vessel" model of the teaching and learning process and encourages the development of student talent by proving a very carefully structured approach to getting students actively involved in constructing their own knowledge. Getting students cognitively, physically, emotionally, and psychologically involved in learning is an important step in turning around the passive and impersonal character of many college classrooms.

Direct Teaching, Lecturing

Our survey of teaching methods suggests that...if we want students to become more effective in meaningful learning and thinking, they need to spend more time in active, meaningful learning and thinking--not just sitting and passively receiving information.

McKeachie (1986)

The obstacles to learning from a lecture were (again) made painfully aware to us (the authors) during a workshop for students and faculty in Norway. While conducting a workshop on cooperative learning for faculty and students at the Norwegian Institute of Technology, Karl was convinced that a short lecture (given in the informal cooperative

3 : 1

Johnson, D. W., Johnson, R., & Smith, K. (1998). **Active Learning: Cooperation In The College Classroom**. Edina, MN: Interaction Book Company. (612) 831-9500; FAX (612) 831-9332.

learning format) on the latest research on learning would be very useful and effective. He asked a focus question at the start, lectured for about 12 minutes, and asked the participants to prepare a summary of the main points and to formulate at least one question. When he finished the short lecture, and asked for a summary, participants did not know what to write. One student jokingly said, "*Karl, what did you say between 'Here's the research' and 'Your task is to create a summary?'*" He got a big laugh, but when we took a break, several of the faculty came to him and said, "*I didn't know what you were talking about. The concepts were somewhat new to me, you were enthusiastic and spoke slowly and clearly, but I really did not understand what you were talking about.*"

After the break, Karl apologized to the workshop participants for wasting their time. It was painful since he thought he had given an excellent lecture. A couple of faculty came to his defense. They said, "*Well, you know, it was a pretty good lecture. It was just kind of new to us.*" But then a student in the back said, "*I understood a little at the beginning, but a lot of lectures are like this for me.*" And a student in the front said (with emphasis), "*This is what it is like for me every day.*"

The look on the faces of those faculty! Perhaps they were reminded that students try to understand what is being presented in a lecture and often feel frustrated by their lack of comprehension. Perhaps Karl should have followed Wilbert McKeachie's advice on lecturing: "*I lecture only when I am convinced it will do more good than harm.*"

In this chapter we shall define lecturing, the problems and enemies of lecturing, the use of informal cooperative learning groups to make students cognitively active during lectures will then be described.

Nature Of Lecturing

The use of lecturing is paradoxical. Lecturing is (and has been) both the most widely criticized of all teaching methods and the most commonly used (Cuban, 1984). Lecturing is particularly popular in the teaching of large introductory sections of courses in a wide variety of disciplines (e.g., psychology, chemistry, mathematics). A **lecture** is an extended presentation in which the instructor presents factual information in an organized and logically sequenced way. It typically results in long periods of uninterrupted instructor-centered, expository discourse that relegates students to the role of passive "spectators." The lecturer presents the material to be learned in more or less final form, gives answers, presents principles, and elaborates on what is being learned. Normally, the lecturer may use reference notes, may use visuals (to enhance the information being presented), may provide students with handouts to help them follow the lecture, and may respond to students' questions as the lecture progresses or at its end.

Given all the criticism of lecturing, why is it still so commonly used? There are several reasons:

Johnson, D. W., Johnson, R., & Smith, K. (1998). **Active Learning: Cooperation In The College Classroom**. Edina, MN: Interaction Book Company. (612) 831-9500; FAX (612) 831-9332.

1. Lecturing is an efficient way to present information. A great deal of material can be presented in a short period of time. Planning time is also efficiently used as it is focused solely on organizing the content to be presented.

2. Lecturing is flexible. It can be adapted to different audiences and time frames can be used in presenting virtually any content area.

3. Lecturing is relatively simple to implement, which makes it especially important to beginning instructors. All a person has to do to teach is stand up in front of the class and talk.

4. Lecturing makes the instructor the center of all communication and attention in the classroom. He or she becomes a "sage on the stage." Students look at the instructor, listen, write down what he or she says, laughs at his or her clever comments, and are impressed by the instructor's insights and knowledge. Lecturing can be very ego-gratifying.

The rationale for and the pedagogy of lecturing are based on (a) theories of the structure and organization of knowledge, (b) the psychology of meaningful verbal learning, and (c) ideas from cognitive psychology associated with the representation and acquisition of knowledge. Jerome Bruner (1960) emphasized that knowledge structures exist and become a means for (a) organizing information about topics, (b) dividing information into various categories, and (c) showing relationships among various categories of information. David Ausubel (1963) believed that meaning emerges from new information only if it is tied into existing cognitive structures and, therefore, instructors should organize information for students, present it in clear and precise ways, and anchor it into cognitive structures formed from prior learning. Ellen Gagne (1985) emphasized that (a) declarative knowledge is represented in interrelated propositions or unifying ideas, (b) existing cognitive structures must be cued so that students bring them from long-term memory into working memory, and (c) students must process new knowledge by coding it and then storing it in their long-term memory. All three of these viewpoints point towards the use of lectures.

Johnson, D. W., Johnson, R., & Smith, K. (1998). **Active Learning: Cooperation In The College Classroom**. Edina, MN: Interaction Book Company. (612) 831-9500; FAX (612) 831-9332.

TABLE 3.1 LECTURING

ADVANTAGES	APPROPRIATE USE	PROBLEMS	ENEMIES
Efficiency	Disseminate Information	Decreasing Student Attention	Preoccupation With Past Or Future
Flexibility	Present Information Not Available Elsewhere	Requires Intelligent, Motivated Auditory Learner	Emotional Moods Such As Anger, Frustration
Simplicity	Present Information Integrated From Many Sources	Promotes Lower-Level Learning Of Factual Information	Student Lack Of Interest In Material Presented
Ego-Gratifying	Guide Students In Understanding Complex Information	Gives Students Same Information, Presented Orally, Impersonally, At Same Pace, No Dialogue	Failure To Understand Material Being Presented
	Arouse Students' Interest In Topic	Students Tend Not To Like It	Feelings Of Alienation From Class & School
	Model Strategies And Procedures Students Need To Use In Independent Practice Help Students Understand Different Perspectives Teach Auditory Learners	Assumes All Students Learn Auditorially, Have High Working Memory, Possess Required Prior Knowledge, Are Good Note-Takers, Have Good Information Processing Strategies And Skills	Entertaining, Clear Presentations That Misrepresent Complexity Of Material

3 : 4

Johnson, D. W., Johnson, R., & Smith, K. (1998). **Active Learning: Cooperation In The College Classroom**. Edina, MN: Interaction Book Company. (612) 831-9500; FAX (612) 831-9332.

Appropriate Use Of Lecturing

The research on lecturing (see reviews by Bligh, 1972; Costin, 1972; Eble, 1983; Henson, 1988; McKeachie, 1967; McKeachie & Kulik, 1975; McMann, 1979; Verner & Dickinson, 1967) indicates that lecturing is appropriate to:

1. **Disseminate information:** Lecturing is appropriate when faculty wish to communicate a large amount of material to many students in a short period of time, update or elaborate on curriculum materials, organize and present material in a particular way, or introduce an area.

2. **Present material that is not available elsewhere:** Lecturing is appropriate when the information is not readily available, original, or too complex and difficult for students to learn on their own.

3. **Expose students in a brief time to content integrated from a variety of sources.** Lecturing is appropriate when faculty need to teach information that must be integrated from many sources and students do not have the time, resources, or skills to find the sources and integrate the information they contain. Ausubel (1963) argues hat effective lectures provide students with information that would take them hours to find on their own.

4. **Expose students in a brief time to content too complex for students to understand and learn on their own.** Lecturing is appropriate when the information studied is so complex that students need guidance and cognitive coaching in order for them to understand it. Concrete examples and organizing complex information in charts, outlines, or hierarchies often help.

5. **Demonstrate/model strategies and procedures students are to use in future assignments.** It sometimes helps students to see strategies and procedures demonstrated so they can imitate the instructor in future assignments.

6. **Expose students in a brief time to several different points of view.** Students often have difficulty in viewing problems from perspectives other than their own. Instructors may need to make explicit different perspectives in viewing material and in approaching problems.

7. **Arouse students' interest in the subject.** When a lecture is presented by a highly authoritative person and/or in a skillful way with lots of humor and examples, students may be intrigued and want to find out more about the subject. Skillful delivery of a lecture includes maintaining eye contact, avoiding distracting behaviors, modulating voice pitch and volume, and using appropriate gestures. Achievement is higher when presentations are clear (Good & Grouws,

3 : 5

Johnson, D. W., Johnson, R., & Smith, K. (1998). **Active Learning: Cooperation In The College Classroom.** Edina, MN: Interaction Book Company. (612) 831-9500; FAX (612) 831-9332.

1977; Smith & Land, 1981), delivered with enthusiasm (Armento, 1977), and delivered with appropriate gestures and movements (Rosenshine, 1968).

8. **Teach students who are primarily auditory learners.** To learn from lectures, students need to be skillful listeners who can organize information acquired auditorially.

Parts Of A Lecture

A lecture has three parts: the introduction, the body, and the conclusion. Proponents of lecturing advise instructors, "*Tell them what you are going to tell them; then tell them; then tell them what you told them.*" First you describe the learning objectives in a way that alerts students to what is to be covered in the lecture. You then present the material to be learned in small steps organized logically and sequenced in ways that are easy to follow. You end with an integrative review of the main points. More specifically, during the **introduction** you will want to:

1. Arouse students' interest by indicating the relevance of the lecture to their goals.

2. Provide motivational cues, such as telling students that the material to be covered is important, useful, difficult, and will be included on a test.

3. Make the objectives of the lecture clear and explicit and set expectations as to what will be included.

4. Use advance organizers by telling students in advance how the lecture is organized. **Advance organizers** are concepts given to the student prior to the material actually to be learned that provide a stable cognitive structure in which the new knowledge can be subsumed (Ausubel, 1963). The use of advance organizers may be helpful when (1) the students have no relevant information to which they can relate the new learning and (2) when relevant cognitive structures are present but are not likely to be recognized as relevant by the learner. Advance organizers provide students with general learning sets that help cue them to key ideas and organize these ideas in relationship to one another. Instructors use advance organizers by announcing the topic as a title, summarizing the major points to be made in the lecture, and defining the terms students might not know. By giving students a cognitive structure in which to fit the material being presented, instructors can improve student comprehension of the material, make it meaningful to them, and improve their ability to recall and apply what they hear.

5. Prompt awareness of students' relevant knowledge by asking questions about knowledge or experience related to the topic. Give and ask for examples. Ask questions to show how the students' prior knowledge relates to the material covered in the lecture. Explicitly relate students' prior knowledge to the topic of the lecture.

Johnson, D. W., Johnson, R., & Smith, K. (1998). **Active Learning: Cooperation In The College Classroom.** Edina, MN: Interaction Book Company. (612) 831-9500; FAX (612) 831-9332.

During the **body** of the lecture, you will want to cover the content while providing a logical organization for the material being presented. There are a variety of ways of organizing the body of a lecture (see Bligh, 1972 for examples). What is important is that the body have a logical organization that is explicitly communicated to students.

Conclude by summarizing the major points, asking students to recall ideas or give examples, and answering any questions.

Despite the popularity of lecturing, there are (a) problems associated with its use and (b) obstacles to lecturing.

Problems With Lecturing

While direct teaching may be appropriately used, there are also problems with direct teaching that must be kept in mind. Much of the research on lecturing has compared lecturing with group discussion. While the conditions under which lecturing is more successful than group discussion have **not** been identified, a number of problems with lecturing have been found.

The first problem with lecturing is that students' attention to what the instructor is saying decreases as the lecture proceeds. Research in the 1960s by D. H. Lloyd, at the University of Reading in Berkshire, England found that student attention levels during lectures followed the pattern of (a) five minutes of settling in, (b) five minutes of readily assimilating material, (c) confusion and boredom with assimilation falling off rapidly and remaining low for the bulk of the lecture, and (d) some revival of attention at the end of the lecture (Penner, 1984). The concentration during lectures of medical students, who presumably are highly motivated, rose sharply and peaked 10 to 15 minutes after the lecture began, and then fell steadily thereafter (Stuart & Rutherford, 1978). J. McLeish in a research study in the 1960s analyzed the percentage of content contained in student notes at different time intervals through the lecture (reported in Penner, 1984). He found that students wrote notes on 41 percent of the content presented during the first fifteen minutes, 25 percent presented in a thirty-minute time period, and only 20 percent of what had been presented during forty-five minutes.

The second problem with lecturing is that it takes an educated, intelligent person oriented toward auditory learning to benefit from listening to lectures. Verner and Cooley (1967) found that in general, very little of a lecture can be recalled except in the case of listeners with above average education and intelligence. Even under optimal conditions, when intelligent, motivated people listen to a brilliant scholar talk about an interesting topic, there can be serious problems with a lecture. Verner and Dickinson (1967, p. 90) give this example:

> "...ten percent of the audience displayed signs of inattention within fifteen minutes. After eighteen minutes one-third of the audience and ten percent of the platform guests were fidgeting. At thirty-five minutes everyone was inattentive; at forty-five

Johnson, D. W., Johnson, R., & Smith, K. (1998). **Active Learning: Cooperation In The College Classroom**. Edina, MN: Interaction Book Company. (612) 831-9500; FAX (612) 831-9332.

minutes, trance was more noticeable than fidgeting; and at forty-seven minutes some were asleep and at least one was reading. A causal check twenty-four hours later revealed that the audience recalled only insignificant details, and these were generally wrong."

The third problem with lecturing is that it tends to promote only lower-level learning of factual information. Bligh (1972), after an extensive series of studies, concluded that while lecturing was as (but not more) effective as reading or other methods in transmitting information, lecturing was clearly less effective in promoting thinking or in changing attitudes. A survey of 58 studies conducted between the years of 1928 and 1967 comparing various characteristics of lectures versus discussions, found that lectures and discussions did not differ significantly on lower-level learning (such as learning facts and principles), but discussion appeared superior in developing higher-level problem- solving capabilities and positive attitudes toward the course (Costin, 1972). McKeachie and Kulik (1975) separated studies on lecturing according to whether they focused on factual learning, higher-level reasoning, attitudes, or motivation. They found lecture to be superior to discussion for promoting factual learning, but discussion was found to be superior to lecture for promoting higher-level reasoning, positive attitudes, and motivation to learn.

Fourth, lecturing is limited by the assumptions that all students need the same information presented orally at the same time and at the same pace, without dialogue with the presenter, and in an impersonal way. Regardless of whether students have different levels of knowledge about the subject being presented, the same information is presented to all at the same time and pace. While students learn and comprehend at different paces, a lecture proceeds at the lecturer's pace. While students who listen carefully and cognitively process the information presented will have questions that need to be answered, lectures typically are one-way communication situations and the large number of classmates inhibit question asking (Stones. 1970). If students cannot ask questions, misconceptions, incorrect understanding, and gaps in understanding cannot be identified and corrected. Lectures can waste student time by telling them things that they could read for themselves. Lecturing by its very nature makes learning impersonal. There is research indicating that personalized learning experiences have more impact on achievement and motivation.

The fifth problem with lecturing is that students tend not to like it. Costin's (1972) review of literature indicates that students like the course and subject area better when they learn in discussion groups than when they learn by listening to lectures. This is important in introductory courses where disciplines often attempt to attract majors.

Finally, there are problems with lecturing as it is based on a series of assumptions about the cognitive capabilities and strategies of students. When you lecture you assume that all students learn auditorially, have high working memory capacity, have all the required prior knowledge, have good note-taking strategies and skills, and are not susceptible to information processing overload.

Johnson, D. W., Johnson, R., & Smith, K. (1998). **Active Learning: Cooperation In The College Classroom.** Edina, MN: Interaction Book Company. (612) 831-9500; FAX (612) 831-9332.

Enemies Of The Lecture

Besides the identified problems with lecturing and direct teaching, there are obstacles to making direct teaching and lecturing effective. We call these obstacles the enemies of the lecture. They are as follows.

1. **Preoccupation with what happened during the previous hour or with what happened on the way to class**. In order for lectures to succeed faculty must take students' attention away from events in the hallway or campus and focus student attention on the subject area and topic being dealt with in class.

2. **Emotional moods that block learning and cognitive processing of information**. Students who are angry or frustrated about something are **not** open to new learning. In order for lectures to work, faculty must set a constructive learning mood. Humor helps.

3. **Disinterest by students who go to sleep or who turn on a tape recorder while they write letters or read comic books**. In order for lectures to work, faculty must focus student attention on the material being presented and ensure that they cognitively process the information and integrate it into what they already know.

4. **Failure to understand the material being presented in the lecture**. Students can learn material incorrectly and incompletely because of lack of understanding. In order to make lectures work there has to be some means of checking the accuracy and completeness of students' understanding of the material being presented.

5. **Feelings of isolation and alienation and beliefs that no one cares about them as persons or about their academic progress**. In order to make lectures work students have to believe that there are other people in the class who will provide help and assistance because they care about the students as people and about the quality of their learning.

6. **Entertaining lectures that misrepresent the complexity of the material being presented**. While entertaining and impressing students is nice, it often does not help students understand and think critically about complex material. To make lectures work, students must think critically and use higher-level reasoning in cognitively processing course content. One of our colleagues is a magnificent lecturer. His explanation of the simplex algorithm for solving linear programming problems is so clear and straightforward that the students go away with the view that it is very simple. Later when they try to solve a problem on their own, they find that they don't have a clue as to how to begin. Our colleague used to blame himself for not explaining well enough. Sometimes he blamed the students. Now he puts small cooperative groups to work on a simple linear programming problem, circulates and checks the progress of each student,

Johnson, D. W., Johnson, R., & Smith, K. (1998). **Active Learning: Cooperation In The College Classroom**. Edina, MN: Interaction Book Company. (612) 831-9500; FAX (612) 831-9332.

provides help where he feels it is appropriate, and only gives his brilliant lectures when the students understand the problem and are ready to hear his proposed solution. Both he and the students are much happier with their increased understanding.

After considering these problems and barriers, it may be concluded that alternative teaching strategies have to be interwoven with lecturing if the lecture method is to be effective. While lecturing and direct teaching have traditionally been conducted within competitive and individualistic structures, they can be made cooperative. Perhaps the major procedure to interweave with lecturing is informal cooperative learning groups.

Informal Cooperative Learning Groups

There are times when instructors need to lecture, show a movie or videotape, give a demonstration, or have a guest speaker. In such cases, informal cooperative learning may be used to ensure that students are active (not passive) cognitively. **Informal cooperative learning** consists of having students work together to achieve a joint learning goal in temporary, ad-hoc groups that last from a few minutes to one class period. Their **purposes** are to focus student attention on the material to be learned, set a mood conducive to learning, help organize in advance the material to be covered in a class session, ensure that students cognitively process the material being taught, and provide closure to an instructional session. Informal cooperative learning groups also ensure that misconceptions, incorrect understanding, and gaps in understanding are identified and corrected, and learning experiences are personalized. They may be used at any time, but are especially useful during a lecture or direct teaching.

During lecturing and direct teaching the instructional challenge for the instructor is to ensure that students do the intellectual work of organizing material, explaining it, summarizing it, and integrating it into existing conceptual networks. This may be achieved by having students do the advance organizing, cognitively process what they are learning, and provide closure to the lesson. Breaking up lectures with short cooperative processing times will give you slightly less lecture time, but will help counter what is proclaimed as the main problem of lectures: *"The information passes from the notes of the professor to the notes of the student without passing through the mind of either one."*

Johnson, D. W., Johnson, R., & Smith, K. (1998). **Active Learning: Cooperation In The College Classroom**. Edina, MN: Interaction Book Company. (612) 831-9500; FAX (612) 831-9332.

PURPOSES OF INFORMAL COOPERATIVE LEARNING

Form a pair. Rank order the following purposes of informal cooperative learning from most important ("1") to least important ("7").

	Focuses student attention on the material to be learned.
	Sets a mood conducive to learning.
	Helps cognitively organize in advance the material to be covered in a class session.
	Ensures that students cognitively process the material being taught.
	Provides closure to an instructional session.
	Allows for identifying and correcting misconceptions, incorrect understanding, and gaps in comprehension.
	Personalizes learning experiences.

FIGURE 3.1 INFORMAL COOPERATIVE LEARNING

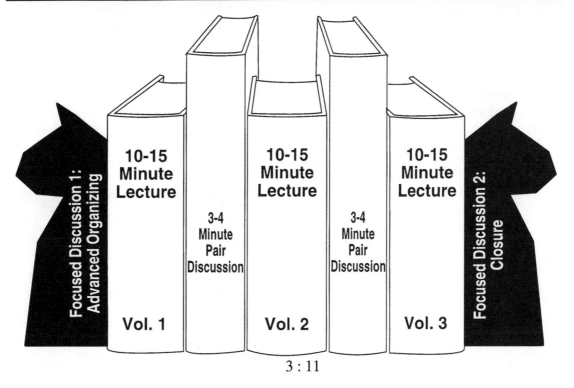

3 : 11

Johnson, D. W., Johnson, R., & Smith, K. (1998). **Active Learning: Cooperation In The College Classroom**. Edina, MN: Interaction Book Company. (612) 831-9500; FAX (612) 831-9332.

Lecturing With Informal Cooperative Learning Groups

The following procedure will help you plan a lecture that keeps students more actively engaged intellectually. It entails having **focused discussions** before and after the lecture (i.e., bookends) and interspersing **pair discussions** throughout the lecture. Two important aspects of using informal cooperative learning groups are to (a) make the task and the instructions explicit and precise and (b) require the groups to produce a specific product (such as a written answer). The procedure is as follows.

1. **Introductory Focused Discussion:** Assign students to pairs. The person nearest them will do. You may wish to require different seating arrangements each class period so that students will meet and interact with a number of other students in the class. Then give the pairs the cooperative assignment of completing the initial (advance organizer) task. Give them only four or five minutes to do so. The discussion task is aimed at promoting **advance organizing** of what the students know about the topic to be presented and **establishing expectations** about what the lecture will cover.

2. **Intermittent Focused Discussions:**

   a. **Lecture Segment One:** Deliver the first segment of the lecture. This segment should last from 10 to 15 minutes. This is about the length of time a motivated adult can concentrate on a lecture. For unmotivated adolescents, the time may be shorter.

   b. **Pair Discussion 1**: Give the students a discussion task focused on the material you have just presented that may be completed within three or four minutes. Its purpose is to ensure that students are actively thinking about the material being presented. The discussion task may be to (a) give an answer to a question posed by the instructor, (b) give a reaction to the theory, concepts, or information being presented, or (c) relate material to past learning so that it gets integrated into existing conceptual frameworks (i.e., elaborate the material being presented). Discussion pairs respond to the task in the following way:

      1. Each student **formulates** his or her answer.

      2. Students **share** their answer with their partner.

      3. Students **listen** carefully to partner's answer.

3 : 12

Johnson, D. W., Johnson, R., & Smith, K. (1998). **Active Learning: Cooperation In The College Classroom**. Edina, MN: Interaction Book Company. (612) 831-9500; FAX (612) 831-9332.

4. Pairs **create** a new answer that is superior to each member's initial formulation through the process of association, building on each other's thoughts, and synthesizing.

Randomly choose two or three students to give 30 second summaries of their discussions. **It is important that students are randomly called on to share their answers after each discussion task**. Such **individual accountability** ensures that the pairs take the tasks seriously and check each other to ensure that both are prepared to answer.

c. **Lecture Segment 2:** Deliver the second segment of the lecture.

d. **Pair Discussion 2:** Give a discussion task focused on the second part of the lecture.

e. Repeat this sequence of lecture segment and pair discussion until the lecture is completed.

3. **Closure Focused Discussion**: Give students an ending discussion task lasting four to five minutes to summarize what students have learned from the lecture. The discussion should result in students integrating what they have just learned into existing conceptual frameworks. The task may also point students toward what the homework will cover or what will be presented in the next class session. This provides closure to the lecture.

Informal cooperative learning ensures students are actively involved in understanding what they are learning. It also provides time for instructors to gather their wits, reorganize notes, take a deep breath, and move around the class listening to what students are saying. Listening to student discussions can give instructors direction and insight into how well students understand the concepts and material being taught (who, unfortunately, may not have graduate degrees in the topic you are presenting).

In the following sections more specific procedures for the initial focused discussion, the intermittent pair discussions, and the closure focused discussion will be given.

Step One: Introductory Focused Discussion

The **first step** in using informal cooperative learning is to require students to meet in ad-hoc informal cooperative discussion pairs or triads (or in permanent base groups) at the beginning of a class session. A four to five minute discussion is used to (a) organize in advance what a student knows about a topic and (b) establish expectations about what the class session will focus on. Ways of structuring introductory focused discussions are discussion pairs, question-and-answer pairs, peer critiques of advanced preparation papers, and progress checks.

Johnson, D. W., Johnson, R., & Smith, K. (1998). **Active Learning: Cooperation In The College Classroom**. Edina, MN: Interaction Book Company. (612) 831-9500; FAX (612) 831-9332.

INTRODUCTORY FOCUSED DISCUSSION PAIRS

To prepare for the class session students may be required to complete a short initial focused discussion task. Plan your lecture around a series of questions. Write the questions on an overhead transparency or on the board.

Task: Answer the questions.

Cooperative: Create, with your partner, one answer for each question, using the following sequence:

1. Each student **formulates** his or her answer.

2. Students **share** their answer with their partner.

3. Students **listen** carefully to partner's answer.

4. Pairs **create** a new answer that is superior to each member's initial formulation through the process of association, building on each other's thoughts, and synthesizing.

   The discussion is aimed at promoting advance organizing of what the students know about the topic to be presented and to set expectations as to what the lecture will cover.

Expected Criteria For Success: Each student able to explain answers.

Individual Accountability: One member from the pair will be randomly chosen to explain the answer. Periodically use the simultaneous explaining procedure of having each group member explain the group's answers to a member of another group.

Expected Behaviors: Explaining, listening, synthesizing by all members.

Intergroup Cooperation: Whenever it is helpful, check procedures, answers, and strategies with another group.

Johnson, D. W., Johnson, R., & Smith, K. (1998). **Active Learning: Cooperation In The College Classroom.** Edina, MN: Interaction Book Company. (612) 831-9500; FAX (612) 831-9332.

QUESTION-AND-ANSWER PAIRS

Task: Answer questions on the homework.

Cooperative: Question-and-answer pairs alternate asking and answering questions on the assigned reading:

1. To prepare for the discussion, students read an assignment and write questions dealing with the major points raised in the assigned reading or other related materials.

2. At the beginning of each class, students are randomly assigned to pairs; one member (Student A) is chosen randomly to ask his or her first question.

3. The partner (Student B) gives an answer. Student A can correct B's answer or give additional information.

4. Student B asks the first member a question and process is repeated.

5. During this time, the instructor goes from dyad to dyad, giving feedback and asking and answering questions.

A similar procedure was promoted by Marcel Goldschmid of the Swiss Federal Institute of Technology in Lausanne (Goldschmid, 1971). A variation on this procedure is the **jigsaw**, in which each student reads or prepares different materials. Each member of the group then teaches the material to the other member and vice versa.

Expected Criteria For Success: Each student writes a paper and edits his or her groupmate's papers.

Individual Accountability: Each student writes out a set of questions on the assignment and must answer his or her partner's questions. The instructor observes to ensure that each student arrived with a set of questions and gives reasonable answers to his or her partner's questions.

Expected Behaviors: Ask and answer questions, giving good explanations.

Intergroup Cooperation: Whenever it is helpful, check answers, procedures, and strategies with another group.

Johnson, D. W., Johnson, R., & Smith, K. (1998). **Active Learning: Cooperation In The College Classroom.** Edina, MN: Interaction Book Company. (612) 831-9500; FAX (612) 831-9332.

ADVANCED PREPARATION PAPERS

To prepare for each class session students may be required to complete a short writing assignment. Even if it is not graded it compels them to organize their thoughts and take some responsibility for how the class goes.

Task: Write a short paper on an aspect of the assigned readings to prepare for class. Before each class session students:

1. Choose as a topic a major theory, concept, research study, or theorist/researcher discussed in the assigned reading.

2. Write a two-page analysis of the chosen topic:

   a. Summarizing the relevant assigned reading.

   b. Adding material from another source (research article or book) to enrich their analysis of the theory, concept, research study, or theorist/researcher.

Cooperative: Students bring four copies of the paper to the class. The members of their base group or discussion pair will read, edit, and criticize the paper. The criteria they will use to do so include the following. Does each paper have a(n):

   a. Introductory statement of the issue focused on.

   b. Summary of the theory or conceptual framework used to understand the issue and a judgment about its significance. *(T = Substantial Theoretical Significance, t = some theoretical significance)*

   c. Clear conceptual definition of concepts and terms.

   d. Summary of what is known empirically.
      (R = Substantial Research Support, r = some research support)

   e. Description of and judgment about practical significance.
      (P = Substantial Practical Significance, p = some practical significance)

   f. Brief description of relevant study that should be conducted.

   g. New information beyond what is contained in the text.

3 : 16

Johnson, D. W., Johnson, R., & Smith, K. (1998). **Active Learning: Cooperation In The College Classroom**. Edina, MN: Interaction Book Company. (612) 831-9500; FAX (612) 831-9332.

Expected Criteria For Success: Each student writes a paper and edits groupmates' papers.

Individual Accountability: Each student writes a paper and signs each paper he or she edits. If each group member uses a different color ink pen the quality of their editing is easily apparent. Periodically use the simultaneous explaining procedure of having each group member explain his or her paper to a member of another group.

Expected Behaviors: Critically evaluating the papers of groupmates.

Intergroup Cooperation: Whenever it is helpful, check editing procedures and strategies with another group.

PROGRESS CHECKS

Students can be given a progress check (similar to a quiz but not graded). A **progress check** consists of questions (multiple choice, short answer, essay) testing students' knowledge of the assigned reading. Students (a) individually complete the progress check (b) retake the progress check and compare answers with a partner from their base group and, if time permits, (c) retake the progress check in the whole base group to broaden the discussion of each question. On any question that the students do not agree, students should identify the page number and paragraph in the text where the correct answer may be found.

Step Two: Intermittent Discussion Pairs

The **second step** in using informal cooperative learning is to structure intermittent discussion pairs during the lecture or class session. Instructors pause every ten to fifteen minutes, ask students to form pairs, and give students a short discussion task to be completed in three or four minutes to ensure that students actively cognitively process the information just presented. The discussion task may be to (a) answer a question posed by the instructor, (b) give a reaction to the theory, concepts, or information being presented, or (c) elaborate (relate material to past learning) on the material being presented. Using intermittent discussion pairs can solve a number of problems inherent in lecturing.

First, it ensures that all students are actively involved in learning the material being presented. Active involvement solves three of the problems with whole class discussions:

Johnson, D. W., Johnson, R., & Smith, K. (1998). **Active Learning: Cooperation In The College Classroom**. Edina, MN: Interaction Book Company. (612) 831-9500; FAX (612) 831-9332.

1. **Lack of response by most students.** Whole-class discussions rarely involve many students. Barnes (1980) found in an observational study of instructor-student interaction that when instructors attempted to solicit student participation through whole-class questioning, students responded only 50 percent of the time.

2. **Domination by a few students.** When faculty do manage to obtain student participation, a very small minority of students tends to dominate. Karp and Yoels (1987) documented that in classes of less than 40 students, four to five students accounted for 75 percent of all interactions and, in classes with more than 40 students, two to three students accounted for over half of the exchanges.

3. **Refusal to ask questions.** In his survey of over 1,000 college students, Stones (1970) found that 60 percent stated that the presence of a large number of classmates would deter them from asking questions, even if the instructor encouraged them to do so.

Second, the use of intermittent discussion pairs facilitates the understanding and retention of material being learned. Students often say, *"I understood it at the time, but I do not remember it now."* Experimental research on human memory (Kappel & Underwood, 1962; Waugh & Norman, 1965) indicates that two types of memory interference build up to cause forgetting during long periods of uninterrupted information processing such as an hour-long lecture. The two types are:

1. **Retroactive interference** which occurs when the information processed toward the end of the lecture interferes with the retention of the information processed at the beginning of the lecture.

2. **Proactive interference** when the information processed at the beginning of the lecture interferes with retention of information processes at the end of the lecture.

By interspersing pair discussions throughout the lecture, long periods of uninterrupted listening and information-processing can be avoided, thus minimizing retroactive and proactive interference.

In addition, the oral and written rehearsal of information soon after it has been received or processed results in greater retention of that information (Atkinson & Shiffrin, 1971; Broadbent, 1970). This is due to the fact that the rate of human forgetting is sharpest immediately after the information is received. Orally rehearsing the information being presented soon after its reception gives the brain an opportunity to consolidate or lock in the memory trace and offsets the rapid rate of forgetting that normally follows just-processed information.

There is evidence that college students do their best in courses that include frequent checkpoints of what they know, especially when the checkpoints occur in small cooperative groups. Ruhl, Hughes, and Schloss (1987) conducted a study on the use of

Johnson, D. W., Johnson, R., & Smith, K. (1998). **Active Learning: Cooperation In The College Classroom**. Edina, MN: Interaction Book Company. (612) 831-9500; FAX (612) 831-9332.

cooperative discussion pairs in combination with lecturing. The study was conducted in separate courses over two semesters. In the two experimental classes the instructor paused for two minutes three times during each of five lectures. The intervals of lecturing between the two-minute pauses ranged from 12 to 18 minutes. During the pauses there was no instructor-student interaction. The students worked in pairs to discuss and rework the notes they took during the lecture. Two types of tests were given: immediate free-recall tests given at the end of each lecture (students were given three minutes to write down everything they could remember from the lecture) and a sixty-five item multiple-choice test measuring long-term retention (administered twelve days after the final lecture). A control group received the same lectures without the pauses and were tested in the same manner. In both courses, students who engaged in the pair discussions achieved significantly higher on the free-recall quizzes and the comprehensive retention test than did the students who did not engage in the pair discussions. The eight-point difference in the means between the experimental and control groups was large enough to make a difference of up to two letter grades, depending on the cutoff points.

Third, the use of intermittent discussion pairs provides students with the opportunity to receive from classmates frequent and immediate feedback. During most lectures, students do not have any opportunity to receive feedback as to the quality and quantity of their comprehension of what is being presented. Frequent and immediate feedback serves to increase students' achievement and motivation to learn (Mackworth, 1970). Classmates can be utilized to give such feedback.

Besides intermittent discussion pairs, instructors may use a number of other active-response strategies as part of lectures. They include asking students to indicate their answer or opinion by "*raise your hand*," "*thumbs up or thumbs down*" or "*clap once if you agree.*"

There are a variety of ways intermittent discussion pairs may be structured. Three of the most common are pair summaries, note-taking pairs, reading pairs, and concept induction pairs.

3 : 19

Johnson, D. W., Johnson, R., & Smith, K. (1998). **Active Learning: Cooperation In The College Classroom**. Edina, MN: Interaction Book Company. (612) 831-9500; FAX (612) 831-9332.

TURN TO YOUR NEIGHBOR SUMMARIES

A common classroom practice is to hold a "*whole-class discussion*." You choose one student or a student volunteers to answer a question or provide a summary of what the lesson has covered so far. The student doing the explaining has an opportunity to clarify and extend what he or she knows through being actively involved in the learning process. The rest of the class is passive. You (the instructor) may ensure that all students are actively learning (and no one is passive) by requiring all students to explain their answers or to summarize simultaneously through the formulate, share, listen, and create procedure.

1. The **task** for students is to explain their answers and reasoning to a classmate and practice the skill of explaining. The **cooperative goal** is to create a joint answer that both members agree to and can explain.

2. **Students formulate an answer to a question** that requires them to summarize what the lesson has covered so far.

3. Students turn to a neighbor (classmate close by) and share their answers and reasoning.

4. **Students listen carefully to their partner's explanation**. They should take notes, nod their head, smile, and encourage their partner to explain the answer and reasoning in detail.

5. **The pair creates a new answer that is superior to their initial formulations** through the processes of association, building on each other's thoughts, and synthesizing.

6. The instructor monitors the pairs and assists students in following the procedure. To ensure individual accountability, you may wish to ask randomly selected students to explain the joint answer they created with their partner.

FORMULATE, SHARE, LISTEN, CREATE

Johnson, D. W., Johnson, R., & Smith, K. (1998). **Active Learning: Cooperation In The College Classroom**. Edina, MN: Interaction Book Company. (612) 831-9500; FAX (612) 831-9332.

COOPERATIVE NOTE-TAKING PAIRS

The notes students take during a lecture are an indicator of what they have learned. Much of the research on lecturing has focused on the value of note-taking, distinguishing between the encoding function of notes and the storage function of notes (Anderson & Armbruster, 1986). Both the encoding (i.e., note-taking assists learning from lectures) and storage (i.e., review of notes is helpful) functions of note-taking increase learning. Taking notes during lectures has been shown to be more effective than listening (Kiewra, 1987), but using the notes for review is more important than the mere fact of taking notes (Kiewra, 1985b).

Students often take notes very incompletely (Hartley & Marshall, 1974; Kiewra, 1985a). There are several reasons why notes may be incomplete:

1. Students with low working memory capacity have difficulty taking notes during lectures, possibly because of difficulties in keeping information available in memory while writing it down (Kiewra & Benton, 1988).

2. The information processing load of a student in a lecture is increased when the student has little prior knowledge of the information (White & Tisher, 1986). When the lecturer uses visual aids frequently a student may become overloaded from the pressure to take notes from visual presentations in addition to the verbal statements.

3. Students who are unskilled in note-taking may take incomplete notes.

4. Students may have a false sense of familiarity with the material presented and, therefore, not bother taking notes.

To improve learning from lectures, students may focus on increasing the quantity and quality of the notes they take and/or improving their methods of reviewing the notes they have taken. Research on improving the quantity and quality of notes taken by students during lectures has often focused on the stimulus characteristics of the lecture itself (e.g, pace of the lecture, use of advance organizers) or on the characteristics of the lecturer (White & Tisher, 1986).

Task: For students to focus on increasing the quantity and quality of the notes they take and/or improving their methods of reviewing the notes they have taken.

3 : 21

Johnson, D. W., Johnson, R., & Smith, K. (1998). **Active Learning: Cooperation In The College Classroom.** Edina, MN: Interaction Book Company. (612) 831-9500; FAX (612) 831-9332.

Cooperative: Two students work together with the common goal of mastering the information being presented.

Procedure: After exposure to a lecture segment, one partner summarizes his or her notes to the other, who in turn adds and corrects. Students may ask each other, "*What have you got in your notes so far?*" "*What are the three key points made by the instructor?*" "*What was the most surprising thing the instructor said?*" The **rule** is that each member must take something from the other's notes to improve his or her own.

Individual Accountability: The notes of a student may be randomly chosen to be examined by the instructor.

Criteria For Success: Complete and accurate notes that have been orally reviewed by each student.

Expected Behaviors: Explaining, listening, synthesizing by all group members.

Intergroup Cooperation: Whenever it is helpful, check procedures, answers, and strategies with another group.

Cooperative note-taking pairs are a tool for structuring active cognitive processing by students during lectures and reducing the information processing load of students. Among other things, it allows for a quick turnaround of what is being learned. Knowledge must be communicated to another person as soon as possible after it is learned if it is to be retained and fully understood. The cooperative note-taking pair procedure results in:

1. The students immediately rehearsing and more deeply processing the information. Appropriate encoding of information in long-term memory requires rehearsal, reorganization, or elaboration of the information. A typical student rarely has the opportunity to rehearse the information from a lecture while that information is still fresh in his or her mind.

2. Students making multiple passes through the material, cognitively processing the information they are learning, and explicitly using metacognitive strategies.

When students are provided with the instructor's lecture notes for review, performance is improved (e.g., Masqud, 1980).

Johnson, D. W., Johnson, R., & Smith, K. (1998). **Active Learning: Cooperation In The College Classroom**. Edina, MN: Interaction Book Company. (612) 831-9500; FAX (612) 831-9332.

READ AND EXPLAIN PAIRS

Whenever you give material to students to read, students may read it more effectively in cooperative pairs than individually.

1. Assign students to pairs (one high reader and one low reader in each pair. Tell students what specific pages you wish them to read. The **expected criterion for success** is that both members are able to explain the meaning of the assigned material correctly.

2. The **task** is to learn the material being read by establishing the meaning of each paragraph and integrating the meaning of the paragraphs. The **cooperative goal** is for both members to agree on the meaning of each paragraph, formulate a joint summary, and be able to explain its meaning.

3. The **procedure** the student pairs follow is:

    a. Read all the headings to get an overview.

    b. Both students silently read the first paragraph. Student A is initially the **summarizer** and Student Be is the **accuracy checker**. Students rotate the roles after each paragraph.

    c. The **summarizer** summarizes in his or her own words the content of the paragraph to his or her partner.

    d. The **accuracy checker** listens carefully, corrects any misstatements, and adds anything left out. Then he or she tells how the material relates to something they already know.

    e. The students move on to the next paragraph, switch roles, and repeat the procedure. They continue until they have read all the assignment. They then summarize and agree on the overall meaning of the entire assigned material.

4. During the lesson the instructor systematically (a) monitors each reading pair and assists students in following the procedure, (b) ensures **individual accountability** by randomly selecting students to summarize what they have read so far, and (c) reminds students that there is **intergroup cooperation** (whenever it is helpful they may check procedures, answers, and strategies with another group).

Johnson, D. W., Johnson, R., & Smith, K. (1998). **Active Learning: Cooperation In The College Classroom**. Edina, MN: Interaction Book Company. (612) 831-9500; FAX (612) 831-9332.

CONCEPT INDUCTION

Concepts may be taught inductively as well as deductively. Concept formation may be done inductively by instructing students to figure out why the examples have been placed in the different boxes.

Tasks: Analyze the examples the instructor places in each box. Identify the concept represented by each box. Then create new examples that may be placed in the boxes.

Cooperative: Students turn to the person next to them and create an answer they can agree on.

Procedure:
1. Draw two (or three) boxes on the chalkboard. Label them Box 1, Box 2, or Box 3.
2. Place one item in each box.
3. Instruct students to use the **formulate, explain, listen, create** procedure to discuss how the items are different.
4. Place another item in each box and repeat. Tell students not to say out loud to another group or the class how the items are different. Each pair must discover it.
5. Once a pair "has it," the members are to make a definition for each box. They then create new examples that may be placed in the boxes.

The procedure for students is:
1. **Formulate** an individual answer.
2. **Share** their answer with their partner.
3. **Listen** carefully to their partner's answer.
4. **Create** a new answer that is superior to their initial formulations through the processes of association, building on each other's thoughts, and synthesizing.

Expected Criteria For Success: Each student must be able to identify the concept represented by each box.

Individual Accountability: One member from the pair will be randomly chosen to explain the answer.

Expected Behaviors: Explaining, listening, synthesizing by all members.

Johnson, D. W., Johnson, R., & Smith, K. (1998). **Active Learning: Cooperation In The College Classroom**. Edina, MN: Interaction Book Company. (612) 831-9500; FAX (612) 831-9332.

❧ Step Three: Closure Focused Discussions ❧

The **third step** in using informal cooperative learning is to (a) assign students to pairs or triads and (b) give them an ending discussion task lasting four to five minutes. The discussion task is aimed at having students summarize what they have learned during the class session, integrate it into existing conceptual networks, and point them towards the homework and the next class session.

During the closure focused discussion, students work in small discussion groups to reconstruct the lecture conceptually. Menges (1988) states that a number of research studies conducted in the 1920's document students' forgetting curve for lecture material. The average student had immediate recall of 62 percent of the material presented in the lecture, but that recall declined to 45 percent after three to four days, and fell to 24 percent after 8 weeks. If students were asked to take an examination immediately after the lecture (systematically reviewing what they had just learned), however, they retained almost twice as much information after 8 weeks, both in terms of factual information and conceptual material. There is every reason to believe that other types of systematic reviews, such as focused discussions and writing assignments, will have similar effects on the retention of the material covered in the lectured.

CLOSURE NOTE-TAKING PAIRS

1. Students are assigned to pairs or chose a nearby person to work with.

2. The **cooperative goal** is to master the information presented during the class session.

3. The **tasks** are to reflect on the class session, review class notes, and ensure the notes are complete and accurate.

4. Member A summarizes the first section of his or her notes to Member B. Member B adds anything left out, corrects anything that is wrong, and relates the information to previously learned material.

5. The roles are reversed and Member B summarizes section two and Member A checks for accuracy. This sequence is repeated until all of the notes are checked.

6. Students may ask each other, *"What have you got in your notes?"* *"What are the key points made by the instructor?"* *"What was the most surprising thing the instructor said today?"*

Johnson, D. W., Johnson, R., & Smith, K. (1998). **Active Learning: Cooperation In The College Classroom**. Edina, MN: Interaction Book Company. (612) 831-9500; FAX (612) 831-9332.

CLOSURE FOCUSED DISCUSSION PAIRS

Tasks: Summarize what has been learned from the lecture and answer questions posed by the instructor that point towards the homework and future class topics.

Cooperative: One set of answers from the pair, both members have to agree, and both members have to be able to explain their answers.

Procedure: The instructor gives an ending discussion task to summarize what students have learned from the lecture. Students should have four or five minutes to summarize and discuss the material covered in the lecture. The discussion should result in students integrating what they have just learned into existing conceptual frameworks. The task may also point students toward what the homework will cover or what will be presented in the next class session. This provides closure to the lecture. The pairs of students may be asked to list:

1. What are the five most important things you learned?

2. What are two questions you wish to ask?

The instructor collects the answers and records them to support the importance of the procedure and to see what students have learned. Handing the papers back periodically with brief comments from the instructor on them helps reinforce this procedure for students.

Individual Accountability: One group member will be randomly selected to explain the group's answers.

Expected Behaviors: Explaining, listening, synthesizing by all members.

Intergroup Cooperation: Whenever it is helpful, check procedures, answers, and strategies with another group.

3 : 26

Johnson, D. W., Johnson, R., & Smith, K. (1998). **Active Learning: Cooperation In The College Classroom**. Edina, MN: Interaction Book Company. (612) 831-9500; FAX (612) 831-9332.

CLOSURE COOPERATIVE WRITING PAIRS

Students can write a "*one-minute paper*" at the end of each teaching session describing (Light, 1990):

1. *"The major point I learned today is..."*

2. *"The main unanswered question I still have is..."*

The one-minute paper (a) helps students focus on the central themes of the course and (b) provides faculty feedback about the success of their teaching.

CLOSURE REVIEW PAIRS

Students are asked to discuss in pairs each of the major topics discussed in class.

1. Assign students to pairs.

2. Give each pair a list of the major topics covered in the class session.

3. The **task** is to recall what they remember (learned) about each topic.

4. The **cooperative goal** is to arrive at one set of learnings about each of the major topics covered in the class session.

5. Procedure: Each pair takes one topic at a time and write down their best answer to the following questions:

   a. What is the topic?   c. What learning activities were used to teach the topic?

   b. Why is it important?   d. What interests you most about the topic?

6. Monitor the pairs. Randomly ask a student to explain a topic. Take notes on which topics seem to be most difficult for students to remember.

7. Ask the pairs to hand in their answers to the list of topics. Read the responses and note which topics were not fully understood. You may wish to review those topics in the next class session.

Johnson, D. W., Johnson, R., & Smith, K. (1998). **Active Learning: Cooperation In The College Classroom**. Edina, MN: Interaction Book Company. (612) 831-9500; FAX (612) 831-9332.

IMPLEMENTATION ASSIGNMENT

Task: For students to make a specific contract with their base group as to how they will apply what they have learned.

Cooperative: Each group member must commit him- or herself to the group to apply what he or she has learned. A binding contract to apply what was learned is negotiated with the group.

Procedure: At the end of the class session each member plans how to apply what he or she has learned. This implementation assignment functions as a learning contract with the base group. Each member discusses with the group and then writes down three specific answers to the questions:

  1. What have I learned?

  2. How will I use it?

  In planning how to implement what they have learned, it is important for students to be as specific as possible about implementation plans and to keep a careful record of their implementation efforts.

Individual Accountability: Each group member may be randomly selected by the instructor to explain his or her implementation plans and results.

Expected Behaviors: Explaining, listening, summarizing by all members.

Other Informal Cooperative Learning Groups

PEER FEEDBACK GROUPS

Students tend to like courses that offer frequent opportunities to revise and improve their work as they go along. Students may learn best when they have a chance to submit an early version of their work, get detailed feedback and criticism, and then hand in a final version for a grade. Any course requirement may go through a peer feedback group before it is formally submitted to the instructor. In a meta-analysis of educational procedures, Walberg (1984) identified feedback as the most powerful predictor of learning. Students need continuous feedback about the adequacy of their performances which may be best provided by classmates.

Johnson, D. W., Johnson, R., & Smith, K. (1998). **Active Learning: Cooperation In The College Classroom**. Edina, MN: Interaction Book Company. (612) 831-9500; FAX (612) 831-9332.

BOOK-ENDS FOR FILMS OR DEMONSTRATIONS

Whenever the class session includes a demonstration (modeling of skills or procedures), video or film, or guest lecturer, informal cooperative learning groups are useful in setting an anticipatory set and processing what was learned. Whenever a demonstration, video or film, or guest speaker is used in a class:

1. Before the demonstration or video:

   a. Present three or four questions that help students organize in advance what they know about the topic and set expectations as to what the demonstration or video will cover.

   b. List several questions that need to be answered or several things students should observe while they watch the demonstration or video.

2. After the demonstration or video has ended:

   a. Present three or four questions that will help students review and organize what they observed and learned.

   b. Combine pairs into groups of four and have the pairs share answers.

COOPERATIVE STUDY GROUPS

The Harvard Assessment Seminars (Light, 1990) compared the grades of students who studied alone with those of students who studied in groups of four to six. Invariably, the students who studied in small groups did better than students who studied alone. The students in small study groups spoke more often, asked more questions, and were generally more engaged than those in the larger groups. Some class time may be allocated to form and organize study groups.

3 : 29

Johnson, D. W., Johnson, R., & Smith, K. (1998). **Active Learning: Cooperation In The College Classroom**. Edina, MN: Interaction Book Company. (612) 831-9500; FAX (612) 831-9332.

ORAL TESTING IN PAIRS

Instructors can ask students to discuss the answer to test questions given orally. Examples of the procedures are:

1. **Multiple-Choice:** To have students recall or apply information that has just been presented, ask students a question (or give them a scenario) with several alternative answers (or responses). Working in pairs, students are to come to an agreement as to which answer is correct. An example from psychology is, "Instructor Smith was in conflict with his Department Chair over whether his scholarly and teaching activities were of sufficient quality for him to be promoted. He tended to go home and be hyper critical of his wife and super strict with his children. A psychoanalyst would view his behavior as an example of: (a) projection, (b) displacement, (c) repression. (correct answer, b. displacement)

2. **Correct Error:** To have students demonstrate their comprehension of the material being presented, give students an erroneous statement. Working in pairs, students are to come to an agreement as to how to correct the statement. An example is, "*Kurt Lewin conducted the classic study on cooperation and competition in 1949.*" (Correct answer: Morton Deutsch conducted the study)

3. **Incomplete Sentence:** To elicit deeper level understanding from students, give them a sentence stem that needs completion. Working in pairs, students are to come to an agreement as to how to complete the sentence. An example is, "*Social interdependence theory may be defined as...*"

HIGHER-LEVEL REASONING PAIRS

1. **In Your Own Words:** Instructors present a major concept or set of ideas and ask students to form pairs and agree on how to restate the concept or set of ideas in their own words (paraphrase).

2. **Developing A Rationale For A Proposition:** To promote higher-level reasoning, instructors may:

   a. Present students with a proposition (e.g., Democracy will promote prosperity).

Johnson, D. W., Johnson, R., & Smith, K. (1998). **Active Learning: Cooperation In The College Classroom.** Edina, MN: Interaction Book Company. (612) 831-9500; FAX (612) 831-9332.

   b. Ask students to form pairs and prepare a rationale to support the proposition. The rationale should be organized in the form of a formal argument (thesis statement, rationale, conclusion).

3. **Compare And Contrast:** To promote deeper-level analysis of the material being presented, instructors may:

   a. Identify two important parallel elements from the lesson (theories, methods, writings, music, art, problems, historical events, cases).

   b. Ask students to form pairs and reach consensus about the similarities and differences between the two elements. An example is, *"Compare and contrast cognitive dissonance and cognitive conflict theory. What are their similarities and differences?"* Alternatively, instructors may ask, *"How are _____ and _____ alike? How are _____ and _____ different?"* A Venn Diagram can then be drawn.

ELEMENT ONE	ELEMENT TWO
Similarities	Differences

4. **Sequencing:** Instructors may present a series of steps (strategy, method, procedure) in random order and ask students to form pairs and reach consensus as to the correct order of the steps.

5. **Reaching A Conclusion:** Instructors may present a data set, a number of events, or a number of opinions and ask students to form pairs and reach consensus about the conclusion that should be drawn from the presented information.

Johnson, D. W., Johnson, R., & Smith, K. (1998). **Active Learning: Cooperation In The College Classroom**. Edina, MN: Interaction Book Company. (612) 831-9500; FAX (612) 831-9332.

COOPERATIVE STUDY GROUPS

The Harvard Assessment Seminars (Light, 1990) compared the grades of students who studied alone with those of students who studied in groups of four to six. Invariably, the students who studied in small groups did better than students who studied alone. The students in small study groups spoke more often, asked more questions, and were generally more engaged than those in the larger groups. Some class time may be allocated to form and organize study groups.

Summary

When lecturing or other direct teaching procedures (such as videos or films, demonstrations, guest speakers) are being used, **informal cooperative learning groups** focus student attention on the material to be learned, set a mood conducive to learning, set expectations as to what will be covered in a class session, ensure that students cognitively process the material being taught, keep students' attention focused on the content, provide an opportunity for discussion and elaboration which promote retention and transfer, make learning experiences personal and immediate, ensure that misconceptions, incorrect understanding, and gaps in understanding are corrected, and provide closure to an instructional session. Students can summarize in three-to-five minute discussions what they know about a topic before and after a class session. Short four-minute discussions in cooperative pairs can be interspersed throughout a lecture.

Besides the use of formal and informal cooperative learning groups, there is a need for a permanent base group that provides relatively long-term relationships among students. It is to this use of cooperative learning that we now turn.

Johnson, D. W., Johnson, R., & Smith, K. (1998). **Active Learning: Cooperation In The College Classroom**. Edina, MN: Interaction Book Company. (612) 831-9500; FAX (612) 831-9332.

INFORMAL COOPERATIVE LEARNING PLANNING FORM

DESCRIPTION OF THE LECTURE

1. **Lecture Topic**: _____

2. **Objectives** (Major Understandings Students Need To Have At The End Of The Lecture):

   a. _____

   b. _____

3. **Time Needed**: _____

4. **Method For Assigning Students To Pairs Or Triads**: _____

5. **Method Of Changing Partners Quickly**: _____

6. **Materials** (such as transparencies listing the questions to be discussed and describing the **formulate, share, listen, create** procedure):

   _____

ADVANCED ORGANIZER QUESTION(S)

Questions should be aimed at promoting **advance organizing** of what the students know about the topic to be presented and **establishing expectations** as to what the lecture will cover.

1. _____

2. _____

3. _____

Johnson, D. W., Johnson, R., & Smith, K. (1998). **Active Learning: Cooperation In The College Classroom**. Edina, MN: Interaction Book Company. (612) 831-9500; FAX (612) 831-9332.

COGNITIVE REHEARSAL QUESTIONS

List the specific questions to be asked every 10 or 15 minutes to ensure that participants understand and process the information being presented. Instruct students to use the **formulate, share, listen, and create** procedure.

1. _____

2. _____

3. _____

4. _____

Monitor by systematically observing each pair. Intervene when it is necessary. Collect data for whole class processing. Students' explanations to each other provide a window into their minds that allows you to see what they do and do not understand. Monitoring also provides an opportunity for you to get the know your students better.

SUMMARY QUESTION(S)

Give an ending discussion task and require students to come to consensus, write down the pair or triad's answer(s), sign the paper, and hand it in. Signatures indicate that students agree with the answer, can explain it, and guarantee that their partner(s) can explain it. The questions could (a) ask for a summary, elaboration, or extension of the material presented or (b) precue the next class session.

1. _____

2. _____

CELEBRATE STUDENTS' HARD WORK

1. _____

2. _____

Johnson, D. W., Johnson, R., & Smith, K. (1998). **Active Learning: Cooperation In The College Classroom**. Edina, MN: Interaction Book Company. (612) 831-9500; FAX (612) 831-9332.

CHAPTER FOUR: COOPERATIVE BASE GROUPS

CHAPTER FOUR:
COOPERATIVE BASE GROUPS

Introduction

In August 1942 U.S. troops landed on Guadalcanal (a island covered by dense, malaria-ridden jungle) and the battle for the Pacific islands began in earnest. Hundreds of thousands of men were killed (24,000 died in the taking of Iwo Jima alone including the reporter, Ernie Pyle) before in June 1945 the Allies took Okinawa, an island within striking distance of the mainland of Japan.

The beautiful island of Okinawa lies equidistant from Manila and Tokyo and was of strategic importance because its fall would leave Formosa (Taiwan) isolated. The first American landings began on April 7. The Machinato Line was hit on April 7; it took six days of fighting to get past it. Massive suicide attacks of Japanese kamikaze pilots on the surrounding American fleet caused the death of 5,000 American sailors. On Okinawa the marines hit the Shuri Line and then faced the final efforts of the Japanese at the edge of the island. When the Japanese defense crumbled, many Japanese soldiers leapt off cliffs to their death rather than surrender. Americans suffered 50,000 casualties while 110,000 Japanese troops died (another 7,000 wounded).

Author William Manchester wrote several years ago in **Life Magazine** about revisiting Sugar Loaf Hill in Okinawa, where 34 years before he had fought as a Marine. He describes how he had been wounded, sent to a hospital and, in violation of orders, escaped from the hospital to rejoin his Army unit at the front. Doing so meant almost certain death. "*Why did I do it?*" he wondered. His heroism is indicative of the power of long-term cooperative groups.

Nature Of Base Groups

The explanation of William Manchester's actions lies in long-term, committed and caring relationships he had developed with the other members of his squad and unit. Such committed relationships do not develop in a few hours or even a few days. They develop from spending long hours working together in which group members depend upon and support each other. In college, therefore, it is important that some of the relationships built through cooperative learning groups are long-term. College has to be more than a series of temporary encounters that last for only a few minutes, a class period, an instructional unit, or a semester. College students could be assigned to permanent cooperative base groups.

Johnson, D. W., Johnson, R., & Smith, K. (1998). **Active Learning: Cooperation In The College Classroom**. Edina, MN: Interaction Book Company. (612) 831-9500; FAX (612) 831-9332.

Base Groups

Types	Functions	Nature
Class (Meet At The Beginning And Ending Of Each Session Or Week)	Provide Academic Support To Members	Heterogeneous in Membership
College (Meet At The Beginning And Ending Of Each Day Or Week)	Provide Personal Support To Members	Meet Regularly (Daily, Bi-Weekly)
	Manage Class Routines And Administrative Requirements	Last For Duration Of Class, Year, Or Until Graduation
	Personalize Class And College Experience	Ensure All Members Are Making Good Academic Progress

Cooperative base groups are long-term, heterogeneous cooperative learning groups with stable membership. Members' primary responsibilities are to (a) provide each other with support, encouragement, and assistance in completing assignments, (b) hold each other accountable for striving to learn, and (c) ensure all members are making good academic progress. Typically, cooperative base groups (a) are heterogeneous in membership (especially in terms of achievement motivation and task orientation), (b) meet regularly (for example, daily or biweekly), and (c) last for the duration of the class (a semester or year) or preferably until the students are graduated.

Types Of Base Groups

There are two ways base groups may be used at the college level. The **first** is to have a base group in each college course. Class base groups stay together only for the duration of the course. The **second** is to organize all students within the college into base groups and have the groups function as an essential component of college life. College base groups stay together for at least a year and preferably for four years or until all members are graduated. The **agendas** of both types of base groups can include:

1. **Academic support tasks:** Base group members encourage each other to master course content and complete all assignments. Members check to see what assignments each member has and what help they need to complete them. The group discusses assignments, answers any questions about assignments, provides information about what a member missed, and plans, reviews, and edits papers. Members can prepare each other to take tests and go over the questions missed afterwards. Members can share their areas of expertise (such as art or computers)

Johnson, D. W., Johnson, R., & Smith, K. (1998). **Active Learning: Cooperation In The College Classroom.** Edina, MN: Interaction Book Company. (612) 831-9500; FAX (612) 831-9332.

with each other. Above all, members monitor each other's academic progress and make sure all members are achieving.

2. **Personal support tasks:** Base group members listen sympathetically when a member has problems with parents or friends, have general discussions about life, give each other advice about relationships, and help each other solve nonacademic problems. Base groups provide interpersonal relationships that personalize the course.

3. **Routine tasks:** The base group provides a structure for managing course procedures such as attendance and homework.

4. **Assessment and evaluation tasks:** The base group provides a structure for assessing and evaluating student academic learning. Many of the more complex and important assessment procedures can best be used in the context of cooperative learning groups.

FORMING BASE GROUPS

Group Size	Four (or three)
Assigning Students	Random Assignment To Ensure Heterogeneity
Arranging Room	Permanent Place For Each Group To Meet
Preparing Materials	Standard Forms Students Use Each Meeting; Group File Folders
Assigning Roles	Runner, Explainer, Accuracy Checker, Encourager

Class Base Groups

The larger the class and the more complex the subject matter, the more important it is to have class base groups. The base groups meet at the beginning and ending of each class session or (if the class session is 50 minutes or less) at the beginning of the first class session each week and at the end of the last class session each week. The members of base groups should exchange phone numbers and information about schedules as they may wish to meet outside of class. All members are expected to contribute actively to the group's work, strive to maintain effective working relationships with other members, complete all assignments and assist groupmates in completing their assignments, and indicate agreement with base group's work by signing the weekly contract. At the **beginning of each session** students meet in base groups to:

4 : 3

Johnson, D. W., Johnson, R., & Smith, K. (1998). **Active Learning: Cooperation In The College Classroom**. Edina, MN: Interaction Book Company. (612) 831-9500; FAX (612) 831-9332.

1. Greet each other and check to see that none of their group is under undue stress. Members ask: *"How are you today?" and "Are we all prepared for class?"*

2. Complete the next task for the membership grid. This helps members get to know each other better. The task is to answer such questions as: *"What is the best thing that has happened to you this week?" "What is your favorite television show?" "Who is your favorite music group?"*

3. Pick up their file folders with an attendance sheet, feedback form, and their assignments from the previous class session (with instructor's comments). The group members record their own attendance by writing the date and their initials in the **Attendance** section of the folder. They pass out the assignments from the previous class session and discuss any comments the instructor has made.

4. Check to see if members have completed their homework or need help in doing so. Members ask: *"Did you do your homework?" "Is there anything you did not understand?"* If extensive help is needed, an appointment is made.

5. In addition to the homework, members review what each member has read and done since the last class session. Each member may be prepared to (a) give a succinct summary of what he or she has read, thought about, and done, (b) share resources they have found, and (c) share copies of assignments they have completed.

6. Students collect each member's work, record it in their **Base Group Progress Report Sheet**, and place the assignments in their file folder. The file folder is returned to the instructor's desk. Periodically, the base groups may be given a checklist of academic skills and assesses which ones each member needs to practice.

Generally, class base groups are available to support individual group members. If a group member arrives late, or must leave early on an occasion, the group can provide information about what that student missed. Group members may assist one another in writing required papers and completing other assignments. They can discuss assigned work, plan papers, review each other's progress, and edit each other's work. Questions regarding the course assignments and class sessions may be addressed in base groups.

The class session closes with students meeting in base groups. **Closing tasks** may be:

1. Ensure all members understand the assignments. Find out what help each member needs to complete the assigned work.
2. Summarize at least three things members learned in today's class session.

3. Summarize how members will use/apply what they have learned.

4. Celebrate the hard work and learning of group members.

Johnson, D. W., Johnson, R., & Smith, K. (1998). **Active Learning: Cooperation In The College Classroom**. Edina, MN: Interaction Book Company. (612) 831-9500; FAX (612) 831-9332.

TABLE 4:1 BASE GROUP AGENDAS

Opening Tasks	Closing Tasks
Greeting And Welcome	Review And Clarify Assignments
Relationship And Group Building Task	Discuss What Was Learned
Check Homework	Discuss Applications Of Learnings
Review Progress: Ongoing Assignments	Celebrate Members' Hard Work

College Base Groups

At the beginning of their freshman year (or any academic year), students should be assigned to base groups. Base groups should stay together for at least a year and ideally, for four years (or until members are graduated). Class schedules should be arranged so members of base groups are assigned to as many of the same classes as possible. In essence, the computer is programmed to assign base groups to classes (whenever possible) rather than individuals.

During the year, base groups meet either twice each day or week. When base groups meet twice a week, they meet first thing in Monday morning and last thing Friday afternoon. **At the beginning of each day students meet in their base groups to:**

1. Congratulate each other for showing up with all their books and materials and check to see that none of their group is under undue stress. The two questions to discuss are: *"Are we all prepared for the day?" and "How are you today?"*

2. Check to see if members are keeping up with their work in their classes or need help and assistance in doing so. The questions to discuss are: *"Tell us how you are doing in each of your classes?" "Is there anything you did not understand?"* If there is not enough time to help each other during the base group meeting, an appointment is made to meet again during free time or lunch. Periodically, the base groups may be given a checklist of academic skills and assess which ones each member needs to practice.

3. Review what members have read and done since the evening before. Members should be able to give a succinct summary of what they have read, thought about, and done. They may come to the group meeting with resources they have found and want to share, or copies of work they have completed and wish to distribute to group members.

4. Get to know each other better and provide positive feedback by discussing such questions as: *"What do you like about each other?" "What do you like about yourself?"* and *"What is the best thing that has happened to you this week?"*

4 : 5

Johnson, D. W., Johnson, R., & Smith, K. (1998). **Active Learning: Cooperation In The College Classroom**. Edina, MN: Interaction Book Company. (612) 831-9500; FAX (612) 831-9332.

At the end of the day students meet in their base groups to ensure everyone is doing their homework, understands the assignments to be completed, and has the help and assistance they need to do their work. In addition, base groups may wish to discuss what members have learned during the day and check to see if all members have plans to do something fun and interesting that evening.

When base groups meet twice each week (perhaps first thing on Monday and last thing on Friday), they meet to discuss the academic progress of each member, provide help and assistance to each other, and hold each member accountable for completing assignments and progressing satisfactorily through the academic program. The **meeting on Monday morning** refocuses the students on college, provides any emotional support required after the weekend, reestablishes personal contact among base group members, and helps students set their academic goals for the week (what is still to be done on assignments that are due, and so forth). Members should carefully review each other's assignments and ensure that members have the help and assistance needed. In addition, they should hold each other accountable for succeeding academically. The **meeting on Friday afternoon** helps students review the week, set academic goals for the weekend (what homework has to be done before Monday), and share weekend plans and hopes.

Quick Base Group Meetings

At times there may be only a few minutes for base groups to meet. Even in as short a time as five to ten minutes, base groups are given four tasks:

1. A quick **self-disclosure task** such as, "*What is the most exciting thing you did during your vacation break? What is the best thing that happened to you last weekend? What is something you are proud of? What is your favorite ice cream?*"

2. An **administrative task** such as what classes to register for next semester.

3. An **academic task** such as, "*You have midterms coming up. As a group, write out three pieces of advice for taking tests. I will type up the suggestions from each group and hand them out next week.*"

4. A **closing task** such as wishing each other good luck for the day or week.

Building A Group Identity

The effectiveness of base groups depends in part on the strength of the group identity. The first week the base groups meet, for example, base groups can pick a name, design a flag, or choose a motto. If a instructor with the proper expertise is available, the groups will benefit from participating in a "challenge course" involving ropes and obstacles. This type of physical challenge that the groups complete together builds cohesion quickly.

4 : 6

Johnson, D. W., Johnson, R., & Smith, K. (1998). **Active Learning: Cooperation In The College Classroom**. Edina, MN: Interaction Book Company. (612) 831-9500; FAX (612) 831-9332.

Base Group Grid

The more personal the relationships among base group members, the greater the social support members can give each other. While students will get to know each other on a personal level while they work together, the process can be accelerated through the use of the base group grid.

Each base group meeting begins with a self-disclosure task in which students complete a column in their base group grid. Examples are, *"What is a positive childhood memory?" "What is your most memorable vacation?" "What is the best book you ever read?" "What is the most important thing you have ever done?" "What is the farthest place (from this room) you have traveled to?"* Members are to write each student's response down in enough detail that they can remember what it is a year later.

Members	Topic 1	Topic 2	Topic 3	Topic 4
Frank				
Helen				
Roger				
David				

Checking And Recording Homework

1. Homework is usually checked in base groups at the beginning of the class session.

2. One member of each group, **the runner**, goes to the instructor's desk, picks up the group's folder, and hands out any materials in the folder to the appropriate members.

3. The group reviews the assignment step-by-step to determine how much of the assignment each member completed and how well each member understands how to complete the material covered. Two roles are utilized: **Explainer** (explains step-by-step how the homework is correctly completed) and **accuracy checker** (verifies that the explanation is accurate and provides coaching if needed). The role of explainer is rotated so that each member takes turns explaining step-by-step how a portion of the homework is correctly completed. The other members are accuracy checkers. The base groups concentrate on clarifying the parts of the assignment that one or more members do not understand.

Johnson, D. W., Johnson, R., & Smith, K. (1998). **Active Learning: Cooperation In The College Classroom**. Edina, MN: Interaction Book Company. (612) 831-9500; FAX (612) 831-9332.

4. At the end of the review the runner records how much of the assignment each member completed, places members' homework in the group's folder, and returns the folder to the instructor's desk.

Base Group Contract Forms

At the end of each class session the base group summarizes what they learned, how they will apply what they have learned, and how they will help each other implement what was learned. In order to help them do so, a set of forms (included at the end of this chapter) may be provided in the folder.

Base Group Folders

The base group folder provides direct communication between students and the instructor. Each base group creates a folder. The folder is a means for managing attendance, assignments, and feedback. In each folder is an **attendance** sheet that each member initials to indicate attendance at the session. The base group folder provides a structure for keeping track of student attendance.

Each class session students place their completed **homework** and other assignments in the folder and turn it in. At the beginning of the following session, the assignments are returned (in the folder) with the instructor's comments on them. Each member receives a score for the quality of the homework completed and the base group as a whole receives a score (the sum of the points each member received). If all base group members complete the assignments at a 100 percent level, every member receives five bonus points. The base group folder provides a procedure for collecting and assessing assignments.

At the end of the session each member fills out a **feedback** form. The forms are collected and placed in the folder. The folder is then returned to the instructor as the session ends. The feedback form may ask for (a) the three most important things the student learned during the session, (b) students favorite part of the session, and (c) the questions students have about the material presented. The base group folder thus provides a structure for obtaining immediate feedback as to students' reactions to each class session.

The folders may be personalized with the group's motto or symbol.

Learning Community

A number of years ago, a speeding car carrying five teenagers slammed into a tree, killing three of them. It was not long before small, spontaneous memorials appeared at the tree. A yellow ribbon encircled its trunk. Flowers were placed nearby on the ground. There were a few goodbye signs. Such quiet testimonies send an important message: When it really matters, we are part of a community, not isolated individuals. We define

Johnson, D. W., Johnson, R., & Smith, K. (1998). **Active Learning: Cooperation In The College Classroom**. Edina, MN: Interaction Book Company. (612) 831-9500; FAX (612) 831-9332.

ourselves in such moments as something larger than our individual selves--as friends, classmates, teammates, and neighbors.

Many students have the delusion that each person is separate and apart from all other individuals. It is easy to be concerned only with yourself. But when classmates commit suicide and when cars slam into trees killing classmates, the shock waves force individuals out of the shallowness of self into the comforting depth of community. In times of crisis, such community may mean the difference between isolated misery and deep personal talks with caring friends.

Being part of a community does not "just happen" when a student enters college. Being known, being liked and respected, and being involved in relationships that provide help and support do not magically happen when the freshman year begins. While many students are able to develop the relationships with classmates and fellow students to provide themselves with support systems, other students are unable to do so. Colleges have to structure student experiences carefully to build a learning community.

Value Of Base Groups

The biggest disease today is not leprosy or tuberculosis, but rather the feeling of being unwanted, uncared for, and deserted by everybody.

Mother Teresa, Nobel Peace Prize, 1979

There are many reasons why cooperative base groups should be used in colleges. As may be seen from Appendix A, like all cooperative efforts, base groups will tend to increase student achievement, build more positive relationships among students, and increase students' psychological health. While these broad outcomes of cooperative efforts are compelling reasons in and of themselves for using base groups, base groups may also be used to increase social support, reduce attrition, and, promote positive attitudes toward education.

Johnson, D. W., Johnson, R., & Smith, K. (1998). **Active Learning: Cooperation In The College Classroom**. Edina, MN: Interaction Book Company. (612) 831-9500; FAX (612) 831-9332.

PURPOSES OF COOPERATIVE BASE GROUPS

Form a pair. Rank order the following purposes of cooperative base groups from most important ("1") to least important ("7").

	Academic Achievement
	Positive Relationships With Other Students
	Psychological Health
	Social Support For Efforts To Achieve Academically
	Social Support For Personal Well-Being
	Less Attrition And Dropping Out Of College
	More Positive Attitudes Toward Achievement And College
	Pro-Social Sense Of Meaning And Purpose In One's Life

Social Support

*A friend is one
to whom one may pour
out all the contents
of one's heart,
chaff and grain together
knowing that the
gentlest of hands
will take and sift it,
keep what is worth keeping
and with a breath of kindness
blow the rest away.*

Arabian Proverb

To discuss the relationship between social support and cooperative base groups, it is necessary to discuss the need for social support, the nature and types of social support, the power of social support, the requirement of long-term relationships, and its essential nature to learning communities.

4 : 10

Johnson, D. W., Johnson, R., & Smith, K. (1998). **Active Learning: Cooperation In The College Classroom**. Edina, MN: Interaction Book Company. (612) 831-9500; FAX (612) 831-9332.

Need For Social Support

Social support comes from relationships. If there are no relationships, there is no social support. Two years ago, a student in the Social Psychology of Education gave David the following feedback. "*This is my last quarter of course work for my doctorate. I have taken 120 quarter hours of courses. This is the first class in which I really got to know other students on a personal level. Why didn't this happen in all my classes?*" College students may be in a similar situation. Many colleges have low levels of social support because:

1. Learning situations are dominated by competitive and individualistic efforts (that promote rivalry, opposition, isolation, and self-centeredness).

2. The college is organized on a mass-production, bureaucratic structure that strives for depersonalized relationships in order to eliminate bias and favoritism. It assumes classmates and instructors are replaceable parts in the education machine and, therefore, "*any classmate or instructor will do.*"

College life can be lonely. Many college students begin college without a clear support group. College students can attend class without talking to other students. Like anyone else, college students can feel isolated, lonely, and depressed. Anyone, no matter how intelligent or creative, can have such feelings. Recently in a Minnesota college district, a popular star athlete committed suicide. Even though he was widely liked, the note he left indicated feelings of loneliness, depression, and isolation. He is not unusual. A recent national survey reported that growing feelings of worthlessness and isolation led 30 percent of America's brightest teenagers to consider suicide, and 4 percent have tried it.

America is in an epidemic of depression and anxiety among our adolescents and young adults (Seligman, 1988). And it seems to be spreading downward as more and more elementary school students are becoming depressed. The stark emptiness of the self and the vacuousness of "me" are revealed when students are faced with a personal crisis.

Isolated and alienated from classmates and faculty breeds depression. Working with others to achieve mutual goals is an essential influence on psychological health. Personal well-being cannot exist without commitment to and responsibility for joint well-being. Contributing to other's well-being increases one's own well-being. Without the sense of belonging, acceptance, and caring that results from cooperative efforts with others, students can remain isolated and vulnerable. In times of crisis, furthermore, being part of cooperative efforts may mean the difference between isolated misery and deep personal talks with caring friends.

Relationships that do develop in colleges may be at best, temporary shipboard romances as students know each other for a semester or year and then move on to different classes and new short-term relationships. Even relationships with instructors may last for only one semester or one year.

4 : 11

Johnson, D. W., Johnson, R., & Smith, K. (1998). **Active Learning: Cooperation In The College Classroom**. Edina, MN: Interaction Book Company. (612) 831-9500; FAX (612) 831-9332.

Nature Of Social Support

There are few things more important to college students than being part of a social support system. **Social support** may be defined as the existence and availability of people on whom one can rely for emotional, instrumental, informational, and appraisal aid. A **social support system** consists of significant others who share a person's tasks and goals and provide resources that enhance the individual's wellbeing and help the individual mobilize his or her resources to deal with challenging and stressful situations (Johnson & Johnson, 1989). Social support is most powerful when it is reciprocated.

There are two types of social support:

1. **Academic Support:** Classmates and faculty provide the assistance and help college students need to succeed academically.

2. **Personal Support:** Classmates and faculty care about and are personally committed to the well-being each student.

Academic Challenge (An Academic Demand That May Be Beyond Student's Capacity To Achieve)		**Social Support** (Significant Others Helping Student Mobilize His / Her Resources To Advance On The Challenge)

The Greater The Social Support, The Greater Academic Challenges May Be

Base Groups And Social Support

To face adversity and deal with challenge, individuals need the support of significant others who share the person's goals. Social support is provided when these significant others show emotional concern for the person's well-being and success, give aid that is instrumental in the person's success, provide information that helps the person succeed, and give feedback that helps the person improve and refine actions that lead to success.

The more social support a student has, the higher the student's achievement will tend to be, the more the student will persist on challenging tasks, the more likely students will be graduated, the healthier psychologically and physically the students will tend to be, the better able students will be to manage stress, and the more likely students will be to challenge their competencies to grow and develop (Johnson & Johnson, 1989). The success of a college depends largely on the social support students have while they are in attendance.

4 : 12

Johnson, D. W., Johnson, R., & Smith, K. (1998). **Active Learning: Cooperation In The College Classroom**. Edina, MN: Interaction Book Company. (612) 831-9500; FAX (612) 831-9332.

THE POWER OF COOPERATIVE BASE GROUPS

RESOURCES	FUNCTIONS: TO INCREASE
1. **Emotional concern** such as attachment, reassurance, and a sense of being able to rely on and confide in a person, all of which contribute to the belief that one is loved and valued.	1. **Achievement and productivity**, including persistence on difficult and challenging tasks.
2. **Instrumental aid** such as direct aid, goods, or services.	2. **Physical health** as individuals involved in close relationships live longer, get sick less often, and recover from illness faster than do isolated individuals.
3. **Information aid** such as facts or advice that may help to solve a problem.	3. **Psychological health**, as close relationships promote adjustment and development by preventing neuroticism and psychopathology, reducing distress, and providing resources such as confidants.
4. **Appraisal aid** such as feedback about degree to which certain behavioral standards are met (information relevant to self-evaluation).	4. **Constructive management of stress and challenges** by providing the caring, resources, information, and feedback needed to cope with stress and by buffering the impact of stress on the individual. Social support and stress are related in that the greater the social support individuals have, the less the stress they experience, and the better able they are to manage the stresses involved in life. The same is true of challenges that test the limits of a student's ability and resolve. There are few challenges that cannot be met when sufficient social support is provided.

Johnson, D. W., Johnson, R., & Smith, K. (1998). **Active Learning: Cooperation In The College Classroom**. Edina, MN: Interaction Book Company. (612) 831-9500; FAX (612) 831-9332.

Long-Term Cooperative Efforts

The longer a cooperative group exists, the more caring their relationships will tend to be, the greater the social support they will provide for each other, the more committed they will be to each other's success, and the more influence members will have over each other. Permanent cooperative base groups provide the arena in which caring and committed relationships can be created that provide the social support needed to improve attendance, personalize the college experience, increase achievement, and improve the quality of college life.

SOCIAL SUPPORT	
ACADEMIC SUPPORT	**PERSONAL SUPPORT**
Encourage And Hold Members Accountable To Complete Assignments, Attend Class, And Achieve Academically	Personalize Class And College Life
Discusses Assignments, Answers Questions, Give Help & Assistance In Understanding Material Being Studied	Listen Sympathetically When A Member Has Problems With Friends Or Parents
Provides Information About What a Late Or Absent Member Missed	Help Each Other Solve Nonacademic Problems
Prepares Members To Take Tests And Go Over Questions Missed Afterwards	Communicate Respect, Liking, And Confidence In One's Ability To Manage One's Challenges
Share Areas Of Expertise (Such As Art Or Computers) With Each Other	Communicate Commitment To One's Well-Being
Monitor Members' Academic Progress And Ensure They Are Achieving	Discuss Personal Beliefs And Experiences

Attrition

Two of the causes of dropping out of college are social alienation and academic alienation. The absence of significant social and intellectual contact often results in departure from college. Base groups provide a means of both preventing and combating dropping out of college. Any student who believes that "*in this college, no one knows me, no one cares about me, no one would miss me when I'm gone,*" is at risk of dropping out. Base groups provide a set of personal and supportive relationships and an academic support system that may prevent many students from dropping out of college through integrating students into college life. **Base groups also provide a means of fighting a**

Johnson, D. W., Johnson, R., & Smith, K. (1998). **Active Learning: Cooperation In The College Classroom**. Edina, MN: Interaction Book Company. (612) 831-9500; FAX (612) 831-9332.

student's inclination to drop out. A faculty member may approach a base group and say, "*Roger thinks he is dropping out of college. Go find and talk to him. We're not going to lose Roger without a fight.*"

Changing Students' Attitudes About Academic Work

There are many students who do not value academic work, do not aspire to do well in college, do not plan to take the more difficult courses, and try to just get by. One of the responsibilities of the faculty is to change the attitudes of these students so that they value college, education, and hard work to learn. In doing so, there are several general principles, supported by research (see Johnson & F. Johnson, 1997), to guide faculty efforts:

1. Attitudes are changed in groups, not individual by individual. Focus your efforts on having students within small groups persuade each other to value education.

2. Attitudes are changed as a result of small group discussions that lead to public commitment to work harder in college and take education more seriously. Attitudes are rarely modified by information or preaching.

3. Messages from individuals who care about, and are committed to, the student are taken more seriously than messages from indifferent others. Build committed and caring relationships between academically-oriented and nonacademically-oriented students.

4. Personally tailor appeals to value education to the student. General messages are not nearly as effective as personal messages. The individuals best able to construct an effective personal appeal are peers who know the student well.

5. Plan for the long term, not sudden conversions. Internalization of academic values will take years of persuasion by caring and committed peers.

6. Support from caring and committed peers is essential to modifying attitudes and behaviors and maintaining the new attitudes and behaviors. Remember, "You can't do it alone. You need help from your friends."

The college experience should inculcate in students a set of attitudes that include valuing education, working hard to learn, taking valuable but difficult courses (such as math, science, and foreign languages), and aspiring to go to graduate school. An important tool for doing so is cooperative base groups. They provide the arena in which academic values may be encouraged and the necessary caring and committed relationships may be developed.

Johnson, D. W., Johnson, R., & Smith, K. (1998). **Active Learning: Cooperation In The College Classroom**. Edina, MN: Interaction Book Company. (612) 831-9500; FAX (612) 831-9332.

Meaning, Purpose, And Psychological Health

The long-term caring and committed relationships promoted by the use of base groups contributes to students' sense of meaning and purpose in college life. Psychological health is increased when an individual believes he or she is striving to achieve meaningful goals and is engaged in meaningful activities. **Meaning** is primarily created from contributing to the wellbeing of others and the common good. The significance of one's actions depend on the degree to which one balances concern for self with concern for others and the community as a whole.

The major barrier to meaning and significance is egocentrism and the focus on one's own well-being at the expense or indifference to the well-being of others. Among many current high school and college students, personal pleasures and pains, successes and failures, occupy center stage in their lives (Conger, 1988; Seligman, 1988). Each person tends to focus on gratifying his or her own ends without concern for others. Physical, psychological, and material self-indulgence has become a primary concern (Conger, 1988; National Association of Secondary College Principals, 1984). Over the past 20 years, self-interest has become more important than commitment to community, country, or God. Young adults have turned away from careers of public service to careers of self-service. Many young adults have a **delusion of individualism**, believing that (a) they are separate and apart from all other individuals and, therefore, (b) others' frustration, unhappiness, hunger, despair, and misery have no significant bearing on their own well-being. With the increase in the past two decades in adolescents' and young adults' concern for personal well-being, there has been a corresponding diminished concern for the welfare of others (particularly the less advantaged) and of society itself (Astin, Green, & Korn, 1987; Astin, Green, Korn, & Schalit, 1986). Self-orientation interferes with consideration of others' needs and concern for others as equally deserving persons.

Meaning does not spring from competitive or individualistic efforts where students strive for outcomes that benefit no one but themselves. Purpose does not grow from egocentric focus on own material gain. Without involvement in interdependent efforts and the resulting concern for others, it is not possible to realize oneself except in the most superficial sense (Conger, 1981; Slater, 1971). Excessive concern for self leads to a banality of life, self-destructiveness, rootlessness, loneliness, and alienation (Conger, 1988). Individuals are empowered, are given hope and purpose, and experience meaning when they contribute to the well-being of others within an interdependent effort. Almost all people, when asked what makes their life meaningful, respond "friends, parents, siblings, spouses, lovers, children, and feeling loved and wanted by others (Klinger, 1977).

Working in cooperative groups provides an opportunity to affect classmates' lives in positive ways. Contributing to the well being of others results in the conviction that what one is doing has meaning and is of some significance. Base groups are especially powerful experiences as students get to know and value their groupmates at such a deep level.

Johnson, D. W., Johnson, R., & Smith, K. (1998). **Active Learning: Cooperation In The College Classroom**. Edina, MN: Interaction Book Company. (612) 831-9500; FAX (612) 831-9332.

Conclusions

Love is loyalty. Love is teamwork. Love respects the dignity of the individual. Heartpower is the strength of your corporation.

Vice Lombardi

In revisiting Sugar Loaf Hill in Okinawa William Manchester gained an important insight. *"I understand at last, why I jumped hospital that long-ago Sunday and, in violation of orders, returned to the front and almost certain death. It was an act of love. Those men on the line were my family, my home. They were closer to me than I can say, closer than any friends had been or ever would be. They were comrades; three of them had saved my life. They had never let me down, and I couldn't do it to them. I had to be with them, rather than let them die and me live with the knowledge that I might have saved them. Men, I now knew, do not fight for flag or country, for the Marine Corps or glory or any other abstraction. They fight for their friends."*

Base groups are long-term heterogeneous cooperative learning groups with stable membership whose primary responsibilities are to provide support, encouragement, and assistance in completing assignments and hold each other accountable for striving to learn. There are two ways base groups may be used. The first is to have a base group in each course. The second is to organize all students within the college into base groups and have the groups function as an essential component of college life. College base groups stay together for at least a year and preferably for four years or until all members are graduated. Base groups focus the power of long-term relationships on supporting academic progress, motivating academic effort, creating positive attitudes toward learning, increasing retention and graduation rates, and providing the caring and commitment necessary for a full and complete college experience.

In order to use cooperative learning effectively, instructors must understand the basic elements that make cooperation work. These basic elements are described in the next chapter. In addition, formal cooperative learning, informal cooperative learning, and cooperative base groups form a "gestalt" that allows instructors to create a learning community within classrooms and colleges. The integrated use of the three types of cooperative learning will be discussed in Chapter 6.

4 : 17

Johnson, D. W., Johnson, R., & Smith, K. (1998). **Active Learning: Cooperation In The College Classroom**. Edina, MN: Interaction Book Company. (612) 831-9500; FAX (612) 831-9332.

BASE GROUP MEETINGS

When: Base groups meet at the beginning and end of each class session.

Opening Tasks: Ask and answer two or more of the following questions:

1. How are you today? What is the best thing that has happened to you since the last class session?

2. Are you prepared for this class session?

3. Did you do your homework? Is there anything about it you do not understand?

4. What have you read, thought about, or done relevant to this course since the last class session?

5. May I read and edit your advanced preparation paper? Will you read and edit mine?

Closing Task: Answer the following questions.

1. Do you understand the assignment? What help do you need to complete it?

2. What are three things you learned in today's class session?

3. How will you use/apply what you have learned?

Celebrate the hard work and learning of group members.

Cooperative: One set of answers from the group, everyone must agree, and everyone must be able to explain.

Individual Accountability: One member of your group will be selected randomly to present your group's answers. At the beginning of the next class session, group members will ask you if you have followed through on your assignments and plans.

Expected Behaviors: Active participating, encouraging, summarizing, and synthesizing.

Intergroup Cooperation: Whenever it is helpful, check procedures, answers, and strategies with another group. When you are finished, compare your answers with those of another group and discuss.

Johnson, D. W., Johnson, R., & Smith, K. (1998). **Active Learning: Cooperation In The College Classroom**. Edina, MN: Interaction Book Company. (612) 831-9500; FAX (612) 831-9332.

BASE GROUP CONTRACT

Write down your major learnings from the assignments and this class session. Then write down how you plan to implement each learning. Share what you learned and your implementation plans with your base group. Listen carefully to their major learnings and implementation plans. You may modify your plans on the basis of your groupmates' plans. Volunteer one thing you can do to help each groupmate implement his or her plans. Utilize the help groupmates offer. Sign each member's plans to seal the contract.

MAJOR LEARNINGS	IMPLEMENTATION PLANS

Date: _____ Participant's Signature: _____

Signatures Of Group Members: _____

_____

Johnson, D. W., Johnson, R., & Smith, K. (1998). **Active Learning: Cooperation In The College Classroom**. Edina, MN: Interaction Book Company. (612) 831-9500; FAX (612) 831-9332.

BASE GROUP PROGRESS REPORT

Name: _____ Group: _____

Class: _____ Level: _____

Date	Assignment	Successes	Problems

Describe Critical Or Interesting Incidents:

Johnson, D. W., Johnson, R., & Smith, K. (1998). **Active Learning: Cooperation In The College Classroom**. Edina, MN: Interaction Book Company. (612) 831-9500; FAX (612) 831-9332.

Chapter Five:

Basic Elements Of Cooperative Learning

Introduction

The Killer Bees is a boys' high college basketball team from Bridgehampton, New York (a small, middle-class town on Long Island) (described in Katzenbach & Smith, 1993). Bridgehampton High College's total enrollment has declined since 1985 from 67 to 41, with less than 20 males attending the high college. There have never been more than 7 players on the team. Yet, since 1980 the Killer Bees have amassed a record of 164 wins and 32 losses, qualified for the state championship playoffs six times, won the state championship twice, and finished in the final four two other times. None of their players was ever really a star and the team was never tall. Not one of the Killer Bees went on to play professional basketball. Although every Killer Bee was graduated and most went on to college, few had the talent to play basketball in college.

How did the Killer Bees become so successful with so few players and so little talent? There are at least three reasons why the Killer Bees consistently won against bigger supposedly more talented opponents. The first is that the Killer Bees' game was "team basketball." They won, not by superior talent, but through superior teamwork. The second reason is that team members adopted an incredible work ethic. They practiced 365 days a year on skill development and teamwork. The third reason was their versatility and flexibility in how they played their opponents. The source of the Killer Bee's focus on team work, hard work, and versatility was a richness and depth of purpose that eludes most teams. Their mission was more than winning basketball games. They were committed to bringing honor and recognition to their community and protecting and enhancing their legacy. They were also committed to each other. The commitment of team members was reciprocated by the community, whose members came to every game and relentlessly cheered the team on.

It is the potential for such performances that make cooperative groups the key to successful education. Teamwork can do for learning what it did for the Killer Bees' basketball performance. The truly committed cooperative learning group is probably the most productive instructional tool educators have. Creating and maintaining truly committed cooperative learning groups, however, is far from easy. In most classrooms they are rare, perhaps because many educators:

Johnson, D. W., Johnson, R., & Smith, K. (1998). **Active Learning: Cooperation In The College Classroom**. Edina, MN: Interaction Book Company.

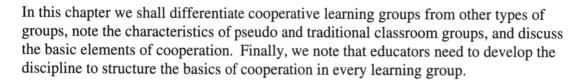

1. Are confused about what:

    a. Is (and is not) a cooperative learning group.

    b. The "basics" that make cooperative learning groups work.

2. Lack the discipline to implement the basics of cooperative efforts in a rigorous way.

In this chapter we shall differentiate cooperative learning groups from other types of groups, note the characteristics of pseudo and traditional classroom groups, and discuss the basic elements of cooperation. Finally, we note that educators need to develop the discipline to structure the basics of cooperation in every learning group.

Making Potential Group Performance A Reality

Not all groups are cooperative groups. Placing people in the same room and calling them a cooperative group does not make them one. Having a number of people work together does not make them a cooperative group. Study groups, project groups, lab groups, committees, task forces, departments, and councils are groups, but they are not necessarily cooperative. Groups do not become cooperative groups simply because that is what someone labels them.

The authors have studied cooperative learning groups for 30 years. We have interviewed thousands of students and instructors in a wide variety of college districts in a number of different countries over three different decades to discover how groups are used in the classroom and where and how cooperative groups work best. On the basis of our findings and the findings of other researchers such as Katzenbach and Smith (1993), we have developed a learning group performance curve to clarify the difference between traditional classroom groups and cooperative learning groups (Figure 5.1).

The learning group performance curve illustrates that how well any small group performs depends on how it is structured. On the performance curve four types of learning groups are described. It begins with the individual members of the group and illustrates the relative performance of these students to pseudo groups, traditional classroom groups, cooperative learning groups, and high-performance cooperative learning groups.

A **pseudo-learning group** is a group whose members have been assigned to work together but they have no interest in doing so. They meet, but do not want to work together or help each other succeed. Members often block or interfere with each other's learning, communicate and coordinate poorly, mislead and confuse each other, loaf, and seek a free ride. The interaction among group members detracts from individual learning without delivering any benefit. The result is that the sum of the whole is less than the

Johnson, D. W., Johnson, R., & Smith, K. (1998). **Active Learning: Cooperation In The College Classroom**. Edina, MN: Interaction Book Company.

potential of the individual members. The group does not mature because members have no interest in or commitment to each other or the group's future.

A **traditional classroom learning group** (see Table 5.1) is a group whose members have accepted that they are to work together, but see little benefit from doing so. Interdependence is low. The assignments are structured so that very little if any joint work is required. Members do not take responsibility for anyone's learning other than their own. Members interact primarily to share information and clarify how the assignments are to be done. Then they each do the work on their own. And their achievements are individually recognized and rewarded. Students are accountable as separate individuals, not as members of a team. Students do not receive training in social skills, and a group leader is appointed who is in charge of directing members' participation. There is no processing of the quality of the group's efforts.

A **cooperative learning group** is more than a sum of its parts. It is a group whose members are committed to the common purpose of maximizing each other's learning. It has a number of defining characteristics. **First,** the group goal of maximizing all members' learning provides a compelling purpose that motivates members to roll up their sleeves and accomplish something beyond their individual achievements. Each member takes responsibility for the performance of him- or herself, all teammates, and the group as a whole. Members believe that "they sink or swim together," and "if one of us fails, we all fail." **Second**, in a cooperative group the focus is both on group and individual accountability. Group members hold themselves and each other accountable for doing high quality work. And they also hold themselves and each other accountable for achieving the overall group goals. **Third**, group members do real work together. They not only meet to share information and perspectives, they produce discrete work-products through members' joint efforts and contributions. And they give whatever assistance and encouragement is needed to promote each other's success. Through promoting each other's success, group members provide both academic and personal support based on a commitment to and caring about each other. **Fourth**, members are taught social skills and are expected to use them to coordinate their efforts and achieve their goals. Both taskwork and teamwork skills are emphasized. All members accept the responsibility for providing leadership. **Finally**, groups analyze how effectively they are achieving their goals and how well members are working together. There is an emphasis on continuous improvement of the quality of their learning and teamwork processes.

A **high-performance cooperative learning group** is a group that meets all the criteria for being a cooperative learning group and outperforms all reasonable expectations, given its membership. What differentiates the high-performance group from the cooperative learning group is the level of commitment members have to each other and the group's success. Jennifer Futernick, who is part of a high-performing, rapid response team at McKinsey & Company, calls the emotion binding her teammates together a form of love (Katzenbach & Smith, 1993). Ken Hoepner of the Burlington Northern Intermodal Team (also described by Katzenbach and Smith, 1993) stated: *"Not only did*

Johnson, D. W., Johnson, R., & Smith, K. (1998). **Active Learning: Cooperation In The College Classroom**. Edina, MN: Interaction Book Company.

we trust each other, not only did we respect each other, but we gave a damn about the rest of the people on this team. If we saw somebody vulnerable, we were there to help." Members' mutual concern for each other's personal growth enables high-performance cooperative groups to perform far above expectations, and also to have lots of fun. The bad news about high-performance cooperative groups is that they are rare. Most groups never achieve this level of development.

TYPES OF GROUPS

Demonstrate your understanding of the different types of groups by matching the definitions with the appropriate group. Check your answers with your partner and explain why you believe your answers to be correct.

	TYPE OF GROUP	DEFINITION
	Pseudo Group	a. A group in which students work together to accomplish shared goals. Students perceive they can reach their learning goals if and only if the other group members also reach their goals.
	Traditional Learning Group	b. A group whose members have been assigned to work together but they have no interest in doing so. The structure promotes competition at close quarters.
	Cooperative Learning Group	d. A group that meets all the criteria for being a cooperative group and outperforms all reasonable expectations, given its membership.
	High- Performance Cooperative Learning Group	c. A group whose members agree to work together, but see little benefit from doing so. The structure promotes individualistic work with talking.

5 : 4

Johnson, D. W., Johnson, R., & Smith, K. (1998). **Active Learning: Cooperation In The College Classroom**. Edina, MN: Interaction Book Company.

FIGURE 5.1 COOPERATIVE EFFORTS

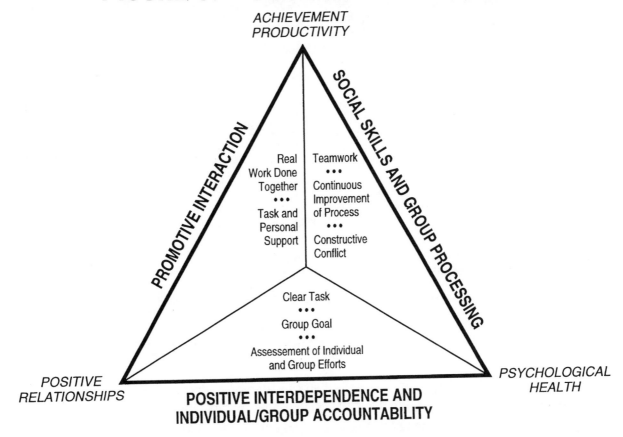

ACHIEVEMENT
PRODUCTIVITY

PROMOTIVE INTERACTION

SOCIAL SKILLS AND GROUP PROCESSING

Real
Work Done
Together
• • •
Task and
Personal
Support

Teamwork
• • •
Continuous
Improvement
of Process
• • •
Constructive
Conflict

Clear Task
• • •
Group Goal
• • •
Assessment of Individual
and Group Efforts

POSITIVE
RELATIONSHIPS

PSYCHOLOGICAL
HEALTH

POSITIVE INTERDEPENDENCE AND
INDIVIDUAL/GROUP ACCOUNTABILITY

FIGURE 5.2 THE LEARNING GROUP PERFORMANCE CURVE

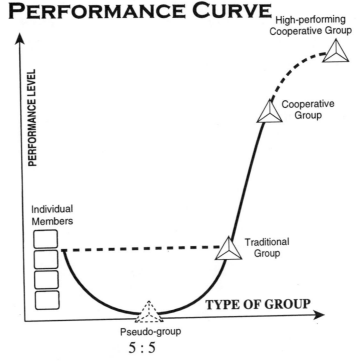

High-performing
Cooperative Group

PERFORMANCE LEVEL

Cooperative
Group

Individual
Members

Traditional
Group

TYPE OF GROUP

Pseudo-group

5 : 5

Johnson, D. W., Johnson, R., & Smith, K. (1998). **Active Learning: Cooperation In The College Classroom**. Edina, MN: Interaction Book Company.

TABLE 1.1 COMPARISON OF LEARNING GROUPS

TRADITIONAL LEARNING GROUPS	COOPERATIVE LEARNING GROUPS
Low interdependence. Members take responsibility only for self. Focus is on individual performance only.	High positive interdependence. Members are responsible for own and each other's learning. Focus is on joint performance.
Individual accountability only.	Both group and individual accountability. Members hold self and others accountable for high quality work.
Assignments are discussed with little commitment to each other's learning.	Members promote each other's success. They do real work together and help and support each other's efforts to learn.
Teamwork skills are ignored. Leader is appointed to direct members' participation.	Teamwork skills are emphasized. Members are taught and expected to use social skills. All members share leadership responsibilities.
No group processing of the quality of its work. Individual accomplishments are rewarded.	Group processes quality of work and how effectively members are working together. Continuous improvement is emphasized.

Forces Hindering Group Performance

Performance and small groups go hand-in-hand. Although cooperative groups outperform individuals working alone, there is nothing magical about groups. There are conditions under which groups function effectively and conditions under which groups function ineffectively. **Potential barriers to group effectiveness** are (Johnson & F. Johnson, 1997):

1. **Lack of Group Maturity:** Group members need time and experience working together to develop into an effective group. Temporary, ad hoc groups usually do not develop enough maturity to function with full effectiveness.

2. **Uncritically Giving One's Dominant Response:** A central barrier to higher-level reasoning and deeper-level understanding is the uncritical giving of members' dominant response to academic problems and assignments. Instead, members should generate a number of potential answers and choose the best one.

3. **Social Loafing--Hiding in the Crowd:** When a group is working on an additive task (group product is determined by summing together individual group members' efforts), and individual members can reduce their effort without other members realizing that they are doing so, many people tend to work less hard. Such social loafing has been demonstrated on a variety of additive tasks such as rope pulling, shouting, and clapping.

Johnson, D. W., Johnson, R., & Smith, K. (1998). **Active Learning: Cooperation In The College Classroom**. Edina, MN: Interaction Book Company.

4. **Free Riding--Getting Something for Nothing:** On disjunctive tasks (if one member does it, all members receive the benefit), there is the possibility of a free ride. When group members realize that their efforts are dispensable (group success or failure depends very little on whether or not they exert effort), and when their efforts are costly, group members are less likely to exert themselves on the group's behalf.

5. **Motivation Losses Due To Perceived Inequity--Not Being a Sucker:** When other group members are free riding, there is a tendency for the members who are working to reduce their efforts to avoid being a "sucker."

6. **Groupthink:** Groups can be overconfident in their ability and resist any challenge or threat to their sense of invulnerability by avoiding any disagreements and seeking concurrence among members.

7. **Lack of Sufficient Heterogeneity:** The more homogeneous the group members, the less each member adds to the group's resources. Groups must develop the right mix of taskwork and teamwork skills necessary to do their work. Heterogeneity ensures a wide variety of resources are available for the group's work.

8. **Lack of Teamwork Skills:** Groups with members who lack the small group and interpersonal skills required to work effectively with others often underperform their most academically able members.

9. **Inappropriate Group Size:** The larger the group, the fewer members that can participate, the less essential each member views their personal contribution, the more teamwork skills required, and the more complex the group structure.

Not every group is effective. Most everyone has been part of a group that wasted time, was inefficient, and generally produced poor work. But there are groups that accomplish wondrous things. Educators must be able to spot the hindering factors and eliminate them by ensuring the basics of cooperation are carefully structured.

Applying The Basics Of Cooperation

Educators fool themselves if they think well-meaning directives to "*work together*," "*cooperate*," and "*be a team*," will be enough to create cooperative efforts among students. There is a discipline to creating cooperation. The "basics" of structuring cooperation are not a series of elements that characterize good groups. They are a regimen that, if followed rigorously, will produce the conditions for effective cooperation. Cooperative learning groups are rare because educators (and students) seek shortcuts to quality groupwork and assume that "*traditional classroom groups will do*."

Johnson, D. W., Johnson, R., & Smith, K. (1998). **Active Learning: Cooperation In The College Classroom**. Edina, MN: Interaction Book Company.

Like persons who wish to lose weight without dieting, they seek easy alternatives to the disciplined application of the basics of effective groups.

The basics of cooperation are not new and startling to most educators. They already have a good idea of what the basics are. The performance potential of learning groups, however, is frequently lost due to educators not applying what they know about cooperative efforts in a disciplined way. The basic components of effective cooperative efforts are positive interdependence, face-to-face promotive interaction, individual and group accountability, appropriate use of social skills, and group processing.

Positive Interdependence: We Instead Of Me

All for one and one for all.

Alexandre Dumas

Within a football game, the quarterback who throws the pass and the receiver who catches the pass are positively interdependent. The success of one depends on the success of the other. It takes two to complete a pass. One player cannot succeed without the other. Both have to perform competently if their mutual success is to be assured. If one fails, they both fail.

The discipline of using cooperative groups begins with structuring positive interdependence (see Johnson & Johnson, 1992b, 1992c). Group members have to know that they "*sink or swim together.*" It is positive interdependence that requires group members to roll up their sleeves and work together to accomplish something beyond individual success. It is positive interdependence that creates the realization that members have two responsibilities: to learn the assigned material and to ensure that all members of their group learn the assigned material. When positive interdependence is clearly understood, it highlights (a) each group member's efforts are required and indispensable for group success (i.e., there can be no "free-riders") and (b) each group member has a unique contribution to make to the joint effort because of his or her resources and/or role and task responsibilities (i.e., there can be no social loafing).

There are three steps in structuring positive interdependence. **The first is assigning the group a clear, measurable task.** Members have to know what they are supposed to do. **The second step is to structure positive goal interdependence** so members believe that they can attain their goals if and only if their groupmates attain their goals. In other words, members know that they cannot succeed unless all other members of their group succeed. Positive goal interdependence ensures that the group is united around a common goal, a concrete reason for being, such as *"learn the assigned material and make sure that all members of your group learn the assigned material."* Positive goal interdependence may be structured by informing group members they are responsible for:

Johnson, D. W., Johnson, R., & Smith, K. (1998). **Active Learning: Cooperation In The College Classroom**. Edina, MN: Interaction Book Company.

1. All members scoring above a specified criterion when tested individually.

2. All members improve their performance over their previous scores:

3. The overall group score (determined by adding the individual scores of members together) being above a specified criterion.

4. One product (or set of answers) successfully completed by the group.

Individuals will contribute more energy and effort to meaningful goals than to trivial ones. Being responsible for others' success as well as for one's own gives cooperative efforts a meaning that is not found in competitive and individualistic situations. The efforts of each group member, therefore, contribute not only to their own success, but also the success of groupmates. When there is meaning to what they do, ordinary people exert extraordinary effort. It is positive goal interdependence that gives meaning to the efforts of group members.

The third step is to supplement positive goal interdependence with other types of positive interdependence. Reward/celebration interdependence is structured when (a) each group member receives the same tangible reward for successfully completing a joint task (if all members of the group score 90 percent correct or better on the test, each will receive 5 bonus points) or (b) group members jointly celebrate their success. Regular celebrations of group efforts and success enhance the quality of cooperation. In order for students to look forward to working in cooperative groups, and enjoy doing so, they must feel that (a) their efforts are appreciated and (b) they are respected as an individual. Long-term commitment to achieve is largely based on feeling recognized and respected for what one is doing. Thus, students' efforts to learn and promote each other's learning need to be (a) observed, (b) recognized, and (c) celebrated. The celebration of individual efforts and group success involves structuring reward interdependence. Ways of structuring positive reward interdependence include:

1. Celebrating their joint success when all members reach criterion.

2. Adding bonus points to all members' academic scores when everyone in the group achieves up to criterion or when the overall group score reaches criterion.

3. Receiving nonacademic rewards (such as extra free time, extra recess time, stickers, stars, or food) when all group members reach criterion.

4. Receiving a single group grade for the combined efforts of group members. This should be cautiously done until all students (and parents) are very familiar with cooperative learning.

5 : 9

Johnson, D. W., Johnson, R., & Smith, K. (1998). **Active Learning: Cooperation In The College Classroom**. Edina, MN: Interaction Book Company.

TYPES OF POSITIVE INTERDEPENDENCE

Positive Goal Interdependence: Students perceive that they can achieve their learning goals if and only if all the members of their group also attain their goals. Members of a learning group have a mutual set of goals that they are all striving to accomplish.

Positive Celebration/Reward Interdependence: Group celebrates success. A joint reward is given for successful group work and members' efforts to achieve.

Positive Resource Interdependence: Each member has only a portion of the information, resources, or materials necessary for the task to be completed and the member's resources have to be combined in order for the group to achieve its goal.

Positive Role Interdependence: Each member is assigned complementary and interconnected roles that specify responsibilities that the group needs in order to complete a joint task.

Positive Identity Interdependence: The group establishes a mutual identity through a name, flag, motto, or song.

Environmental Interdependence: Group members are bound together by the physical environment in some way. An example is putting people in a specific area in which to work.

Positive Fantasy Interdependence: A task is given that requires members to imagine that they are in a life or death situation and must collaborate in order to survive.

Positive Task Interdependence: A division of labor is created so that the actions of one group member have to be completed if the next team member is to complete his or her responsibility.

Positive Outside Enemy Interdependence: Groups are placed in competition with each other. Group members then feel interdependent as they strive to beat the other groups and win the competition.

Johnson, D. W., Johnson, R., & Smith, K. (1998). **Active Learning: Cooperation In The College Classroom**. Edina, MN: Interaction Book Company.

Role interdependence is structured when each member is assigned complementary and interconnected roles (such as reader, recorder, checker of understanding, encourager of participation, and elaborator of knowledge) that specify responsibilities that the group needs in order to complete the joint task. Roles prescribe what other group members expect from a person (and therefore the person is obligated to do) and what that person has a right to expect from other group members who have complementary roles. In cooperative groups responsibilities are often divided into (a) roles that help the group achieve its goals and (b) roles that help members maintain effective working relationships with each other. Such roles are vital to high-quality learning. The role of checker, for example, focuses on periodically asking each groupmate to explain what is being learned. Rosenshine and Stevens (1986) reviewed a large body of well-controlled research on teaching effectiveness and found "checking for comprehension" to be one specific teaching behavior that was significantly associated with higher levels of student learning and achievement. While the instructor cannot continually check the understanding of every student (especially if there are 30 or more students in the class), the instructor can engineer such checking by having students work in cooperative groups and assigning one member the role of checker.

Resource interdependence is structured when each member has only a portion of the information, materials, or resources necessary for the task to be completed and members' resources have to be combined in order for the group to achieve its goal. Ways of structuring resource interdependence include:

1. Limiting the resources given to the group. Only one pencil, for example, may be given to a group of three students.

2. Jigsawing materials so that each member has part of a set of materials. A group could be given the assignment of writing a biography of Abe Lincoln and information on Lincoln's childhood given to one member, information on Lincoln's early political career given to another, information on Lincoln as president given to a third, and information on Lincoln's assassination given to the fourth member.

3. Having each member make a separate contribution to a joint product. Each member, for example, could be asked to contribute a sentence to a paragraph, an article to a newsletter, or a chapter to a "book."

Identity interdependence is structured when the group establishes a mutual identity through a name or a group symbol such as a motto, flag, or song. Outside enemy interdependence (striving to perform higher than other groups) and fantasy interdependence (striving to solve hypothetical problems such as how to deal with being shipwrecked on the moon). Task interdependence is structured by creating a division of labor so that the actions of one group member have to be completed if the next group member is to complete his or her responsibilities. Environmental interdependence exists

Johnson, D. W., Johnson, R., & Smith, K. (1998). **Active Learning: Cooperation In The College Classroom**. Edina, MN: Interaction Book Company.

when group members are bound together by the physical environment in some way (such as a specific area to meet in).

The heart of cooperative efforts is positive interdependence. Without positive interdependence, cooperation does not exist. Positive interdependence may focus on joint outcomes or on the mutual effort required to achieve the group's goals. Positive goal and reward interdependence (with the related identity, outside enemy, fantasy, and environmental interdependence) result in members realizing that all group members (Johnson & Johnson, 1989a):

1. Share a common fate where they all gain or lose on the basis of the overall performance of group members. One result is a sense of personal responsibility (a) for the final outcome and (b) to do their share of the work.

2. Are striving for mutual benefit so that all members of the group will gain. There is recognition that what helps other group members benefits oneself and what promotes one's own productivity benefits the other group members.

3. Have a long-term time perspective so that long-term joint productivity is perceived to be of greater value than short-term personal advantage.

4. Have a shared identity based on group membership. Besides being a separate individual, one is a member of a team. The shared identity binds members together emotionally and creates an expectation for a joint celebration based on mutual respect and appreciation for the success of group members. The experience creates a positive cathexis so that group members like each other. Feelings of success are shared and pride is taken in other members' accomplishments as well as one's own.

Positive resource, role, and task interdependence result in individuals realizing that the performance of group members is mutually caused. No member is on his or her own. Each person views him- or herself as instrumental in the productivity of other group members and views other group members as being instrumental in his or her productivity. Members realize that their efforts are required in order for the group to succeed (i.e., there can be no "free- riders') and that their potential contribution to the group as being unique (because of their role, resources, or task responsibilities). Each member shares responsibility for other members' productivity (mutual responsibility) and is obligated to other members for their support and assistance (mutual obligation). As a result of the mutual causation, cooperative efforts are characterized by positive inducibility in that group members are open to being influenced by each other and substitutability in that the actions of group members substitute for each other so that if one member of the group has taken the action there is no need for other members to do so. There is a mutual investment in each other.

Johnson, D. W., Johnson, R., & Smith, K. (1998). **Active Learning: Cooperation In The College Classroom**. Edina, MN: Interaction Book Company.

The authors have conducted a series of studies investigating the nature of positive interdependence and the relative power of the different types of positive interdependence (Frank, 1984; Hwong, Caswell, Johnson, & Johnson, 1993; Johnson, Johnson, Stanne, & Garibaldi, 1990; Johnson, Johnson, Ortiz, & Stanne, 1991; Lew, Mesch, Johnson, & Johnson, 1986a, 1986b; Mesch, Johnson, & Johnson, 1988; Mesch, Lew, Johnson, & Johnson, 1986). Six questions concerning positive interdependence have been addressed by our research. The **first** question is whether group membership in and of itself is sufficient to produce higher achievement and productivity or whether group membership and positive interdependence are required. The results of Hwong, Caswell, Johnson, and Johnson (1993) indicate that positive interdependence is necessary. Knowing that one's performance affects the success of groupmates seems to create "responsibility forces" that increase one's efforts to achieve.

The **second** question is whether interpersonal interaction is sufficient to increase productivity or whether positive interdependence is required. Debra Mesch and Marvin Lew conducted a series of studies in which they investigated whether the relationship between cooperation and achievement was due to the opportunity to interact with peers or positive goal interdependence. Their results are quite consistent. The individuals achieved higher under positive goal interdependence than when they worked individualistically but had the opportunity to interact with classmates (Lew, Mesch, Johnson, & Johnson, 1985a, 1985b; Mesch, Johnson, & Johnson, 1988; Mesch, Lew, Johnson, & Johnson, 1985).

The **third** question is whether goal or reward interdependence is most important in promoting productivity and achievement. The results of the Mesch and Lew studies indicate that while positive goal interdependence is sufficient to produce higher achievement and productivity than an individualistic effort, the combination of goal and reward interdependence is even more effective. The impact of the two types of outcome interdependence seem to be additive.

The **fourth** question is whether different types of reward interdependence have differential effects on productivity. Michael Frank's (1984) study indicates not. Both working to achieve a reward and working to avoid the loss of a reward produced higher achievement than did individualistic efforts.

The **fifth** question is whether goal or resource interdependence is most important in enhancing productivity and achievement. Johnson and Johnson (in press) found goal interdependence promoted higher achievement than did resource interdependence. The study by Johnson, Johnson, Stanne, and Garibaldi indicated that while goal interdependence in and of itself increased achievement, the combination of goal and resource interdependence increased achievement even further. Compared with individualistic efforts, the use of resource interdependence alone seemed to decrease achievement and lower productivity.

Johnson, D. W., Johnson, R., & Smith, K. (1998). **Active Learning: Cooperation In The College Classroom**. Edina, MN: Interaction Book Company.

Finally, there is a question as to whether positive interdependence simply motivates individuals to try harder or facilitates the development of new insights and discoveries through promotive interaction. The latter position is supported by the fact that some studies have found that members of cooperative groups use higher level reasoning strategies more frequently than do individuals working individualistically or competitively.

In summary, our research indicates that positive interdependence provides the context within which promotive interaction takes place, group membership and interpersonal interaction among students do not produce higher achievement unless positive interdependence is clearly structured, the combination of goal and reward interdependence increases achievement over goal interdependence alone, and resource interdependence does not increase achievement unless goal interdependence is present also.

Individual Accountability/Personal Responsibility

What children can do together today, they can do alone tomorrow.

Vygotsky

Among the early settlers of Massachusetts there was a saying, "*If you do not work, you do not eat.*" Everyone had to do his or her fair share of the work. **The discipline of using cooperative groups includes structuring group and individual accountability. Group accountability** exists when the overall performance of the group is assessed and the results are given back to all group members to compare against a standard of performance. **Individual accountability** exists when the performance of each individual member is assessed, the results given back to the individual and the group to compare against a standard of performance, and the member is held responsible by groupmates for contributing his or her fair share to the group's success. On the basis of the feedback received, (a) efforts to learn and contribute to groupmates' learning can be recognized and celebrated, (b) immediate remediation can take place by providing any needed assistance or encouragement, and (c) groups can reassign responsibilities to avoid any redundant efforts by members.

The purpose of cooperative groups is to make each member a stronger individual in his or her own right. Individual accountability is the key to ensuring that all group members are in fact strengthened by learning cooperatively. After participating in a cooperative lesson, group members should be better prepared to complete similar tasks by themselves. There is a pattern to classroom learning. **First**, students learn knowledge, skills, strategies, or procedures in a cooperative group. **Second**, students apply the knowledge or perform the skill, strategy, or procedure alone to demonstrate

Johnson, D. W., Johnson, R., & Smith, K. (1998). **Active Learning: Cooperation In The College Classroom**. Edina, MN: Interaction Book Company.

their personal mastery of the material. Students learn it together and then perform it alone.

Individual accountability results in group members knowing they cannot "hitch-hike" on the work of others. When it is difficult to identify members' contributions, when members' contributions are redundant, and when members are not responsible for the final group outcome, members sometimes engage in social loafing or seek a free ride (Harkins & Petty, 1982; Ingham, Levinger, Graves, & Peckham, 1974; Kerr & Bruun, 1981; Latane, Williams & Harkins, 1979; Moede, 1927; Petty, Harkins, Williams, & Latane, 1977; Williams, 1981; Williams, Harkins, & Latane, 1981). Common ways to structure individual accountability include:

1. Keeping the size of the group small. The smaller the size of the group, the greater the individual accountability.

2. Giving an individual test to each student.

3. Giving random oral examination. Students are randomly selected to present his or her group's work to you (in the presence of the group) or to the entire class.

4. Observing each group and recording the frequency with which each member contributes to the group's work.

5. Assigning one student in each group the role of checker. The **checker** asks other group members to explain the reasoning and rationale underlying group answers.

6. Having students teach what they learned to someone else. When all students do this, it is called simultaneous explaining.

Positive Interdependence And Accountability

In cooperative situations, group members share responsibility for the joint outcome. Each group member takes **personal responsibility** for (a) contributing his or her efforts to accomplish the group's goals and (b) helping other group members do likewise. The greater the positive interdependence structured within a cooperative learning group, the more students will feel personally responsible for contributing their efforts to accomplish the group's goals. The shared responsibility adds the concept of ought to members' motivation--one **ough**t to do one's share, contribute, and pull one's weight. The shared responsibility also makes each group member personally accountable to the other group members. Students will realize that if they fail to do their fair share of the work, other members will be disappointed, hurt, and upset.

Johnson, D. W., Johnson, R., & Smith, K. (1998). **Active Learning: Cooperation In The College Classroom**. Edina, MN: Interaction Book Company.

Face-To-Face Promotive Interaction

In an industrial organization it's the group effort that counts. There's really no room for stars in an industrial organization. You need talented people, but they can't do it alone. They have to have help.

John F. Donnelly, President, Donnelly Mirrors

The discipline of using cooperative groups includes ensuring that group members meet face-to-face to work together to complete assignments and promote each other's success. Group members need to do real work together. Promotive interaction exists when individuals encourage and facilitate each other's efforts to complete tasks in order to reach the group's goals. Through promoting each other's success, group members build both an academic and a personal support system for each member. There are three steps to encouraging promotive interaction among group members. **The first is to schedule time for the group to meet.** As simple as this step seems, many learning groups are not given sufficient meeting time to mature and develop. **The second step is to highlight the positive interdependence that requires members to work together to achieve the group's goals.** It is positive interdependence that creates the commitment to each other's success. **The third step is to encourage promotive interaction among group members.** Monitoring groups and celebrating instances of members' promotive interaction is one way to do so.

While positive interdependence in and of itself may have some effect on outcomes, it is the face-to-face promotive interaction among individuals fostered by the positive interdependence that most powerfully influences efforts to achieve, caring and committed relationships, and psychological adjustment and social competence (Johnson & Johnson, 1989a). Promotive interaction is characterized by individuals providing each other with efficient and effective help and assistance, exchanging needed resources such as information and materials and processing information more efficiently and effectively, providing each other with feedback in order to improve subsequent performance, challenging each other's conclusions and reasoning in order to promote higher-quality decision making and greater insight into the problems being considered, advocating the exertion of effort to achieve mutual goals, influencing each other's efforts to achieve the group's goals, acting in trusting and trustworthy ways, being motivated to strive for mutual benefit, and a moderate level of arousal characterized by low anxiety and stress. Members do real work together.

5 : 16

Johnson, D. W., Johnson, R., & Smith, K. (1998). **Active Learning: Cooperation In The College Classroom**. Edina, MN: Interaction Book Company.

Interpersonal and Small Group Skills

I will pay more for the ability to deal with people than any other ability under the sun.

John D. Rockefeller

Placing socially unskilled students in a group and telling them to cooperate does not guarantee that they are able to do so effectively. We are not born instinctively knowing how to interact effectively with others. Interpersonal and small group skills do not magically appear when they are needed. Students must be taught the social skills required for high quality collaboration and be motivated to use them if cooperative groups are to be productive. The whole field of group dynamics is based on the premise that social skills are the key to group productivity (Johnson & F. Johnson, 1997).

The fourth arena in the disciplined use of cooperative groups is teaching group members the small group and interpersonal skills they need to work effectively with each other. In cooperative learning groups students are required to learn academic subject matter (**taskwork**) and also to learn the interpersonal and small group skills required to function as part of a group (**teamwork**). If the teamwork skills are not learned, then the taskwork cannot be completed. If group members are inept at teamwork, their taskwork will tend to be substandard. On the other hand, the greater the members' teamwork skills, the higher will be the quality and quantity of their learning. Cooperative learning is inherently more complex than competitive or individualistic learning because students have to simultaneously engage in taskwork and teamwork. In order to coordinate efforts to achieve mutual goals, students must (a) get to know and trust each other, (b) communicate accurately and unambiguously, (c) accept and support each other, and (c) resolve conflicts constructively (Johnson, 1991, 1993; Johnson & F. Johnson, 1997).

The more socially skillful students are, and the more attention instructors pay to teaching and rewarding the use of social skills, the higher the achievement that can be expected within cooperative learning groups. In their studies on the long-term implementation of cooperative learning, Marvin Lew and Debra Mesch (Lew, Mesch, Johnson & Johnson, 1986a, 1986b; Mesch, Johnson, & Johnson, 1988; Mesch, Lew, Johnson, & Johnson, 1986) investigated the impact of a reward contingency for using social skills as well as positive interdependence and a contingency for academic achievement on performance within cooperative learning groups. In the cooperative skills conditions students were trained weekly in four social skills and each member of a cooperative group was given two bonus points toward the quiz grade if all group members were observed by the instructor to demonstrate three out of four cooperative skills. The combination of positive interdependence, an academic contingency for high performance by all group members, and a social skills contingency promoted the highest achievement.

Johnson, D. W., Johnson, R., & Smith, K. (1998). **Active Learning: Cooperation In The College Classroom**. Edina, MN: Interaction Book Company.

HOW VALUABLE ARE SOCIAL SKILLS?

Given below are six of the more important outcomes of being socially skilled. Form a pair. Rank order the outcomes from most important ("1") to least important ("6").

RANK	OUTCOME OF SOCIAL SKILLS
	Personal development and identity: Our identity is created out of relationships with others. As we interact with others we note their responses to us, we seek feedback as to how they perceive us, and we learn how to view ourselves as others view us. Individuals who have few interpersonal skills have distorted relationships with others and tend to develop inaccurate and incomplete views of themselves.
	Employability, productivity and career success: Social skills may be even more important than education and technical skills to employability, productivity, and career success. Recent national surveys found that (a) when hiring new employees, employers value interpersonal and communication skills, responsibility, initiative, and decision-making skills and (b) 90 percent of the people fired from their jobs were fired for poor job attitudes, poor interpersonal relationships, inappropriate behavior, and inappropriate dress. In the real world of work, the heart of most jobs, especially the higher-paying, more interesting jobs, is getting others to cooperate, leading others, coping with complex power and influence issues, and helping solve people's problems in working with others.
	Quality of life: There is no simple recipe for creating a meaningful life, but the research indicates that for almost everyone a necessary ingredient for a high quality of life is some kind of satisfying, close, personal, intimate relationship.
	Physical health: Positive, supportive relationships have been found to be related to living longer lives, recovering from illness and injury faster and more completely, and experiencing less severe illnesses. Physical health improves when individuals learn the interpersonal skills necessary to take more initiative in their relationships and become more constructive in the way they deal with conflict. Loneliness and isolation kill. High quality relationships create and extend life.
	Psychological health: When individuals do not have the interpersonal skills to build and maintain positive relationships with others, psychological illness results. The inability to establish acceptable relationships often leads to anxiety, depression, frustration, alienation, inadequacy, helplessness, fear, and loneliness. The ability to build and maintain positive, supportive relationships, on the other hand, is related to psychological health and adjustment, lack of neuroticism and psychopathology, reduction of psychological distress, coping effectively with stress, resilience, self-reliance and autonomy, a coherent and integrated self-identity, high self-esteem, general happiness, and social competence.
	Ability to cope with stress: Positive and supportive relationships help individuals cope with stress by providing caring, information, resources, and feedback. Supportive relationships decrease the number and severity of stressful events, reduce anxiety, and help with the appraisal of the nature of the stress and one's ability to deal with it constructively. Discussions with supportive peers help individuals perceive the meaning of the stressful event, regain mastery over their lives, and enhance their self-esteem.

Johnson, D. W., Johnson, R., & Smith, K. (1998). **Active Learning: Cooperation In The College Classroom**. Edina, MN: Interaction Book Company.

Group Processing

Take care of each other. Share your energies with the group. No one must feel alone, cut off, for that is when you do not make it.

Willi Unsoeld, Renowned Mountain Climber

The final phase of the discipline of using cooperative groups is structuring group processing. Effective group work is influenced by whether or not groups reflect on (process) how well they are functioning. A **process** is an identifiable sequence of events taking place over time, and **process goals** refer to the sequence of events instrumental in achieving outcome goals (Johnson & F. Johnson, 1997). **Group processing** may be defined as reflecting on a group session to (a) describe what member actions were helpful and unhelpful and (b) make decisions about what actions to continue or change. The **purpose** of group processing is to clarify and improve the effectiveness of the members in contributing to the collaborative efforts to achieve the group's goals.

There are **five steps** in structuring group processing in order to improve continuously the quality of the group's taskwork and teamwork (see Johnson, Johnson, & Holubec, 1993a). **The first step is to assess the quality of the interaction among group members as they work to maximize each other's learning.** The easiest way to conduct such assessments of the "process" of how the group gets its work done is for the instructor to observe the cooperative learning groups as they work. The instructor systematically moves from group to group and uses a formal observation sheet or checklist to gather specific data on each group. The frequency with which targeted social skills are used can be recorded.

PROCESSING STARTERS

1. Name three things your group did well in working together. Name one thing your group could do even better.

2. Think of something that each group member did to improve group effectiveness. Tell them what it is.

3. Tell your group members how much you appreciate their help today.

4. Rate yourself from 1 (low) to 10 (high) on (name a cooperative skill like encouraging participation, checking for understanding). Share your rating with your group and explain why you rated yourself the way you did. Plan how to increase the frequency with which group members use this skill.

Johnson, D. W., Johnson, R., & Smith, K. (1998). **Active Learning: Cooperation In The College Classroom**. Edina, MN: Interaction Book Company.

Systematic observation allows instructors to attain a "window" into students' minds. Listening to students explain how to complete the assignment to groupmates provides better information about what students do and do not know and understand than do correct answers on tests or homework assignments. Listening in on students' explanations provides valuable information about how well the students understand the instructions, the major concepts and strategies being learned, and the basics of working together effectively. Wilson (1987, p.18) conducted a three-year, teaching-improvement study as part of a college faculty development program. Both faculty and students agreed that faculty needed help on knowing if the class understood the material or not.

Instructors are not the only ones who can observe groups and record data about their functioning. A student observer can be appointed for each learning group (rotating the responsibility for each lesson). And at the end of a lesson, each group member can fill out a checklist as to the frequency with which they engaged in each targeted social skill. It is often helpful to assess the quality of the overall group product so groups can compare how well they performed with specific patterns of interaction among members.

The second step in examining the process by which the group does its work is to give each learning group feedback. Instructors need to allocate some time at the end of each class session for each cooperative group to process how effectively members worked together. Group members need to describe what actions were helpful and unhelpful in completing the group's work and make decisions about what behaviors to continue or change. The data collected can be taken from the checklists and placed in a Pareto chart to focus the discussion on current levels of effectiveness and how to improve the quality of the group's work. Individual efforts that contribute to the group's success need to be recognized and celebrated. Such small group processing (a) enables learning groups to focus on maintaining good working relationships among members, (b) facilitates the learning of cooperative skills, (c) ensures that members receive feedback on their participation, (d) ensures that students think on the meta-cognitive as well as the cognitive level, and (e) provides the means to celebrate the success of the group and reinforce the positive behaviors of group members. Some of the keys to successful small group processing are allowing sufficient time for it to take place, providing a structure for processing (such as "List three things your group is doing well today and one thing you could improve"), emphasizing positive feedback, making the processing specific rather than general, maintaining student involvement in processing, reminding students to use their cooperative skills while they process, and communicating clear expectations as to the purpose of processing.

Group processing provides a structure for group members to hold each other accountable for being responsible and skillful group members. In order to contribute to each other's learning, group members need to attend class, be prepared (i.e., have done the necessary homework), and contribute to the group's work. A student's absenteeism and lack of preparation often demoralizes other members. Productive group work requires members to be present and prepared, and there should be some peer

Johnson, D. W., Johnson, R., & Smith, K. (1998). **Active Learning: Cooperation In The College Classroom**. Edina, MN: Interaction Book Company.

accountability to be so. When groups "process," they discuss any member actions that need to be improved in order for everyone's learning to be maximized.

The third step is for groups to set goals as to how to improve their effectiveness. Members suggest ways the teamwork could be improved and the group decides which suggestions to adopt. Discussing group functioning is essential. A common teaching error is to provide too brief a time for students to process the quality of their collaboration. Students do not learn from experiences that they do not reflect on. If the learning groups are to function better tomorrow than they did today, members must receive feedback, reflect on how their actions may be more effective, and plan how to be even more skillful during the next group session.

The fourth step is to process how effectively the whole class is functioning. In addition to small group processing, instructors should periodically conduct whole-class processing sessions. At the end of the class period the instructor can then conduct a whole-class processing session by sharing with the class the results of his or her observations. If each group had a student observer, the observation results for each group may be added together to get an overall class total.

The fifth step is to conduct small-group and whole-class celebrations. It is feeling successful, appreciated, and respected that builds commitment to learning, enthusiasm about working in cooperative groups, and a sense of self-efficacy about subject-matter mastery and working cooperatively with classmates.

Stuart Yager examined the impact on achievement of (a) cooperative learning in which members discussed how well their group was functioning and how they could improve its effectiveness, (b) cooperative learning without any group processing, and (c) individualistic learning (Yager, Johnson, & Johnson, 1985). The results indicate that the high-, medium-, and low-achieving students in the cooperation-with-group-processing condition achieved higher on daily achievement, post-instructional achievement, and retention measures than did the students in the other two conditions. Students in the cooperation-without-group-processing condition, furthermore, achieved higher on all three measures than did the students in the individualistic condition. Johnson, Johnson, Stanne, and Garibaldi (1990) conducted a follow-up study comparing cooperative learning with no-processing, cooperative learning-with-instructor processing (instructor specified cooperative skills to use, observed, and gave whole-class feedback as to how well students were using the skills), cooperative learning with instructor and student processing (instructor specified cooperative skills to use, observed, gave whole-class feedback as to how well students were using the skills, and had learning groups discuss how well they interacted as a group), and individualistic learning. Forty-nine high ability Black American high college seniors and entering college freshmen at Xavier University participated in the study. A complex computer-assisted problem-solving assignment was given to the students. All three cooperative conditions performed higher than did the individualistic condition. The combination of instructor and student processing resulted

Johnson, D. W., Johnson, R., & Smith, K. (1998). **Active Learning: Cooperation In The College Classroom**. Edina, MN: Interaction Book Company.

in greater problem-solving success than did the other cooperative conditions. Julie Archer-Kath (Archer-Kath, Johnson, & Johnson, in press) studied the impact of the combination of group and individual feedback with group feedback only on student performance and attitudes. Fifty-six eighth-grade midwestern students studying German were used as subjects. The investigators found that the combination of group and individual feedback resulted in higher achievement motivation, actual achievement, and more positive attitudes toward each other, the subject area, the instructor, and themselves.

Positive Interdependence And Intellectual Conflict

The greater the positive interdependence within a learning group, the greater the likelihood of intellectual disagreement and conflict among group members. When members of a cooperative learning group become involved in a lesson, their different information, perceptions, opinions, reasoning processes, theories, and conclusions will result in intellectual disagreement and conflict. When such controversies arise, they may be dealt with constructively or destructively, depending on how they are managed and the level of interpersonal and small group skills of the participants. When managed constructively, controversy promotes uncertainty about the correctness of one's conclusions, an active search for more information, a reconceptualization of one's knowledge and conclusions and, consequently, greater mastery and retention of the material being discussed and the more frequent use of higher-level reasoning strategies (Johnson & Johnson, 1979, 1989, 1992a). Individuals working alone in competitive and individualistic situations do not have the opportunity for such intellectual challenge and, therefore, their achievement and quality of reasoning suffer.

Reducing Problem Behaviors

When students first start working in cooperative learning groups they sometimes engage in unhelpful behaviors. Whenever inappropriate student behavior occurs, your first move should be toward strengthening the perceived interdependence.

Student Is Not Participating Or Bringing Work Or Materials		
Jigsaw Materials	Assign Student Role Essential For Group Success	Reward Group If All Members Achieve Up To Criterion To Increase Peer Pressure To Participate

Johnson, D. W., Johnson, R., & Smith, K. (1998). **Active Learning: Cooperation In The College Classroom**. Edina, MN: Interaction Book Company.

A Student Is Talking About Everything But The Assignment	
Give A Reward The Student Or Group Finds Especially Attractive	Structure Task So Steady Contributions Are Required For Group Success

A Student Is Working Alone And Ignoring The Group Discussion	
Limit Resources In The Group (If There Is Only One Pencil, The Member Will Be Unable To Work Alone)	Jigsaw Materials So That The Students Cannot Complete The Assignment Without Other Members' Information

A Student Is Refusing To Let Other Members Participate		
Jigsaw Resources	Assign Other Members Essential Roles (Such As Reader, Recorder, Summarizer)	Reward Group On Basis Of The Lowest Two Scores By Group Members

Summary

In certain groups, such as sports teams and combat units, there are factors such as contagious excitement, strong norms favoring maximal effort, and intense feelings of commitment, loyalty, and obligation, group members often demonstrate levels of motivation and effort far beyond what would be expected from an individual acting alone. During a basketball game in 1989, for example, Jay Burson, a player on the Ohio State University team, continued to play in a game after he had suffered a broken neck. There are many examples where people like Jay Burson doubled their efforts or placed themselves in great jeopardy because of their devotion and loyalty to other group members and the group.

Cooperative learning groups and student learning are inextricably connected. The truly committed cooperative learning group is probably the most productive instructional tool instructors have at their disposal, provided that instructors know what cooperative efforts are and have the discipline to structure them in a systematic way. Despite the fact that most educators are familiar with cooperative learning groups, many educators are imprecise in their thinking about cooperative efforts. For that reason, gaining a clear understanding of (a) what a cooperative learning group is and is not and (b) the basics of making cooperative efforts effective, can provide insights useful for strengthening the

Johnson, D. W., Johnson, R., & Smith, K. (1998). **Active Learning: Cooperation In The College Classroom**. Edina, MN: Interaction Book Company.

performance of cooperative learning groups. Imprecise thinking about cooperative learning groups, however, pales in comparison to the lack of discipline most educators bring to using cooperative learning groups in instructional situations.

Not all groups are cooperative groups. Groups can range from pseudo learning groups to traditional classroom groups to cooperative learning groups to high-performance cooperative learning groups. High-performance cooperative learning groups are rare. Most cooperative groups never reach this level. Many educators who believe that they are using cooperative learning are, in fact, using traditional classroom groups. There is a crucial difference between simply putting students in groups to learn and in structuring cooperation among students. Cooperation is not having students sit side-by-side at the same table to talk with each other as they do their individual assignments. Cooperation is not assigning a report to a group of students where one student does all the work and the others put their names on the product as well. Cooperation is not having students do a task individually with instructions that the ones who finish first are to help the slower students. Cooperation is much more than being physically near other students, discussing material with other students, helping other students, or sharing material among students, although each of these is important in cooperative learning.

Educators can examine any learning group and decide where on the group performance curve it now is. Pseudo learning groups and traditional classroom groups are characterized by group immaturity, members uncritically giving their dominant response in completing assignments, members engaging in social loafing and free riding, members losing motivation to learn, groupthink, homogeneity of skills and abilities, and inappropriate group size and resources. Cooperative learning groups are characterized by members perceiving clear positive interdependence, holding each other personally and individually accountable to do his or her fair share of the work, promoting each other's learning and success, appropriately using the interpersonal and small group skills needed for successful cooperative efforts, and processing as a group how effectively members are working together. These five essential components must be present for small group learning to be truly cooperative.

Creating cooperative learning groups is not easy. It takes daily, disciplined application of the basics of cooperative efforts. These basics are tough standards and present a difficult implementation challenge to instructors. At the same time, working hard to ensure that the basics are present in each learning group will accelerate instructors' efforts to ensure that all students are achieving up to their full potential.

Understanding how to implement the five basic elements in formal cooperative learning lessons, informal cooperative learning activities, and cooperative base groups sets the stage for using all three in an integrated way. That is the topic of the next chapter.

Johnson, D. W., Johnson, R., & Smith, K. (1998). **Active Learning: Cooperation In The College Classroom**. Edina, MN: Interaction Book Company.

Chapter Six:
Integrated Use Of All Types Of Cooperative Learning

Introduction

Pull together. In the mountains you must depend on each other for survival.

Willi Unsoeld, Mountain Climber

Structuring cooperative learning in classrooms involves integrating the use of the three types of cooperative learning groups. Each course may have a mixture of cooperative formal, informal, and base groups. Given below are two examples of how the different ways of using cooperative learning may be used. The examples are followed by a discussion of personalizing the learning environment of the class.

Table 6.1 Integrated Use Of All Types Of Cooperative Learning For 50 Minute Session		
Step	Activity	Time
1	Welcome And Opening Base Group Meeting	10
2	Choice 1: Direct Teaching, Informal Cooperative Learning	35
3	Choice 2: Work In Formal Cooperative Learning Groups	35
4	Choice 3: Direct Teaching, Formal Coop Learning Groups	35
5	Choice 4: Academic Controversy	35
6	Closing Base Group Meeting	5

Johnson, D. W., Johnson, R., & Smith, K. (1998). **Active Learning: Cooperation In The College Classroom**. Edina, MN: Interaction Book Company.

Table 6.2 Weekly Schedule For 50 Minute Class Sessions

Session 1		Session 2		Session 3	
Time	Activity	Time	Activity	Time	Activity
15	Base Group Meeting	5	Base Group Meeting	5	Base Group Meeting
30	Lecture With Informal CL	35	Formal CL Groups Work On Assignment Or Controversy	15	Formal CL Groups Work On Assignment
5	Base Group Meeting	5	Base Group Meeting	10	Lecture With Informal CL
				15	Base Group Meeting

Fifty-Minute Class Session

The types of cooperative learning may be used in an integrated way either on a class session (see Table 6.1) or a weekly (see Table 6.2) basis. Given below is a description of using the four types of cooperative learning in an integrated way during one class session. It involves an instructor welcome, an opening base group meeting, a choice among formal cooperative learning, informal cooperative learning, or academic controversy, and a closing base group meeting.

Instructor Welcome

The instructor formally starts the class by welcoming the students and instructing them to meet in their base groups.

Opening Base Group Meeting

The introduction and warm-up for the class are provided within base groups. The initial **base group** meeting includes the following tasks:

1. Greet each other and check to see that none of their group is under undue stress. Members ask: *"How are you today?"* and *"Are we all prepared for class*?"

Johnson, D. W., Johnson, R., & Smith, K. (1998). **Active Learning: Cooperation In The College Classroom**. Edina, MN: Interaction Book Company.

2. Check to see if members have completed their homework or need help in doing so. Members ask: *"Did you do your homework?" "Is there anything you did not understand?"*

3. Share resources they have found or copies of work they have completed and wish to distribute to their base group members.

4. Deepen their relationships by discussing such questions as: *"What is the best thing that has happened to you this week?" "What is your favorite television show?"*

Base group activities must be completed within about 5 minutes. Regularly structuring this time is essential for helping students get into a good learning mood, communicating high expectations about completing homework and helping others, and providing a transition between the student's (and instructor's) previous hour and the current class session.

Choice 1: Direct Teaching With Informal Cooperative Learning

Direct teaching begins and ends with a focused discussion in an informal cooperative learning group and has paired discussions interspersed throughout the lecture (see Chapter 5). During the discussions students:

1. **Formulate** an answer individually (30 seconds).

2. **Share** your answer with your partner (1 minute).

3. **Listen** carefully to your partner's answer (1 minute).

4. **Create** an answer that is superior to your individual answers (1 minute).

Students are slow and awkward at following this procedure initially but once they become familiar with it they work intensely. Again, this is an important time for the instructor to circulate among the students, listen in, and learn what they already know about the topic. In the long run it is important to vary the type of informal cooperative learning groups, using simultaneous explanation pairs one day and cooperative note-taking pairs another.

Choice 2: Formal Cooperative Learning Groups

If a group assignment is given, it is carefully structured to be cooperative (see Chapter 3). The instructor notes the objectives of the lesson, makes a series of preinstructional decisions, communicates the task and the positive interdependence, monitors the groups

Johnson, D. W., Johnson, R., & Smith, K. (1998). **Active Learning: Cooperation In The College Classroom.** Edina, MN: Interaction Book Company.

as they work and intervenes when needed, and evaluates students' learning and has groups process how effectively members are working together. Formal cooperative learning groups are used when the instructor wishes to achieve an instructional objective that includes conceptual learning, problem solving, or the development of students' critical thinking skills. Formal cooperative learning groups are needed for simulations of first-hand experiences, role playing, or the sharing of expertise and resources among members.

Choice 3: Short Direct Teaching And Short Group Assignment

The third choice for the instructor is to use a combination of direct teaching with informal cooperative learning and an assignment to be completed in formal cooperative learning groups. The group assignment may be carried over into the following class period.

Choice 4: Academic Controversy

The instructor's fourth choice is to conduct an academic controversy about an issue being studied. Students come prepared to present the best case possible for their assigned position, critically analyze the opposing position, learn the material supporting both sides, and come to their best reasoned judgment about the issue.

Closing Base Group Meeting

The class session ends in a base group meeting in which members list three or four major learnings and one or two questions about the material covered. The summaries and questions are handed in as the students leave. Commenting on what was learned and answering a few of the questions sends a message to the students that the activity is important. The summaries and questions provide the instructor with valuable information about what the students are learning. Finally, members of the base groups should celebrate their hard work and success.

Ninety-Minute Class Session

The basic structure of a 90-minute period is essentially the same as for the 50-minute period except it is easier both to lecture and have cooperative learning groups complete an assignment within one class session. Class begins with a base group meeting, the instructor gives a lecture using informal cooperative learning groups to ensure that students are cognitively active while the instructor disseminates information, conducts a formal cooperative learning activity to promote problem-solving and higher-level learning, and closes the class with a second base group meeting.

Johnson, D. W., Johnson, R., & Smith, K. (1998). **Active Learning: Cooperation In The College Classroom**. Edina, MN: Interaction Book Company.

Table 6.3 Integrated Use Of All Types Of Cooperative Learning For 90 Minute Session

Step	Activity	Time
1	Opening Base Group Meeting	10
2	Direct Teaching With Informal Cooperative Learning	25
3	Work On Assignment In Formal Cooperative Learning	40
4	Direct Teaching With Informal Cooperative Learning	10
5	Closing Base Group Meeting	5

Instructor Welcome

The instructor formally starts the class by welcoming the students and instructing them to meet in their base groups.

Opening Base Group Meeting

The base group meetings can be longer (up to 15 minutes) and more complex activities can be conducted. Valuable information can be gleaned by eavesdropping on the base groups and noting which parts of the assignment caused difficulty.

Direct Teaching With Informal Cooperative Learning

Direct teaching may follow. In using a variety of informal cooperative learning group procedures, faculty need to structure carefully the five basic elements of cooperative learning within the learning situation.

Complete Assignment In Formal Cooperative Learning Groups

Formal cooperative learning groups become the heart of longer class periods. Students take increasing responsibility for each other's learning, and the instructor takes increasing responsibility for guiding this process. Faculty should structure positive interdependence in a variety of ways and give students the opportunity to promote each other's learning face-to-face. It is helpful to use a variety of formal cooperative learning procedures, such as jigsaw, problem- solving, joint projects, and peer composition (see Chapter 3). Occasional reporting by the students to the whole class (by randomly calling on

Johnson, D. W., Johnson, R., & Smith, K. (1998). **Active Learning: Cooperation In The College Classroom**. Edina, MN: Interaction Book Company.

individual students to report for their group) can help the instructor guide the overall flow of the class. Carefully monitor the cooperative groups and use formal observation sheets to collect concrete data on group functioning to use during whole class and small group processing.

As an alternative to formal cooperative learning, an instructor may structure an academic controversy about an issue being studied. Students come prepared to present the best case possible for their assigned position, critically analyze the opposing position, learn the material supporting both sides, and come to their best reasoned judgment about the issue.

Direct Summary With Informal Cooperative Learning

At the end of the class session instructors will wish to call the class together and summarize what was covered and point towards what will be covered in the next class session. In doing so, students should be asked to consider one or two issues phrased as questions. Informal cooperative learning is used. The instructor poses a question, students **formulate** their answer to the question, turn to another student and **share** their answer, **listen** to their partner's answer, and **create** a new answer that is better than either one.

Closing Base Group Meeting

The class session closes with students meeting in base groups. Closing tasks include:

1. Ensuring all members understand the assignment? Find out what help each member needs to complete it?

2. Summarizing at least three things members learned in today's class session?

3. Summarizing how members will use/apply what they have learned?

4. Celebrating the hard work and learning of group members.

Examples Of Integrated Use Of Cooperative Learning

We need colleges in which great lessons are common place occurrences. Great lessons result from the hard work of instructors and in order to have a college in which great lessons are commonplace, instructors have to be skilled in using formal and informal cooperative learning procedures as well as cooperative base groups. In order for such

Johnson, D. W., Johnson, R., & Smith, K. (1998). **Active Learning: Cooperation In The College Classroom**. Edina, MN: Interaction Book Company.

colleges to exist, instructors must adopt a set of beliefs, prepare lessons carefully, and then polish and polish and polish and polish each lesson until the lesson flows smoothly from beginning to middle to end (Stevenson & Stigler, 1992).

Stevenson and Stigler (1992) compared teaching methods in the United States, Japan, Taiwan, and China. They concluded that great lessons were far more commonplace in Japan, Taiwan, and China than in the United States and identified a number of **destructive teaching patterns**. The **first** is giving students solitary work. Students in the United States were found to spend nearly 50 percent of their time working alone, isolated from classmates and the instructor. They worked on their own, at their desks, doing solitary activities such as filling in workbooks or handout sheets and reading. In Japan, Taiwan, and China, students worked as a whole class as a unit with the instructor as a leader and in small groups. The **second** is the teaching pattern of 30 minutes of instructor lecturing followed by 20 minutes of having students individually complete work sheets. The Asian instructors rarely lectured. Instead, they planned lessons in which there was a continual flow and change from whole class to small groups to individual practice to small groups to whole class and so forth. All classroom activities were logically sequenced to ensure that the academic objectives of the lesson were reached.

On the basis of their comparison of colleges in the United States, Japan, Taiwan, and China, Stevenson and Stigler (1992) conclude that there are a number of **pre-beliefs** that differentiate good from poor instructors. **First**, good instructors believe that high achieving students are made, not born (they avoid the genetic fallacy). They see achievement being determined by student effort (not ability) and sustained time-on-task in instructor-led lessons presented in a thoughtful, relaxed, and nonauthoritarian manner. **Second**, good instructors believe that great instructors are made, not born (they avoid the genetic fallacy). They see great lessons resulting from instructor effort in planning, conducting, and continual polishing and polishing lessons. **Third**, good instructors see their role as (a) planning and conducting coherent, well orchestrated lessons (not giving lectures) and (b) serving as a knowledgeable guide, not a dispenser of information or an arbiter of correctness.

Carefully prepared and conducted lessons have a beginning, middle, and an end. Stevenson and Stigler (1992) call this "lesson coherence." To **begin** the lesson the instructor presents a practical, real world, problem or provocative issue that intellectually challenges students. Everything that follows is organized around solving the problem. The problem is presented first. Then concepts and rules are presented second. Instructors pose provocative questions and allow students adequate time for reflection.

The student is the protagonist who meets challenges and resolves problems during the lesson. As the protagonist, students must construct knowledge, rather than the instructor doing so. During the **middle** of the lesson instructors (a) lead students from what is known to what is unknown, (b) direct students' attention to the critical part of the

Johnson, D. W., Johnson, R., & Smith, K. (1998). **Active Learning: Cooperation In The College Classroom**. Edina, MN: Interaction Book Company.

problem, (c) provide variety by alternating whole class work, small group discussions, and individual application of what is being learned, and (d) have students present and defend the solutions and products they create. The emphasis is on students producing, explaining, and evaluating solutions to problems (not on rote mastery of facts and procedures). Instructors vary teaching procedures so that the procedures are responsive to differences in student's prior experience. And instructors interweave instruction, practice, and evaluation into a coherent whole. Concrete representations are used to teach abstract concepts. The emphasis is on students constructing multiple solutions by generating ideas and evaluating their correctness. Student errors are used an index of what still needs to be learned.

The lesson **ends** with (a) students presenting what they have learned and defending their reasoning and (b) a review what has been learned and how it relates to the problem or issue posed at the beginning of the lesson.

Such carefully prepared and conducted lessons require the integrated use of the three types of cooperative learning. Using a mixture of cooperative formal (whole class, small groups, pairs), informal (pairs, triads), and base groups in a lesson provides so many important aspects of good instruction that they all cannot be mentioned here. Using the three types of cooperative learning in an integrated way:

1. Helps instructors build coherent lessons with a clear beginning, middle, and end.

2. Allows instructors to present more difficult problems, material, and intellectual challenges for students to solve.

3. Allows students to construct their own knowledge.

4. Provides variety, which engages and maintains students' interest and attention.

5. Allows many different learning modes (auditory, visual, kinesthetic) to be used within one lesson.

6. Requires students to actively explain and defend their reasoning and conclusions to groupmates.

7. Allows groupmates to assess the quality of a student's understanding and reasoning and provide immediate remediation if is needed. Students use the own and their groupmates' errors as indications of what still needs to be learned.

8. Helps ensure that students are exposed to multiple strategies and procedures for solving problems and completing assignments.

Johnson, D. W., Johnson, R., & Smith, K. (1998). **Active Learning: Cooperation In The College Classroom**. Edina, MN: Interaction Book Company.

9. Increases students' motivation to achieve as a result of the social support and group identification.

A typical lesson follows. The instructor formally starts the class by welcoming the students and having meet in their base groups to greet each other, review what has happened in the previous class sessions, and focus students' attention on what is to be learned. The problem or issue to be studied is introduced, using informal cooperative learning groups. If direct teaching (such as a whole class demonstration) is necessary, it is conducted with informal cooperative learning groups. Formal cooperative learning groups are then used to solve the problem presented or complete the assignment given. Members of different learning groups then meet and each student explains his or her group's reasoning and conclusions. Students may apply what they have learned by individually working on a set of similar problems or using the strategies to complete a similar assignment, and then meet in their formal cooperative learning group to assess their success and receive more help if it is needed. At the end of the class session students meet in their base groups to summarize and synthesize what they have learned.

Example One

An example of the integrated use of the cooperative learning procedures is as follows. Students arrive at class and meet in their **base groups** to welcome each other, complete a self-disclosure task (such as "what is each member's favorite television show"), check each student's homework to make sure all members understand the academic material and are prepared for the class session, and tell each other to have a great day.

The instructor then begins a lesson on the limitations of being human. To help students cognitively organize in advance what they know about the advantages and disadvantages of being human, the instructor uses **informal cooperative learning.** The instructor asks students to form a triad and ponder, *"What are five things you cannot do with your human limitations that a Billion Dollar Being might be designed to do?"* Students have four minutes to do so. In the next ten minutes, the instructor explains that while the human body is a marvelous system, we (like other organisms) have very specific limitations. We can not see bacteria in a drop of water or the rings of Saturn unaided. We can not hear as well as a deer or fly like an eagle. Humans have never been satisfied being so limited and, therefore, we have invented microscopes, telescopes, and our own wings. The instructor then instructs students to turn to the person next to them and answer the questions, *"What are three limitations of humans, what have we invented to overcome them, and what other human limitations might we be able to overcome?"*

Formal cooperative learning is now used in the lesson (for the Billion-Dollar Being lesson, see **Topics in Applied Science**, Jefferson County Colleges, Golden, Colorado). The instructor has the 32 students count off from 1 to 8 to form groups of four randomly. Group members sit so they can face each other and face the instructor. Each member is assigned a role: researcher/runner, summarizer/time-keeper, collector/recorder, and

Johnson, D. W., Johnson, R., & Smith, K. (1998). **Active Learning: Cooperation In The College Classroom**. Edina, MN: Interaction Book Company.

technical advisor (role interdependence). Every group gets one large 2 feet by three feet piece of paper, a marking pen, a rough draft sheet for designing the Being, an assignment sheet explaining the task and cooperative goal structure, and four student self-evaluation checklists (resource interdependence). The **task** is to design a Billion-Dollar Being that overcomes the human limitations thought of by the class and the group. The group members are to draw a diagram of the Being on the scratch paper and when they have something they like, transfer it to the larger paper. The instructor establishes **positive goal interdependence** by asking for one drawing from the group that all group members contribute to and can explain. The **criterion for success** is to complete the diagram in the 30-minute time limit. The instructor ensures **individual accountability** by observing each group to ensure that members are fulfilling their roles and that any one member can explain any part of the Being at any time. The instructor informs students that the **expected social skills** to be used by all students are encouraging each other's participation, contributing ideas, and summarizing. She defines the skill of encouraging participation and has each student practice it twice before the lesson begins. While students work in their groups, the instructor **monitors** by systematically observing each group and intervening to provide academic assistance and help in using the interpersonal and small group skills required to work together effectively. At the end of the lesson the groups hand in their diagrams of the Billion Dollar Being to be assessed and **evaluated.** Group members then **process** how well they worked together by identifying actions each member engaged in that helped the group succeed and one thing that could be added to improve their group next time.

The instructor uses **informal cooperative learning** to provide closure to the lesson by asking students to meet in new triads and write out six conclusions about the limitations of human beings and what we have done to overcome them.

At the end of the class session the **cooperative base groups** meet to review what students believe is the most important thing they have learned during the day, what homework has been assigned, what help each member needs to complete the homework, and to tell each other to have a fun afternoon and evening.

Example Two

An example of the integrated use of the types of cooperative learning is as follows. Students start the college day by meeting in their **base groups** to welcome each other, complete a self-disclosure task (such as "what is each member's favorite television show"), check each student's homework to make sure all members understand the academic material and are prepared for the day, and tell each other to have a great day. The instructor then begins a lesson on world interdependence. The instructor has a series of objects and wants students to identify all the countries involved in creating the objects. To help students cognitively organize in advance what they know about the world economy the instructor uses **informal cooperative learning** by asking students to turn to

Johnson, D. W., Johnson, R., & Smith, K. (1998). **Active Learning: Cooperation In The College Classroom.** Edina, MN: Interaction Book Company.

the person seated next to them and identify the seven continents and one product that is produced in each continent. They have four minutes to do so.

Formal cooperative learning is now used in the lesson. The objectives for the lesson are for students to learn about global economic interdependence and to improve their skill in encouraging each other's participation. The instructor has her 30 students count off from 1 to 10 to form triads randomly. They sit so they can either face each other or face the instructor. The instructor hands out the objects that include a silk shirt with plastic buttons, a cup of tea (a saucer and cup with a tea bag and a lump of sugar in it), and a walkman and earphones (with a cassette tape of a Nashville star) made by Phillips (a European company). She assigns members of each triad the roles of hypothesizer (who hypothesizes about the number of products in each item and where they came from), a reference guide (who looks up each hypothesized country in the book to see what products it exports), and a recorder. After each item the roles are rotated so that each student fulfills each role once.

The instructor introduces world economic interdependence by noting that:

1. A hand-held calculator most often consists of electronic chips from the U.S., is assembled in Singapore or Indonesia, placed in a steel housing from India, and stamped with a label "Made in Japan" (the trees and chemicals from which the paper and ink in the label are all made and are processed elsewhere and the plastic in the keys and body are all made elsewhere) on arrival in Yokohama.

2. Modern hotels in Saudi Arabia are built with room modules made in Brazil, construction labor from South Korea, and management from the United States.

3. The global economic interdependence is almost beyond imagining.

The instructor then assigns the **academic task** of identifying how many countries contributed to the production of each object. She establishes **positive goal interdependence** by stating that it is a cooperative assignment and, therefore, all members of the group must agree on an answer before it is recorded and all members must be able to explain each of the group's answers. The criteria for success was to hand in a correctly completed report form and for each member to score 90 percent or better on the test to be given the next day on world economic interdependence. She establishes **positive reward interdependence** by stating that if the record sheet is accurate, each member will receive 15 points and if all members of the group achieve 90 percent or better on the test, each member will receive 5 bonus points. **Individual accountability** is established by the roles assigned and the individual test. In addition, the instructor will observe each group to make sure all students are participating and learning. The instructor informs students that the **expected social skill** to be used by all students is encouraging each other's participation. She defines the skill and has each student practice it twice before the lesson begins.

Johnson, D. W., Johnson, R., & Smith, K. (1998). **Active Learning: Cooperation In The College Classroom.** Edina, MN: Interaction Book Company.

While students work in their groups, the instructor **monitors** by systematically observing each group and intervening to provide academic assistance and help in using the interpersonal and small group skills required to work together effectively. At the end of the lesson the groups hand in their report forms to be **evaluated** and **process** how well they worked together by identifying three things members did to help the group achieve and one thing that could be added to improve their group next time.

Next, the instructor then uses a **generic cooperative lesson structure** to teach vocabulary. Studying vocabulary words is a routine that occurs every week in this class. Instructors tell students to move into their vocabulary pairs, take the vocabulary words identified in the world interdependence lesson, and for each word (a) write down what they think the word means, (b) look it up in the text and write down its official definition, (c) write a sentence in which the word is used, and (d) learn how to spell the word. When they have done that for each word, the pair is to make up a story in which all of the words are used. Pairs then exchange stories and carefully determine whether all the words are used appropriately and spelled correctly. If not, the two pairs discuss the word until everyone is clear about what it means and how it should be used.

The instructor uses **informal cooperative learning** to provide closure to the lesson by asking students to meet with a person from another group and write out four conclusions they derived from the lesson and circle the one they believed was the most important.

At the end of the day the **cooperative base groups** meet to review what students believe is the most important thing they have learned during the day, what homework has been assigned, what help each member needs to complete the homework, and to tell each other to have a fun afternoon and evening.

The Evolution of Cooperative Learning

In implementing cooperative learning, instructors need a time-line to guide their efforts. Although a few instructors take cooperative learning strategies and change their classrooms overnight, most instructors engage in a slower, more evolutionary approach. Both the collaborative skills of the students and the instructional skills of the instructors take time to develop and build. Generally, the stages instructors pass through in becoming proficient in structuring learning situations cooperatively are:

1. **Nonuse.** Instructors have not heard of cooperative learning or are under pressures that prevent consideration of new instructional strategies.

2. **Decision to use and initial preparation.** Instructors learn enough about cooperative learning to be interested in trying it. They plan their first lesson.

Johnson, D. W., Johnson, R., & Smith, K. (1998). **Active Learning: Cooperation In The College Classroom**. Edina, MN: Interaction Book Company.

Months	Non Use	To Use	Decision	Initial Use	Beginning Use	Mechanical Use	Routine Use
1							
2							
3							
4							
5							
6							
7							
8							
9							
10							
11							
12							
13							
14							
15							
16							
17							
18							

Year One (Months 1–9) · Year Two (Months 10–18)

Figure 6.1 Evolutionary Implementation

Johnson, D. W., Johnson, R., & Smith, K. (1998). **Active Learning: Cooperation In The College Classroom**. Edina, MN: Interaction Book Company.

3. **Initial use.** Instructors are using cooperative learning less than 10 percent of the time. They are attempting to deal with the initial "start-up" issues of:

   a. Logistical issues of moving furniture and making transitions in and out of cooperative learning, getting students to sit together and engage in such "forming" (see Chapter 5) behaviors as "using quiet voices," and getting students to turn and look at the instructor when instructions are given.

   b. Communication issues of clearly defining the positive interdependence and individual accountability so that students understand what actions are appropriate and inappropriate.

4. **Beginning use.** Instructors use cooperative learning between 10 and 20 percent of the time. Issues they focus on typically are:

   a. Instructor monitoring issues of determining how effectively students collaborate and counting frequencies of positive behaviors to share with the whole class or individual groups.

   b. Student monitoring and processing issues of training students to observe the collaborative interaction of group members and process how effectively their group is functioning. This can be done with any age student. Instructors have had kindergarten and first-grade students observing their group for "who talks," "who takes turns," and "who asks someone else to speak."

   c. Teaching students the collaborative skills they need to function effectively in cooperative learning groups. Instructors will move from "forming" to "functioning" skills. They may wish to emphasize the "formulating and fermenting" skills after students have mastered the basics of working collaboratively. Some care has to be taken in translating the skills into phrases and actions that are appropriate for the age and the background of the students being taught.

5. **Mechanical use.** Instructors follow the general procedures for implementing cooperative learning in a step-by- step fashion, planning each lesson, and reviewing recommended procedures before each lesson. Instructors at this point are usually using cooperative learning from 20 to 50 percent of the time. Some of the issues instructors deal with are:

   a. Using a variety of ways to structure positive interdependence and individual accountability, to monitor and process, and to evaluate.

   b. Expanding the use of cooperative learning from one subject area or class to several subject areas or classes.

Johnson, D. W., Johnson, R., & Smith, K. (1998). **Active Learning: Cooperation In The College Classroom**. Edina, MN: Interaction Book Company.

    c. Thinking in terms of curriculum units (rather than single lessons) being cooperative, and in terms of alternating among cooperative, competitive, and individualistic learning rather than the isolated use of cooperative learning.

    d. Teaching collaborative and academic skills simultaneously.

6. **Routine use.** Instructors automatically structure cooperative learning situations without conscious thought or planning. The concurrent focus on academic and collaborative skills happens spontaneously. Instructors are usually using cooperative learning more than 50 percent of the time and are dealing with the following issues:

    a. Integrating cooperative, competitive, and individualistic lessons.

    b. Varying how cooperative learning is structured according to tasks, students, and circumstances.

    c. Integrating cooperative learning with other teaching strategies in their repertoire.

    d. Applying collaborative skills and understanding of positive interdependence to faculty relationships and other settings.

It may take a year for instructors to develop into mechanical users of cooperative learning and it often takes up to two years for instructors to become firmly routine users (see Figure 6.1). In planning how you will progress from beginning to routine use of cooperative learning the following advice may be helpful:

1. **Do not try to move too fast.** Start with a single lesson. Move to conducting at least one cooperative lesson per day and then to modifying a curriculum unit to be primarily cooperative. Finally, think of integrating cooperative, competitive, and individualistic learning within a class or subject area.

2. **Persevere!** Do not stop growing in your use of cooperative learning. Lay out a long-range plan and stay with it. Especially persevere with students who have a hard time collaborating with peers.

3. **Seek support** from one or more colleagues and engage in joint sharing of successes, problems, new ideas, and curriculum modification.

4. **Plan carefully** for the start of each college year so that cooperative learning is emphasized right away.

Johnson, D. W., Johnson, R., & Smith, K. (1998). **Active Learning: Cooperation In The College Classroom**. Edina, MN: Interaction Book Company.

Personalizing The Learning Environment

Learning is a personal experience. The more frequently cooperative learning is used, the more personalized the learning will be. Haines and McKeachie (1967) demonstrated that students in classes stressing competition for grades showed more tension, self-doubt, and anxiety than did students working in cooperative learning groups. There are a number of ways that the learning environment may be personalized.

First, monitor cooperative groups closely. Circulate among the groups, systematically observe, and often stop to (a) join in and interact with group members or (b) intervene within a group . The more attentive instructors are to individual students the more effective and personal the teaching. It is easier to make a direct comment to a student in a small group than in a whole- class setting.

Second, work to establish classroom norms that promote individuality, creativity, and sensitivity to students' needs. All students need to feel respected, free, and motivated to make the maximum contributions of what they are capable.

Third, demonstrate a willingness to learn from students. Every instructor- student interaction carries potential for learning for both the instructor and students. When faculty accept and learn from students' contributions, the learning experience becomes more personal for the students.

Fourth, present students with a realistic assessment of what they have learned and with high expectations as to what they can learn if they make the effort. Faculty offer students a tension between present and future, actuality and possibility. Schneider, Klemp, and Kastendiek (1981) concluded that effective instructors (a) believe that average students are competent, (b) identify and affirm students' capabilities, (c) express the view that students are capable of change, and (d) accept student suggestions for changes in learning plans when the changes are consistent with the students' learning objectives. Daloz (1987) found that students described effective instructors as "*giving me confidence in myself,*" "*kept pushing me and telling me I could do it,*" and "*having faith in me even when I did not.*" Through their expectations of students, faculty can communicate where students are and what they can become without allowing either to eclipse the other.

Fifth, send them out of class feeling happy. John Wooden, the basketball coach at UCLA for many years, wrote out a detailed lesson plan for every one of his practices. At the end of each lesson plan he wrote "Send the players to the showers happy." Similarly, Durward Rushton (a principal in Hattisburg, Mississippi) states that each student should feel personally **secure**, have a sense of **belonging**, and experience some **success** each class session (SBS). Instructors should adopt similar attitudes toward creating a positive atmosphere for each class session. One step to doing so is eliminating put-downs. Being put-down by a instructor is the most common response given to the question "*What is*

Johnson, D. W., Johnson, R., & Smith, K. (1998). **Active Learning: Cooperation In The College Classroom.** Edina, MN: Interaction Book Company.

your most memorable experience from high school?" (Kohl, personal communication, 1989). Many students are afraid to contribute in class, some for lack of confidence, others because they fear their ideas are not worthy. The simple procedure of saying something positive about every student's comment, question, or answer to a question has remarkable power for transforming a classroom.

A simple means for promoting a personalized learning environment is having students (and you) wear name tags to help students learn each other's names. Instructors often comment that for their students, the most important word in the English language is their name. Name tagging is a simple procedure that makes a profound difference in the atmosphere of the classroom. Students immediately "warm-up" to their colleagues and seem to appreciate the opportunity to meet and greet each other. The short time that this activity consumes is more than compensated by the improvement in the learning mood of the students. On the first day have students complete a name tag. In the center the student (and instructor) places his or her name (actually the way he or she prefers to be addressed) in print large enough to be read 20 feet away. In the corners are placed other information about the student, such as, birthplace, favorite place, hobbies, favorite artist, something they're looking forward to, and major or profession. Finally, surrounding their name they are asked to place two or three adjectives that describe them. The students are then given about 10 minutes to meet and learn something about as many other students in the class as possible.

Cooperate And Graduate

The message in many colleges where cooperative learning is being implemented is "*Succeeding in this class is hard work, difficult, and takes considerable effort. You do not have to do the work alone. Work together, help each other.*" Our motto is "*Helping and sharing are not cheating during learning time.*" During testing time, of course, it's a different matter. At testing time we want to see what individuals can do. Students typically perform better on individual tests, however, after their group has prepared them. Succeeding academically results from group, not individual, efforts.

Conclusions

Formal cooperative learning, informal cooperative learning, and cooperative base groups form a "gestalt" that allows instructors to present coherent lessons in which all activities lead to the achievement of mutual learning goals. The integrated use of the three types of cooperative learning provides the context in which competitive and individualistic activities may be used effectively.

6 : 17

Johnson, D. W., Johnson, R., & Smith, K. (1998). **Active Learning: Cooperation In The College Classroom.** Edina, MN: Interaction Book Company.

Integrated Use Of All Types Of Cooperative Learning

Task: Plan a day (week) with cooperative learning being used 100 percent of the time. The objective is to provide on overall gestalt as to how the four different types of cooperative learning and a wide variety of the lesson structures may be used in an integrated way.

Cooperation: Find a partner who teaches the same grade level and subject area as you do. Develop one plan for the two of you, both of you must agree that the plan will work, and both of you must be able to implement the plan.

Individual Accountability: Each person will have to present the plan to a member of another group.

Expected Behaviors: Explaining, listening, synthesizing by all members.

Intergroup Cooperation: Whenever it is helpful, check procedures and plans with other groups.

Note: Now that it has been established that cooperative learning may be used 100 percent of the day, the issue of the supplemental use of competitive and individualistic learning becomes relevant. The next chapter focuses on that issue.

6 : 18

Johnson, D. W., Johnson, R., & Smith, K. (1998). **Active Learning: Cooperation In The College Classroom**. Edina, MN: Interaction Book Company.

EPSY 5150: THE SOCIAL PSYCHOLOGY OF EDUCATION

David W. Johnson, 60 Peik Hall, 624-7031

Overview of the Course

This is an introductory course that will cover broad areas in social psychology with specific emphasis in education. Most topics will be teasers in the sense that entire courses could be developed around many of the areas we will discuss in one hour. Hopefully you will leave this course wanting to delve further into specific topics in social psychology. In this course you will be expected to become acquainted with the major theories, research, and "names" in the field. Class sessions will be spent in lectures, discussions, and experiential exercises.

Textbook

Brehm, S., & Kassin, S. (1996). **Social psychology**. Boston, MA: Houghton-Mifflin.

Johnson, D. W. (1970). **Social Psychology of Education**. Edina, MN: Interaction Book Company.

Course Requirements

1. Attend class.

2. Be prepared for and actively involved in class discussions and activities.

3. Read assigned material for each class session.

4. Write preparation papers.

5. Write a research review paper discussing some aspect of social psychological theory and research and design a relevant research study.

6. Write a perspective-reversal paper on a current social issue.

Johnson, D. W., Johnson, R., & Smith, K. (1998). **Active Learning: Cooperation In The College Classroom**. Edina, MN: Interaction Book Company.

7. Pass the examinations.

8. Participate in a base group and make sure that all group members pass the tests, write acceptable papers, and generally make satisfactory progress in achieving the academic goals of the course.

Tests

1. The **Group Discussion Test** consists of a meeting of your base group to discuss the content of the assigned reading. Each group will be expected to provide copies of the questions they discussed, an outline of their answers and procedures, and their subjective evaluation of the learning resulting from the experience. A more detailed handout on the group discussion test will be distributed. The test will take place during the next to last class session.

2. The **Basic Concepts Quizzes** will be composed of multiple choice or matching items drawn from readings, lectures, and class discussions. Successful performance is considered to be 90 percent of the questions answered correctly. Any group whose members do not answer 90 percent of the questions correctly will be required to indicate competence on incorrect items. These quizzes will take place weekly.

3. The **Basic Concepts Final Examination** will be given the final day of class. It represents the bottom line of the course. Anyone taking the course has to be able to pass this test at a 90 percent correct level.

Papers

1. **Class Preparation Papers**: Each week write a one to two page paper on a theory, research study, concept, idea, theorist, or researcher in the reading assignment.

2. **Perspective-Reversal Paper**: Take a social issue, such as alienation, racism, sexism, pollution, or corruption in government and write a five or six page paper applying social psychological concepts, research, and theory to its solution. In writing the paper, take a viewpoint (perspective, frame of reference) opposite to your own and construct the paper to support that opposite viewpoint.

3. **Research Review Paper**: Write a (1) research review in an area of interest in social psychology (required of all MA and PhD degree students) or (2) project applying some aspect of social psychology to a practical situation (alternative for nondegree students). This paper should be approximately 12 pages long.

Johnson, D. W., Johnson, R., & Smith, K. (1998). **Active Learning: Cooperation In The College Classroom**. Edina, MN: Interaction Book Company.

Grading

Grades will be determined on the basis of learning contracts. A certain minimum amount of work is expected of all students in graduate level course. The alternative learning contracts are:

Grade D: Course Requirements 1, 2, 3, 7, 8.

Grade C: Course Requirements 1, 2, 3, 4, 7, 8.

Grade B: Course Requirements 1, 2, 3, 4, 5, 7, 8.

Grade A: All Course Requirements (1 - 8).

All work must meet standards for acceptable performance level. On the final day of classes students must submit a written statement of the contract they are working to fulfill along with the required proof of meeting the contract. Although students will be given grades of "I" if necessary, it is highly discouraged. Absolutely no incompletes will be given for uncompleted group tests.

Class Sessions

Week 1   Introduction to the Course; Social Self

Week 2   Perceiving Persons; Perceiving Groups

Week 3   Interpersonal Attraction; Intimate Relationships

Week 4   Helping Others; Aggression; Conflict

Week 5   Social Influence Theories, Conformity

Week 6   Attitude Acquisition and Change

Week 7   Social Interdependence: Cooperative, Competitive, Individualistic Efforts

Week 8   Equity and Attribution Theories; Social Psychology of Law & Health

Week 9   Group Discussion Test

Week 10   Basic Concepts Test; Summary; Evaluation of Course

Johnson, D. W., Johnson, R., & Smith, K. (1998). **Active Learning: Cooperation In The College Classroom**. Edina, MN: Interaction Book Company.

Basic Course Requirements

The basic assumption of this course is that learning results from a continuing process of rational discourse. Within the course there are both opportunities and responsibilities. Your **opportunity** is to learn. Your **responsibilities** are to maximize your learning from the course (i.e., improve your intellectual understanding), maximize the learning of your classmates, and to apply what you learn to your work and personal life. To take advantage of the opportunity and to meet your responsibilities you are to:

1. **Master the basic concepts, theories, research studies, and researchers.** You are expected to know more after you have finished the course than you did before.

2. **Think critically about the course content** and topics to achieve understanding and insights.

3. **Explain precisely to several classmates your learnings, insights, and conclusions.** Your learning is not complete until you teach what you know to someone else and can describe precisely what you have learned.

4. **Ask others to share their knowledge**, conclusions, and insights with you. When they do so, listen carefully, elaborate by explaining how what you have just learned from them fits in with previous knowledge learned, and thank them.

5. **Engage in intellectual controversy** by taking positions counter to those of your classmates, developing clear rationales from the material in the texts, challenging their reasoning and conclusions, and arguing the issues until you are logically persuaded. Review the rules for constructive controversy before doing so.

6. **Get your work done on time.** You cannot deprive classmates of their opportunity and obligations to help you improve your understanding, conclusions, and insights.

7. Plan how to apply what you have learned to improve the quality of your work and personal life. **You should be able to describe precisely how you can use what you have learned in this class.**

6 : 22

Johnson, D. W., Johnson, R., & Smith, K. (1998). **Active Learning: Cooperation In The College Classroom.** Edina, MN: Interaction Book Company.

Preparation Papers

1. Your **task** is to write a short paper (one to two pages) on an aspect of the assigned readings to prepare for class. Before each class session:

   a. Choose a major theory, concept, idea, or person discussed in the assigned reading.

   b. Write a one to two page analysis of it (1) summarizing the relevant assigned readings and (2) adding relevant material from another source (book, journal, magazine, newspaper) to enrich the analysis.

2. Bring five copies of the paper to the class:

   a. Give a copy of your paper to each member of your base group and to the professor.

   b. Present a three minute summary of your paper. While you do, the other members will be completing an assessment form to give you feedback on the quality of your presentation.

3. Before the next class session the members of the cooperative base group read, edit, and criticize the paper. They complete an assessment form for each member's paper. Members then sign each member's paper. The signature means that they have read the paper and have provided feedback to improve their groupmates' writing skills. The criteria they will use are on the form. The criteria include:

   a. An introductory statement of the issue focused on.

   b. A summary of the theory or conceptual framework used to understand the issue and a judgment about its significance.
   (T = Substantial Theoretical Significance, t = some theoretical significance)

   c. Clear conceptual definition of concepts and terms.

   d. Summary of what is known empirically.
   (R = Substantial Research Support, r = some research support)

   e. Description of and judgment about practical significance.
   (P = Substantial Practical Significance, p = some practical significance)

   f. Brief description of a relevant study that should be conducted to advance knowledge about the issue.

6 : 23

Johnson, D. W., Johnson, R., & Smith, K. (1998). **Active Learning: Cooperation In The College Classroom**. Edina, MN: Interaction Book Company.

    g. New information beyond what is contained in the text.

4. The cooperative groups summarize what they have learned from members' papers and how it applies to the topic of the class sesson.

Preparation Paper Assessment Form

Name: _____ **Date:** _____

Title Of Paper: _____

Points Possible	Criteria	Points Earned
10	Has A Clear, Accurate, Descriptive Title	
10	Begins With A Position Statement	
10	Each Paragraph Is Indented	
10	Each Paragraph Begins With A Topic Sentence	
10	Capitalization, Appearance, Punctuation, Spelling	
10	Includes Information From Two Or More Sources	
10	Includes Persuasive Supporting Sentences	
10	Includes Analysis And Critical Thinking	
10	Ends With Conclusions	
10	Other:	
100	**Total**	

Write specific suggestions on how to improve the paper on the back of this page.

1. Complete this form for each member's preparation paper and give to that member.

2. Take the forms for your preparation paper and add the totals together.

3. Divide by the number of forms received to calculate the mean rating.

4. Record the results on your quality chart for writing preparation papers.

6 : 24

Johnson, D. W., Johnson, R., & Smith, K. (1998). **Active Learning: Cooperation In The College Classroom**. Edina, MN: Interaction Book Company.

Presenting Your Preparation Paper

Each week you will make a three-minute presentation of your preparation paper. The objectives of your presentation are to (a) inform and teach the other group members the material in your preparation paper and (b) communicate the excitement and interest you feel towards the issue covered. Your presentation should contain at least two modalities (such as oral and visual). If possible, give the group members an active role in the presentation. You will be presenting to your group while members of other groups are also presenting, so there will be some background noise.

Oral Presentations Rubric

Name: _____ **Date:** _____

Title Of Presentation: _____

Criterion	Rating	Comments
Addresses Subject, Scholarly, Informative		
Organized (introduction, body, conclusion)		
Creative Reasoning And Persuasiveness		
Intriguing (audience wants to find out more)		
Interesting, Transitions, Easy To Follow, Concise		
Volume, Enunciation, Eye Contact, Gestures		
Involving (audience active, not passive)		
Visual Aids, Props, Music		
Other:		
Total		

For each criterion, rate the presentation between 1 (very poor) to 5 (very good).

Johnson, D. W., Johnson, R., & Smith, K. (1998). **Active Learning: Cooperation In The College Classroom**. Edina, MN: Interaction Book Company.

Peer Editing Of Research Review Papers

The research review paper required for this class needs to be written in conjunction with your base group. You are required to hand in a paper revised on the basis of the reviews by your base groups members. The procedure for writing the paper is as follows.

1. Students are assigned to a base group. Each is individually responsible for writing a paper reviewing the research in an area related to the content of the course.

2. Each member describes to the base group what he or she is planning to write. Base group members listen carefully and probe with a set of questions.

3. Students search individualistically for the research articles they need to write their papers, keeping an eye out for material useful to other members of their base group.

4. Students write their papers individualistically. Cooperative papers are allowed if they clearly reflect twice the work of an individual's paper (if an individual's paper is 10 pages long, a paper written by a pair should be 20 pages long).

5. When completed, students proofread each other's compositions, making corrections in capitalization, punctuation, spelling, language usage, topic sentence usage, making suggestions for better organizing and conceptualizing the review, and generally making suggestions about how to improve other aspects of the research review. If peer reviewer suggest major revisions, serious consideration should be given to re-writing the paper to ensure that it is acceptable to the instructor.

6. Each student submits to the instructor a copy of the research review paper, a copy of the reviews, and a written response to the peer reviews. The response should be thoughtful replies to the comments of the peer reviewers.

Students are evaluated in two ways: Does their research review paper meet the criteria for adequacy? Do the research reviews of the other base group members meet the criteria for adequacy?

When the research reviews are completed, the base group discusses how effectively they worked together (listing the specific actions they engaged in to help each other), plan what behaviors they are going to emphasize in the next peer-editing situation, and thank each other for the help and assistance received.

Johnson, D. W., Johnson, R., & Smith, K. (1998). **Active Learning: Cooperation In The College Classroom**. Edina, MN: Interaction Book Company.

Base Groups

Base groups are long-term, heterogeneous cooperative learning groups with stable membership whose primary responsibility is to provide each student the support, encouragement, and assistance they need to make academic progress. Base groups personalize the work required and the course learning experiences. During this course you will be a part of a base group consisting of four participants. These base groups will stay the same during the entire course. The members of your base group should exchange phone numbers and information about schedules as you may wish to meet outside of class. **The base group functions as a support group for members that:**

1. Gives assistance, support, and encouragement for mastering the course content and skills and provides feedback on how well the content and skills are being learned.

2. Gives assistance, support, and encouragement for thinking critically about the course content, explaining precisely what one learns, engaging in intellectual controversy, getting the work done on time, and applying what is learned to one's own life.

3. Provides a set of interpersonal relationships to personalize the course and an arena for trying out the cooperative learning procedures and skills emphasized within the course.

4. Provides a structure for managing course evaluation.

You have three major responsibilities:

1. Master and appropriately implement the theories, concepts, and body of knowledge (as well as skills) emphasized in the course.

2. Ensure that all members of your base group master and appropriately implement the theories, concepts, and body of knowledge (as well as skills) emphasized in the course.

3. Ensure that all members of the class master and appropriately implement the theories, concepts, and body of knowledge (as well as skills) emphasized in the course. In other words, if your group is successful, find another group to help until all members of the class are successful.

At the beginning of each session class members meet in their base groups to:

1. Congratulate each other for living through the time since the last class session and check to see that none of their group is under undue stress.

6 : 27

Johnson, D. W., Johnson, R., & Smith, K. (1998). **Active Learning: Cooperation In The College Classroom**. Edina, MN: Interaction Book Company.

2. Check to see if members have completed their homework or need help and assistance in doing so.

3. Review what members have read and done since the last class session. Members should be able to give a brief, terse, succinct summary of what they have read, thought about, and done. They may come to class with resources they have found and want to share, or copies of work they have completed and wish to distribute to their base group members.

The basic concepts tests and the group discussion final examination will be conducted in base groups. Base group members are responsible for personally completing the tests at a 90 percent correct level and ensuring that all other members do likewise.

Base groups are available to support individual group members. If a group member arrives late, or must leave early on an occasion, the group can provide information about what that student missed. Additionally, group members may assist one another in writing the required papers for the class. The assignments may be discussed in the base groups, papers may be planned, reviewed, and edited in base groups, and any questions regarding the course assignments and class sessions may be first addressed in the base group. If the group is not able to resolve the issue, it should be brought to the attention of the instructor or the teaching assistant.

All members are expected to contribute actively to the class discussions, work to maintain effective working relationships with other participants, complete all assignments, assist classmates in completing their assignments, express their ideas, not change their minds unless they are persuaded by logic or information to do so, and indicate agreement with the base group's work by signing the weekly contract.

Johnson, D. W., Johnson, R., & Smith, K. (1998). **Active Learning: Cooperation In The College Classroom**. Edina, MN: Interaction Book Company.

Group Discussion Test

For the **group discussion test** you will meet with your base group and discuss the content of the assigned reading. Find a comfortable spot for your group to meet. The **purpose** of the group discussion test is to have a thorough, intellectually stimulating, creative, fun, and practically useful discussion of the assigned texts. More specifically, the **task** is to demonstrate mastery and deeper-level understanding of the assigned readings. This task is to be accomplished **cooperatively**. You are to generate one set of answers for the group and all members must agree with and be able to explain the answers. During the group test group members should focus on:

1. Integrating relevant theory, research, and practical experiences.

2. Analyzing in depth possible answers to the question in order to achieve insights.

3. Thinking divergently.

4. Critically examining each other's reasoning and engaging in constructive controversy.

5. Making the examination a fun and enjoyable experience for everyone.

To structure this process a number of discussion questions are attached. These questions are aimed at being **integrative** in the sense that material from many different chapters and books are relevant to answering them. So will be your personal and practical experiences and background. The **responsibilities of each group member** are to:

1. Choose two of the suggested discussion questions. For each question think carefully about the answer. Make sure that your answer combines material from many different chapters of the assigned texts as well as your own relevant personal experiences and background. Learn the answer to the questions thoroughly as you will be the **group expert** on what the text books have to say about the issue highlighted in the question.

2. Plan how to lead a group discussion on the question that will require higher-level reasoning, critical thinking, conceptual integration of material from many different chapters of the assigned texts, and a working knowledge of the specific relevant theories and research findings. In order to do so you will need to prepare for each group member (a) a typed outline of the answer to the question with the relevant page numbers in the assigned text books and (b) copies of relevant written information to facilitate discussion. As members of your group may be visual rather than auditory learners, **prepare visuals** such as diagrams, charts, and cartoons to help them learn, think critically about, and conceptually integrate the relevant theory, research, and practical experiences.

Johnson, D. W., Johnson, R., & Smith, K. (1998). **Active Learning: Cooperation In The College Classroom**. Edina, MN: Interaction Book Company.

3. Be prepared to (a) contribute to the discussion of each question and (b) learn, think critically about, and conceptually integrate relevant theory, research, and experiences.

The group discussion test should last for at least three hours. Cover at least one question from each member. Since each member is prepared to lead a discussion on two questions, flip a coin to select which question will be part of the examination. **Guidelines** are:

1. Come prepared with the texts, materials, lecture notes, and pen and paper.

2. Stick to the questions. It is easy to go off on tangents.

3. Cite specific theories, research, and concepts. Refer to specific pages. Avoid broad generalizations. Describe personal experiences that contradict current knowledge.

4. Refer to personal experiences. Comparing the theories and research findings against your personal experiences is valuable and often allows for integration of concepts.

5. Set time limits for each question and stick to these limits rigidly.

6. Encourage disagreement and controversy. Support viewpoints and positions with theory and research. Follow rules of constructive controversy.

7. Take responsibility for both task and maintenance actions. Your group has a definite task to accomplish (i.e., demonstrate understanding of the field of social psychology), but the discussion should be enjoyable as well as a productive learning experience.

8. All members must participate actively to (a) contribute to the learning of others and (b) demonstrate overtly to the other members of the group that he or she has read the texts and mastered the content of the course.

To verify that the group test did take place and that the criteria for passing were met by all group members, each member will be required to sign the certification form. Make sure that there are no "free-loaders." Do not sign off for a group member unless he or she arrived at the examination fully prepared and participated actively in the discussion of each question. If any group member is absent, the group is to determine whether the absence was excusable and what the member has to do to make up the test.

The group will be expected to hand in a **report** consisting of the certification form, a listing of the questions discussed, a summary of the answers and conclusions generated by the discussion, a copy of the outline and materials the group member used to lead the discussion, a description of the procedures followed, and a subjective evaluation of the learning resulting from the experience.

Johnson, D. W., Johnson, R., & Smith, K. (1998). **Active Learning: Cooperation In The College Classroom.** Edina, MN: Interaction Book Company.

Group Exam Certification Form

We, the undersigned, certify that we have participated in the group discussion examination and have met the following criteria:

1. We understand the basic concepts, theories, and bodies of research presented in the texts and lectures.

2. We know the major theorists and researchers discussed in the texts and lectures.

3. We can apply the theories and research findings to practical situations.

4. We can conceptualize a research question and design a research study to test our hypotheses.

5. We have submitted our choice of questions and a brief summary of each answer we have formulated as a group.

Name	Signature	Date

Basic Concepts Test

This course covers a body of knowledge that includes concepts, theories, research studies, and researchers. To complete this course, a mastery of the basic content is required. The **basic concepts test** is composed of multiple-choice, matching, and short answer test items drawn from the readings, lectures, and class discussions. Each student will take the test individually. **Until all members of the base group complete the exam successfully (90 percent of the tests answered correctly), however, no member will receive a grade for the course.** Any student who does not score 90 percent or better on the test will be required to meet with his or her base group and receive remedial help, until they can demonstrate competence on 90 percent of the test items.

Johnson, D. W., Johnson, R., & Smith, K. (1998). **Active Learning: Cooperation In The College Classroom**. Edina, MN: Interaction Book Company.

Individual Portfolio

Points Possible	Criteria	Points Earned
	Attendance	
	Self-Assessments (Knowledge, Writing, Presenting)	
	Preparation Papers	
	Feedback From Group Members On Writing	
	Presentations Of Preparation Papers	
	Feedback From Group Members On Presenting	
	Research Review Paper	
	Feedback From Group Members On Research Paper	
	Perspective-Reversal Paper	
	Feedback From Group Members On PR Paper	
	Individual Basic Concepts Test	
	Total	

Johnson, D. W., Johnson, R., & Smith, K. (1998). **Active Learning: Cooperation In The College Classroom**. Edina, MN: Interaction Book Company.

Group Portfolio

Points Possible	Criteria	Points Earned
	Attendance (All Members)	
	Group Self-Assessment	
	All Preparation Papers Written & Feedback Given	
	All Presentations Made & Feedback Given	
	All Research Papers Written & Feedback Given	
	All Perspective Papers Written & Feedback Given	
	Group Test Taken, All Members Present	
	All Members Pass Basic Concepts Test	
	Total	

6 : 33

Johnson, D. W., Johnson, R., & Smith, K. (1998). **Active Learning: Cooperation In The College Classroom**. Edina, MN: Interaction Book Company.

Student Information Sheet

Course_____ **Quarter & Year**_____

Name_____ **Group Number**_____

Phone Number_____ **Degree Working Towards**_____

Present Profession_____

Motivation For Taking This Course:

Johnson, D. W., Johnson, R., & Smith, K. (1998). **Active Learning: Cooperation In The College Classroom**. Edina, MN: Interaction Book Company.

Chapter Seven:

Group Processing

Introduction

In 1979 a commuter aircraft crashed while landing at an airport on Cape Cod in Massachusetts (reported in Norman, 1992). The pilot died and the co-pilot and six passengers were seriously injured. As the plane was landing, the copilot noted that the plane seemed to be too low, and he told the pilot. The pilot, however, did not respond. The copilot remarked that the glide path seemed rather steep, but the pilot did not respond. The copilot remarked that the descent rate seemed excessive. The pilot did not respond. The pilot, who was also president of the airline, and who had just hired the copilot, hardly ever responded. He was the strong, silent type. He was in charge, and that was that. United States airlines regulations require pilots and copilots to respond to one another, but what was the co-pilot to do. He was new to the company, and the captain was his boss. Moreover, the captain often flew low. What the copilot failed to notice was that the captain was "incapacitated." That is technical term meaning that the captain was unconscious and probably dead from a heart attack. At the investigation the copilot testified that (a) he made all the required call-outs except the "no contact" call and (b) the pilot did not acknowledge any of the calls. Because the captain rarely acknowledged calls, the lack of response did not alert the copilot to the fact that the pilot was dead. It seems strange. They were flying along and the pilot died. You would think the copilot would have noticed.

TEAM
T = Together
E = Everyone
A = Achieves
M = More

What was not established in the cockpit of that plane was a procedure for group processing. The pilot and copilot never discussed the process of flying the plane, did not analyze the nature of their interaction, and did not reflect on their effectiveness as a team. Consequently, when an emergency occurred, the copilot was slow to recognize it. If cooperative learning groups are to function effectively, and student achievement is to be maximized, regular group processing is a necessity.

This chapter presents a framework for ensuring that group processing takes place in an effective manner (see Figure 7.1). We define group processing, discuss procedures for structuring group processing, and give practical suggestions for making group processing effective.

Active Learning: Cooperation in the College Classroom, Interaction Book Company, 7208 Cornelia Drive, Edina, MN 55435, (612) 831-9500, FAX (612) 831-9332

Figure 7.1 Small Group And Whole Class Processing

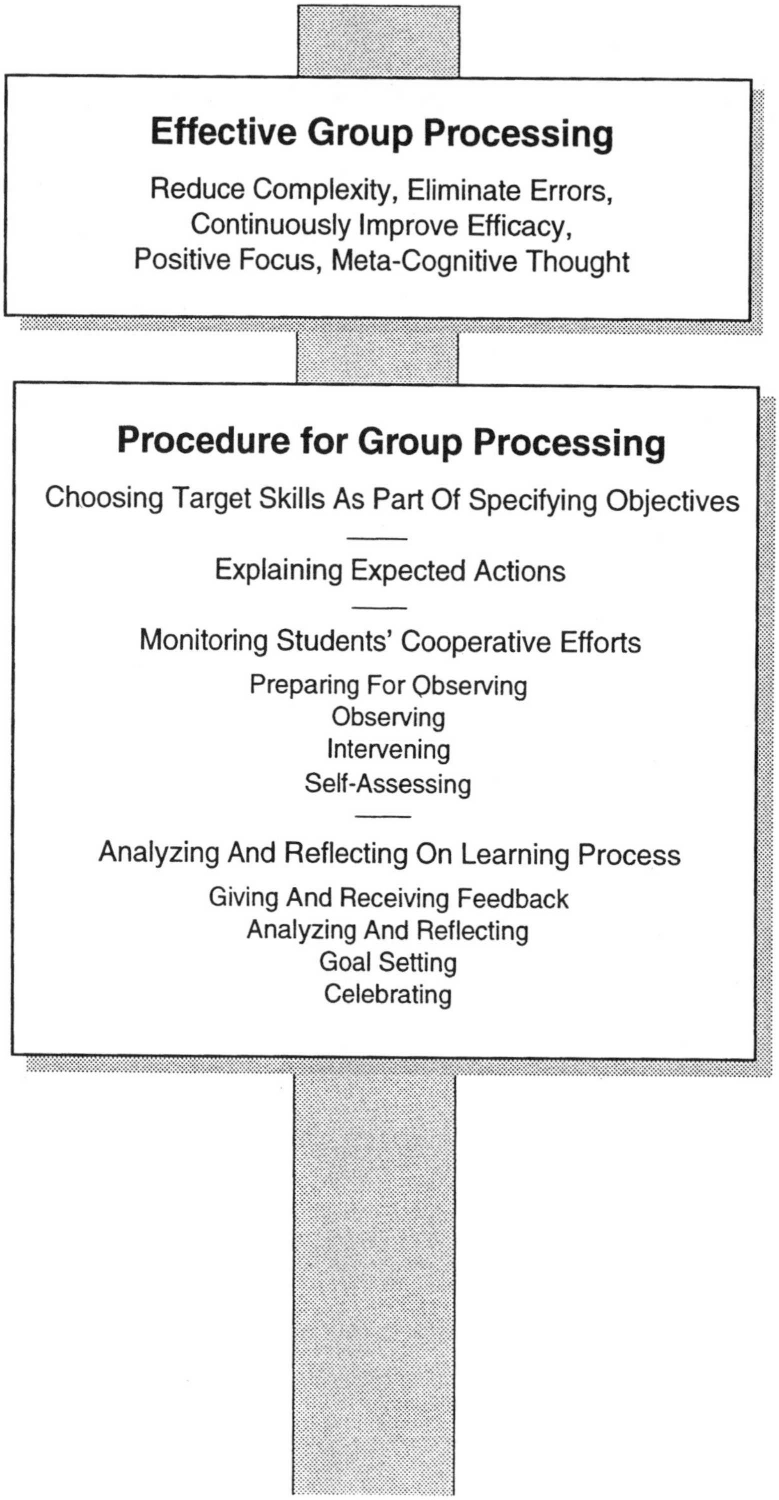

Effective Group Processing

Reduce Complexity, Eliminate Errors,
Continuously Improve Efficacy,
Positive Focus, Meta-Cognitive Thought

Procedure for Group Processing

Choosing Target Skills As Part Of Specifying Objectives

———

Explaining Expected Actions

———

Monitoring Students' Cooperative Efforts

Preparing For Observing
Observing
Intervening
Self-Assessing

———

Analyzing And Reflecting On Learning Process

Giving And Receiving Feedback
Analyzing And Reflecting
Goal Setting
Celebrating

7 : 2

Active Learning: Cooperation in the College Classroom, Interaction Book Company, 7208 Cornelia Drive, Edina, MN 55435, (612) 831-9500, FAX (612) 831-9332

The Nature Of Group Processing

We don't seek to be one thousand percent better at any one thing. We seek to be one percent better at one thousand things.

Jan Carlzon, President, Scandinavian Air Systems

Group members should examine the process they are using to complete assignments and continuously improve it. A **process** is an identifiable sequence of actions (or events) taking place over time aimed at achieving a given goal (Johnson & F. Johnson, 1997). **Group processing** is members reflecting on the group's work and members' interaction to clarify and improve members' efforts to achieve the group's goals and maintain effective working relationships by (a) describing what member actions were helpful and unhelpful and (b) making decisions about what actions to continue or change. The **purposes** of group processing are to:

1. Improve continuously the quality of the group's taskwork and teamwork.

2. Increase individual accountability by focusing attention on each member's responsible and skillful actions to learn and to help groupmates learn.

> **Group Processing**
> Receive Feedback
> Analyze And Reflect
> Set Improvement Goals
> Celebrate

3. Streamline the learning process to make it simpler (reducing complexity).

4. Eliminate unskilled and inappropriate actions (error-proofing the process).

Monitoring	Processing
Prepare For Observation	Students & Groups Receive Feedback
Observe, Supervise Student Observers	Reflect On What Was Helpful And Unhelpful
Summarize Results In Graphs	Set Goals For Improvement
Intervene To Improve Learning	Celebrate Hard Work And Success

Monitoring prepares the way for processing. During monitoring you (the instructor) prepare for observation, observe and supervise the students and visitors who are observing, and summarize and organize the observations (often in charts and graphs) to give to students and other stakeholders. When it is needed, you intervene to improve students' taskwork and teamwork.

7 : 3

Active Learning: Cooperation in the College Classroom, Interaction Book Company, 7208 Cornelia Drive, Edina, MN 55435, (612) 831-9500, FAX (612) 831-9332

At the end of the sesson, students should engage in group processing. **You (the instructor) structure group processing by** (a) setting aside time for students to reflect on their experiences in working with each other and (b) provide procedures for students to use in discussing group effectiveness (such as, "*List three things your group is doing well today and one thing you could improve*"). You may provide several minutes or so at the end of each group session for immediate processing and a longer period of time every five group sessions or so for a more detailed discussion of the process the group is using to maximize members' learning. Students reflect on and analyze the group session to (a) describe what member actions were helpful and unhelpful in contributing to the joint efforts to achieve the group's goals and (b) make decisions about what actions to continue or change. Group processing occurs at two levels; there is both small group processing and whole-class processing. There are four parts to group processing.

1. **Feedback:** Ensure each student, group, and class receives (and gives) feedback on the effectiveness of taskwork and teamwork.

2. **Reflection:** Ensure students analyze and reflect on the feedback they receive.

3. **Improvement Goals:** Help individuals and groups set goals for improving the quality of their work.

4. **Celebration:** Encourage the celebration of members' hard work and the group's success.

Giving Personal Feedback In A Helpful, Non Threatening Way

_____ 1. Focus feedback on behavior (not on personality traits).

_____ 2. Be descriptive (not judgmental).

_____ 3. Be specific and concrete (not general or abstract).

_____ 4. Make feedback immediate (not delayed).

_____ 5. Focus on positive actions (not negative ones).

_____ 6. Present feedback in a visual (such as a graph or chart) as well as auditory fashion (not just spoken words alone).

Active Learning: Cooperation in the College Classroom, Interaction Book Company, 7208 Cornelia Drive, Edina, MN 55435, (612) 831-9500, FAX (612) 831-9332

Giving And Receiving Feedback

You take the first step in structuring group processing when you ensure that learning groups and individual students receive feedback on the quality of their taskwork and teamwork so they can continuously improve both. **Feedback** is information on actual performance that individuals compare with criteria for ideal performance. When feedback is given skillfully, it generates energy, directs the energy toward constructive action, and transforms the energy into action towards improving the performance of the teamwork skills. Student performance improves and the discrepancy between actual and real performance decreases. Increased self-efficacy tends to result. Students tend to feel empowered to be even more effective next time. The following checklist may help in assessing the effectiveness of feedback.

Feedback Checklist

Feedback	Yes	No, Start Over
Is Feedback Given?		Was Not Given Or Received, Start Over
Is Feedback Generating Energy In Students?		Students Are Indifferent, Start Over
Is Energy Directed Towards Identifying & Solving Problems So Performance Is Improved?		Energy Used To Resist, Deny, Avoid Feedback, Start Over
Do Students Have Opportunities To Take Action To Improve Performance?		No, Students Are Frustrated & Feel Like Failures, Start Over

Reflecting On And Analyzing Feedback

You take the second step in structuring group processing when you have students reflect on and analyze the group session they have just completed to discover what helped and what hindered the quality of learning and whether specific behaviors had a positive or negative effect. Varying the procedures for analyzing and reflecting on the data collected about members interactions keep group processing vital and interesting. Ways of doing so include having each group:

1. Plot in a chart the data on members' interaction. Two of the most helpful charting procedures are the Bar Chart and the Run Chart.

2. Do a mind-map representing the secrets to his or her success.

3. Rate themselves on a series of dimensions on a bar chart.

Active Learning: Cooperation in the College Classroom, Interaction Book Company, 7208 Cornelia Drive, Edina, MN 55435, (612) 831-9500, FAX (612) 831-9332

4. Give each member 60 seconds to identify three things other members did to help groupmates learn.

5. Discuss the effective use of teamwork skills by members (*"How did other group members encourage participation?" "How did other group members check for understanding?"*). Each group member gives his or her response and then consensus is achieved through discussion.

Ensuring Every Group Member Receives Positive Feedback

1. Having each group focus on one member at a time. Members tell the target person one thing he/she did that helped them learn or work together effectively. The focus is rotated until all members have received positive feedback.

2. Having members write a positive comment about each other member's participation on an index card. The students then give their written comments to each other so that every member will have, in writing, positive feedback from all the other group members.

3. Having members comment on how well each other member used the social skills by writing an answer to one of the following statements. The students then give their written statements to each other.

❑ *I appreciate it when you...*

❑ *I admire you for...*

❑ *I enjoy it when you...*

❑ *You really helped the group when you...*

This procedure may also be done orally. In this case students look at the member they are complementing, use his or her name, and give their comments. The person receiving the positive feedback makes eye contact and says nothing or "thank you." Positive feedback should be directly and clearly expressed and should **not** be brushed off or denied.

7 : 6

Active Learning: Cooperation in the College Classroom, Interaction Book Company, 7208 Cornelia Drive, Edina, MN 55435, (612) 831-9500, FAX (612) 831-9332

Summarizing Observation Data: Example

Imagine you have finished observing a cooperative learning group with four members. You can either provide direct feedback to each student or you can show them the data and ask them to reach their own conclusions about their participation. If you decide to give direct feedback, you might say:

Helen contributed ten times, Roger seven times, Edythe five times, and Frank twice. Frank encouraged others to participate ten times, Edythe five times, and Roger and Helen twice. Roger summarized five times, Frank twice, and Helen and Edythe once.

If you decided to let the students reach their own conclusions, you might say:

Look at the totals in the rows and columns. What conclusions could you make about:
a. Your participation in the lesson.
b. The effectiveness of the group in completing the assignment.

In summarizing, you might say:

Each of you will wish to set a personal goal for how you can be even more effective tomorrow than you were today. What actions did you engage in most and least? What actions were most and least appropriate and helpful under the circumstances (summarizing right after someone else summarized may be inappropriate and unhelpful)? What actions would have helped the group work more effectively? Decide on a personal goal to increase your effectiveness and share it with the other group members.

Observation Form

Students	Contributes Ideas	Encourages Others To Contribute	Integrates, Summarizes	Totals
Frank	II	IIIII IIIII	II	14
Helen	IIIII IIIII	II	I	13
Roger	IIIII II	II	IIIII	14
Edythe	IIIII	IIIII	I	11
Totals	24	19	9	52

Active Learning: Cooperation in the College Classroom, Interaction Book Company, 7208 Cornelia Drive, Edina, MN 55435, (612) 831-9500, FAX (612) 831-9332

Avoiding Negative Feedback

Working cooperatively in a pair, rank order the following consequences of negative feedback from most important ("1") to least important ("2").

_____	1. It confirms their apprehension about being evaluated and students will resist being observed in the future.
_____	2. Criticism carries more weight than does praise. One critical remark often outweighs dozens of positive comments.
_____	3. People bring more past history to criticism than to praise. Negative feedback taps into past rejection and failure.
_____	4. Weaknesses take more words to explain than do strengths.
_____	5. Trust is easy to destroy but hard to build. Criticism often destroys trust.

Processing Without Observation Data

Students need to reflect on and analyze the group session they just completed in order to discover what helped and what hindered the quality of learning and whether specific behaviors had a positive or negative effect. Such reflection and analysis is generally structured by the instructor. **When there is no observational data for the group to analyze or time is very short:**

1. Give group members 30 seconds to identify three things other members did to help others learn. Every member is heard from in a short period of time.

2. Give group members a series of questions concerning their effective use of skills ("*How did other group members encourage participation?*" "*How did other group members check for understanding?*"). Each group member gives his or her response and then consensus is achieved through discussion.

3. Make the last question on an assignment sheet a group-processing question. This signals that the group processing is an integral part of one's learning.

A good way for instructors to stay in touch with the functioning of each learning group is to have each group summarize its processing and place its summary in a folder with its completed academic work. The folder is handed in to the instructor each class session.

Varying the procedures for processing keeps group processing vital and interesting. At the end of the processing, group members should set goals for improving the effectiveness of the group.

Active Learning: Cooperation in the College Classroom, Interaction Book Company, 7208 Cornelia Drive, Edina, MN 55435, (612) 831-9500, FAX (612) 831-9332

Processing Starters

1. Name three things your group did well in working together. Name one thing your group could do even better.

2. Think of something that each group member did to improve group effectiveness. Tell them what it is.

3. Tell your group members how much you appreciate their help today.

4. Rate yourself from 1 (low) to 10 (high) on (name a cooperative skill like encouraging participation, checking for understanding). Share your rating with your group and explain why you rated yourself the way you did. Plan how to increase the frequency with which group members use this skill.

Whole Class Processing

In addition to small group processing, you should periodically conduct whole-class processing sessions.

1. **You can share your observations with the whole class.** Charting the data to get a continuous record of class improvement is always a good idea. You make a large chart on which you record the frequency with which students' performed each targeted skill. Students can see how much they improved over time. You may wish to give the class a reward when the class total exceeds a preset criterion of excellence. Not only does such a chart visually remind students of the skills they should practice while working in their groups, but continuous improvement becomes a challenge that promotes class cooperation.

2. **You can add together the observation results of the student observers for an overall class total.** You may wish to chart this data.

3. You can ask students to (a) describe things they did to help each other learn, (b) discuss members' answers in the group for a minute or two and arrive at a consensus on an answer, and (c) share their group's answer with the class as a whole. Since this procedure takes some time, three questions may be as many as you will wish to ask.

Students do not learn from experiences that they do not reflect on. If the learning groups are to function better tomorrow than they did today, members must receive feedback, reflect on how the effectiveness of their actions may be improved, and plan how to be even more skillful during the next group session.

Active Learning: Cooperation in the College Classroom, Interaction Book Company, 7208 Cornelia Drive, Edina, MN 55435, (612) 831-9500, FAX (612) 831-9332

Setting Goals For Improved Functioning

You take the third step in structuring group processing when you encourage students to set improvement goals. After analyzing the observational and self-assessment data, reflecting on its meaning, and giving each other feedback, **group members set improvement goals specifying how they will act more skillfully in the next group session.** Students should publicly announce the behavior they plan to increase. They should write the goal down and review it at the beginning of the next group session. Goal setting is the link between how students did today and how well they will do tomorrow. Goal setting can have powerful impact on students' behavior as there is a sense of ownership of and commitment to actions that a student has decided to engage in (as opposed to assigned behaviors). **Some procedures for goal setting are:**

1. Have students set specific behavioral goals for the next group session. Have each student pick a specific social skill to use more effectively (an "I" focus) and/or have the group reach consensus about which collaborative skill all group members will practice in the next session (a "we" focus). The group can be required to hand in a written statement specifying which social skill each member is going to emphasize during the next work session.

2. In a whole-class processing session, ask each group to agree on one conclusion to the statement, "*Our group could do better on social skills by...,*" and tell their answer to the entire class. You write the answers on the board under the title "goals." At the beginning of the next cooperative learning lesson, you publicly read over the goal statements and remind students what they agreed to work on during this session.

3. Have each student write an answer to one of the following questions before the next cooperative learning session:

    a. "Something I plan to do differently next time to help my group is..."

    b. "The social skill I want to use next time is..."

    c. "I can help my group next time by..."

    d. "Two things I will do to help my group next time are..."

    e. "One social skill I will practice more consistently next time is..."

4. As an optional activity, have students plan where, outside of class, they can apply the social skills they are learning in class. Ask them to make connections between the cooperative learning groups and the rest of their lives. Have them specify times in the hallway, playground, home, church, or community where they can use the same social skills they are learning in class. Both "I" and "we" focuses are useful.

Active Learning: Cooperation in the College Classroom, Interaction Book Company, 7208 Cornelia Drive, Edina, MN 55435, (612) 831-9500, FAX (612) 831-9332

Celebrating

You take the fourth step in structuring group processing when you have group members celebrate their success and members' efforts to learn. Group processing ends with students celebrating their hard work and the success of their cooperative learning group. Celebrations are key to encouraging students to persist in their efforts to learn (Johnson & Johnson, 1994). Long-term, hard, persistent efforts to learn come more from the heart than from the head. Being recognized for efforts to learn and to contribute to groupmates' learning reaches the heart more effectively than do grades or tangible rewards. Both small-group and whole-class celebrations should take place. Small group processing provides the means to celebrate the success of the group and reinforce the positive behaviors of group members. Individual efforts that contribute to the group's success are recognized and encouraged. Members' actions aimed at helping groupmates learn are perceived, respected, and recognized. It is feeling successful, appreciated, and respected that builds commitment to learning, enthusiasm about working in cooperative groups, and a sense of self-efficacy about subject-matter mastery and working cooperatively with classmates.

A common teaching error is to provide too brief a time for students to process the quality of their cooperation. Students do not learn from experiences that they do not reflect on. If the learning groups are to function better tomorrow than they did today, students must receive feedback, reflect on how their actions may be more effective, and plan how to be even more skillful during the next group session.

Common Problems, Possible Solutions

If you have one of these problems, what will you do? Working with a partner, rank order the alternatives from most effective to least effective.

1. **"I do not have enough time to do processing."** When time is running out, try one of these:

   _____ Have students turn to their partners and tell them one thing they did that helped them learn that day (positive feedback).

   _____ Sample the class by having a few students tell the class one thing a partner did that helped them learn that day.

   _____ Have students thank their partners and shake hands or give high-fives.

   _____ Do the processing and assign the rest of the lesson as homework or assign the processing questions as homework.

Active Learning: Cooperation in the College Classroom, Interaction Book Company, 7208 Cornelia Drive, Edina, MN 55435, (612) 831-9500, FAX (612) 831-9332

_____ Do yesterday's processing at the start of today's cooperative group. Challenge students to improve their group from yesterday.

2. "Students are not specific enough in their answers." Vague answers may mean trust is low or students are still learning to process. Try having the group write and turn in answers to specific questions, such as:

_____ What are three ways each member helped the group today?

_____ What are three things your group did well in working together? What's one thing that would make your group even better?

_____ What social skills did each member use in the group today? What is one social skill each member will use next time?

_____ How did you help the group today? How will you help even more next time?

3. "Some students do not help or use poor cooperative skills with the processing."

_____ Have students individually and privately write their answers to processing questions so they have time to think about it. Have them give these directly to you so they can be more candid than if they were giving feedback in the group.

_____ Assign roles during processing (such as recorder, question-asker, encourager) so everyone has a structured, positive job.

_____ Give students positive sentence starters ("_It helped me today when you..._" "_One thing I appreciate about you is..._").

_____ Have the class brainstorm ways in which members can help in groups. Make a list so students are visually reminded of what to say when giving positive feedback and processing.

_____ Occasionally, sit with a group and guide their processing (modeling), then ask students to rotate leading processing in a similar way.

_____ Formally observe or have a student observer and have the group discuss the resulting data ("What behaviors did we do well? How could we improve?").

Active Learning: Cooperation in the College Classroom, Interaction Book Company, 7208 Cornelia Drive, Edina, MN 55435, (612) 831-9500, FAX (612) 831-9332

Continuously Improving Quality Of Social Skills

To improve the quality of learning in cooperative groups, the process of working together needs to be carefully examined to (a) streamline the learning process to make it simpler (reducing complexity), (b) eliminate unskilled and inappropriate actions (error-proofing the process), and (c) improve continuously students' skills in working as part of a team.

High quality work is based on the continuous improvement of teamwork (and taskwork) skills. You engineer a process through which students assess the current levels of their social skills and plan how to increase them:

❑ Decide which social skill is going to be emphasized in the lesson.

❑ Operationally define the social skill with a T-Chart and teach the social skill to students.

❑ Prepare an observation form, appoint observers, explain the observation form.

❑ Conduct the lesson, observing each of the learning groups, and coaching the student observers. **Observation** is aimed at recording and describing members' behavior as it occurs in the group, that is, to provide objective data about the interaction among group members. The behavior of group members is observed so that students may be given feedback about their participation in the group and so that inferences can be made about the ways in which the group is functioning.

❑ Complete the lesson and structure the procedure for processing how members use the social skill. The data gathered by you and the observers are analyzed as are the self-assessments by the members of how often and how well they individually performed the targeted social skills. The data are recorded and displayed on charts so that individual students and the groups can track their improvement in using the social skill and make informed decisions as to how students' teamwork can be improved. After small group processing, you conduct whole class processing in which you share your feedback to the class as a whole. Class charts are used to record and display the progress in mastering the social skill. Students set goals for improving their social skills during the next group meeting. Finally, the group members celebrate their hard work in mastering social skills.

Processing Quickies

Our group is really good at...	The best thing that happened was...
Words to describe our group are...	Today our group discovered...
Today I helped my group by...	We are a super team because...
Today I learned...	Next time we will be better at...

Active Learning: Cooperation in the College Classroom, Interaction Book Company, 7208 Cornelia Drive, Edina, MN 55435, (612) 831-9500, FAX (612) 831-9332

Summary

Group processing is the key to continuous improvement. Without group processing, ineffective practices will tend to continue and the potential of the learning group will tend not to be realized. There are four steps to ensuring that students engage in effective group processing. Students must receive feedback on the effectiveness of their actions in trying to learn and help groupmates learn. Students must reflect on the feedback. Students then set improvement goals specifying how they will act more skillfully in the next group session. Finally, students celebrate their hard work and the success of their learning group.

Some of the keys to successful small group processing are allowing sufficient time for it to take place, providing a structure for processing (such as "*List three things your group is doing well today and one thing you could improve*"), emphasizing positive feedback, making the processing specific rather than general, maintaining student involvement in processing, reminding students to use their cooperative skills while they process, and communicating clear expectations as to the purpose of processing.

In order to improve the quality of the group's work, it is also necessary to assess what each group member is learning academically. That is the focus of the next chapter.

7 : 14

Active Learning: Cooperation in the College Classroom, Interaction Book Company, 7208 Cornelia Drive, Edina, MN 55435, (612) 831-9500, FAX (612) 831-9332

Group Processing: Purposeful Reading

Read the first question. Find the answer in the text. Discuss the answer with your partner until both of you agree and are able to explain it. Relate the answer to previous learning. Move to the next question and repeat the procedure.

Questions

1. What is group processing?

2. What are the four purposes of group processing?

3. What are the four stages of group processing?

4. What is feedback?

5. What are three ways to ensure that all students receive positive feedback?

6. What are the pitfalls of negative feedback?

7. What are three ways to process without observation data?

8. What are three ways to conduct whole class processing?

9. What are four procedures for setting improvement goals?

10. Why are group celebrations important?

11. What are the three obstacles to group processing? What are three ways each obstacle may be overcome?

12. How do you continuously improve the quality of the use of social skills?

Active Learning: Cooperation in the College Classroom, Interaction Book Company, 7208 Cornelia Drive, Edina, MN 55435, (612) 831-9500, FAX (612) 831-9332

Ways To Promote Effective Processing

1. Give students time. Remember they are learning a new skill and must pass through the stages of awkward, phony, mechanical, and automatic.

2. Remember that to build trust, you must build safety. You do this by daily asking students to share the positive things about each other's participation and building a positive feedback environment.

3. Students do not automatically know the social skills needed for effective functioning. Have frequent discussions of helpful group behaviors. Display a poster of those behaviors in the classroom so students have a constant visual reminder of what to do. When teaching a specific social skill, remember to post the appropriate T-chart.

4. Emphasize problems in working together that are expected and are opportunities for growth and development. After emphasizing the positives within the group, teach the groups to tackle problems as problem-solving tasks. Teach them to define the problem, generate three possible solutions, pick one solution, try it, and if that does not work, try another. Continue until the problem is solved. Go through this procedure with groups until they learn to do it without you.

5. Ask students specific (instead of general) questions about their group effectiveness. Instead of asking *"How well did you work together?"* ask questions like:
   a. As a group, name three things the group did well in working together. Name one thing that would make your group even better. Make a plan for improvement.
   b. As a group, list three ways each group member helps the group.
   c. As a group, make a list of the social skills all group members have mastered. Pick a social skill to work on until all members can add it to the list.
   d. Individually, write three things you like about working in your group. Write one thing that would make your group even better. Write what you will do to help.
   e. Individually, write three ways you helped the group today.
   f. Individually, make a list of all the social skills you have mastered. Pick a social skill to add to the list. Plan how to master it. Practice the skill until you can add it to the mastery list.
   g. Tell each group member something he or she did that helped you.
   h. Tell each group member something you appreciate about him or her.

6. Periodically, have whole-class discussions on how well the groups are working. Ask students to tell you specific things that help them learn and work together well. Ask for suggestions of skills to work on to make the groups even better. Have the class pick one as a goal to work on. When they achieve mastery, celebrate!

Active Learning: Cooperation in the College Classroom, Interaction Book Company, 7208 Cornelia Drive, Edina, MN 55435, (612) 831-9500, FAX (612) 831-9332

Chapter Eight:
Assessment And Evaluation

Conducting Assessments

In the time of change, learners inherit the earth, while the learned find themselves beautifully equipped to deal with a world that no longer exists.

Eric Hoffer

In 1955 Edward Banfield lived for nine months in a small town in southern Italy that he called "Montegrano" (Johnson & Johnson, 1996). What Banfield noticed most was the town's alienated citizenry, grinding poverty, and pervasive corruption. He concluded that the primary source of Montegrano's plight was the distrust, envy, and suspicion that characterized its inhabitants' relations with each other. They viewed communal life as little more than a battleground. Town members consistently refused to help one another unless it would result in material gain. Many actually tried to prevent their neighbors from succeeding, believing that others' good fortune would inevitably undercut their own. Consequently, they remained socially isolated and impoverished, unable to cooperate to solve common problems or pool their resources and talents to build viable economic enterprises.

Montegrano's citizens were not inherently more selfish or foolish than people elsewhere. But for a number of complex historical and cultural reasons, they lacked the norms, habits, attitudes, and networks that encourage people to work together for the common good. They lacked what Alexis de Tocqueville called "the habits of the heart." Habits of the heart include taking responsibility for the common good, trusting others to do the same, being honest, having self-discipline, reciprocating good deeds, and perfecting the skills necessary for cooperation and conflict management. The relationship between democracy and such habits is supported by the fact that in the United States, since the early 1960s voter turnout in national elections has fallen by a quarter and the number of citizens saying that *most people can be trusted* has dropped by more than a third.

There is far more to assessment than giving students grades (Johnson & Johnson, 1996). It is vital to assess what students know, understand, and retain over time (academic learning). It is equally important to assess (a) the quality and level of their reasoning processes and (b) their skills and competencies (such as oral and written communication skills and skills in using technology). In today's complex and every changing world, a

Johnson, D. W., Johnson, R., & Smith, K. (1998). **Active Learning: Cooperation in the Collge Classroom.** Edina, MN: Interaction Book Company. (612) 831-9500, FAX (612) 831-9332

broad view of education is needed rather than a narrow focus on the memorization of facts. More than ever, colleges need to focus on teaching students appropriate work habits (such as completing work on time and striving for quality work and continuous improvement) and attitudes (such as a love of learning, desire to read good literature, commitment to democracy).

Your Assessment Plan

Given below are generic assessment targets and procedures. In planning your assessment program, check the targets that you wish to assess and then check the procedures you wish to use. Match the procedures with the targets so it is clear how you will assess each target.

What Is Assessed	Procedures Used To Assess
_____ Academic Learning	_____ Goal Setting Conferences
_____ Reasoning Process/Strategies	_____ Standardized Tests
_____ Skills & Competencies	_____ Instructor-Made Tests
_____ Attitudes	_____ Written Compositions
_____ Work Habits	_____ Oral Presentations
	_____ Projects
	_____ Portfolios
	_____ Observations
	_____ Questionnaires
	_____ Interviews
	_____ Learning Logs & Journals
	_____ Student Management Teams

In achieving these complex and long-term responsibilities of the college, instructors need to conduct three types of assessments: **diagnostic** (diagnose students' present level of knowledge and skills), **formative** (monitor progress toward learning goals to help form the instructional program), and **summative** (provide data to judge the final level of students' learning). These assessments need to focus on both the process and the

Johnson, D. W., Johnson, R., & Smith, K. (1998). **Active Learning: Cooperation in the Collge Classroom.** Edina, MN: Interaction Book Company. (612) 831-9500, FAX (612) 831-9332

outcomes of learning and instruction. Assessments need to take place in more authentic settings as well as in the classroom. The number of stakeholders in education have increased as the world economic and the interdependence among nations have increased. And the stakes of many of the assessments have increased, as students' futures are more and more determined by what they have learned and how many years of formal education they have completed. As the seriousness of educators' responsibilities have increased, so has the need to use a wider variety of assessment procedures.

Essential Definitions

Form a pair and match the correct definition with each concept. Combine with another pair and check answers.

Concept	Definition
____ 1. Instruction	a. Change within a student that is brought about by instruction.
____ 2. Learning	b. Judging the merit, value, or desirability of a measured performance.
____ 3. Rubric	c. Standards against which the quality and quantity of performances are assessed (what counts or is important).
____ 4. Assessment	d. Structuring of situations in ways that help students change, through learning.
____ 5. Criteria	e. Collecting information about the quality or quantity of a change in a student, group, instructor, or administrator.
____ 6. Evaluation	f. Articulation of gradations of quality and quantity for each criterion, from poor to exemplary.

Assessment Issues

Purpose	Focus	Setting	Stakeholders	Stakes
Diagnostic	Process Of Learning	Artificial (Classroom)	Students-Parents	Low
Formative	Process Of Instruction	Authentic (Real-World)	Instructors, Administrators	High
Summative	Outcomes Of Learning		Policy-Makers	
	Outcomes Of Instruction		Colleges, Employers	

Johnson, D. W., Johnson, R., & Smith, K. (1998). **Active Learning: Cooperation in the Collge Classroom.** Edina, MN: Interaction Book Company. (612) 831-9500, FAX (612) 831-9332

Meaningful Assessment

Involvement In Process		Use Of Outcomes	
Less Meaning	**More Meaning**	**Less Meaning**	**More Meaning**
Isolated Goals	Interdependent Goals	Individual Celebration	Joint Celebration
Work Alone	Joint Effort With Others	New Isolated Goals	New Interdependent Goals
Self-Assess Only	Assess Other's Work As Well As One's Own		
Receive Feedback Only	Both Give And Receive Feedback		

Making Assessments Meaningful And Manageable

The two major issues educators face in conducting effective and responsible assessments are making the assessments (Johnson & Johnson, 1996):

1. Meaningful to the various stakeholders.

2. Manageable so they will actually get done.

Many educators forget that a strong motivating force for students is to increase their competencies in a way that benefits those they care about. Such personal meaning is created by three factors:

1. **Structuring positive interdependence among students**. It is positive interdependence that creates positive relationships among students, a commitment to each other's learning and well-being, a desire to contribute to the common good, the motivation to strive to be one's best for the sake of others as well as oneself, and the conviction that there is more to life than selfish self-interest.

2. **Involve students in the learning and assessment processes**. Students need to be involved in formulating their learning goals, choosing the paths for achieving the goals, assessing their progress and success, planning how to improve, and implementing their plan, serious management problems arise.

3. **Ensure assessment data is organized in a way that it may be used**. Useful results help students to seek remediation for what they misunderstood, reviews to

8 : 4

Johnson, D. W., Johnson, R., & Smith, K. (1998). **Active Learning: Cooperation in the Collge Classroom.** Edina, MN: Interaction Book Company. (612) 831-9500, FAX (612) 831-9332

fill in gaps in what they know, and new learning experiences to take the next steps to advance their knowledge and skills.

These three issues are interrelated. Positive interdependence creates the context for involvement. The involvement creates the ownership of the learning and assessment processes and the motivation to use the assessment results to improve one's understanding and competencies. The more clearly the results point towards the next steps to be taken to increase the quality and quantity of the learning, the more likely students are to engage in the assessment process. Implementing plans to improve learning requires the help of collaborators, which returns the cycle to positive interdependence.

Serious management problems arise in involving students in formulating their learning goals, choosing the paths for achieving the goals, assessing their progress and success, planning how to improve, and implementing their plan. One instructor working by him- or herself can no longer manage the entire assessment system. The most natural sources of help for instructors are students and colleagues. Students provide the most help because they are available at all times. To be constructive participants in the assessment process, however, students need to be organized into cooperative learning groups. Students oriented toward competition or only their own individualistic efforts resist contributing to others' continuously improvement. To organizational theorists such as Deming, competitive and individualistic structures are "forces for destruction." To provide quality assessment, students have to be as committed to classmates' learning and academic success as they are to their own. Such commitment only comes from clear positive interdependence.

Meaningful Assessments		
Positive Interdependence	**Involvement**	**Useful Results**
Common Purpose	Setting Goals, Planning Paths To Achieve Goals, Assessing Progress, Planning For Improvement, Implementing Plans	Clarify Of Next Steps To Improve
Positive Relationships	Ownership	Use Of Results
Meaning	**Meaning**	**Meaning**

8 : 5

Johnson, D. W., Johnson, R., & Smith, K. (1998). **Active Learning: Cooperation in the Collge Classroom.** Edina, MN: Interaction Book Company. (612) 831-9500, FAX (612) 831-9332

Cooperative learning groups provide the setting, context, and environment in which assessment becomes part of the instructional process and students learn almost as much from assessing the quality of their own and their classmates' work as they do from participating in the instructional activities.

1. Cooperative learning allows assessment to be integrated into the learning process. **Continuous assessment requires continuous monitoring and support, which can best be done within cooperative learning groups.**

2. The new assessment practices are so labor intensive that students who are sincerely committed to each other's learning and success may need to be involved.

3. Cooperative learning groups allow more modalities to be used in the learning and assessment process while focusing on more diverse outcomes.

4. Cooperative learning groups allow groupmates to be sources of information in addition to the instructor and the curriculum materials.

5. Involving groupmates in assessment reduces possible biases resulting from the instructor being the sole source of feedback and the heavy reliance on reading and writing as assessment modalities.

6. Cooperative learning groups provide each student help in analyzing assessment data, interpreting the results, and implementing improvement plans.

It is difficult to imagine a class in which cooperative learning groups do not help make the assessment system more manageable or how a comprehensive assessment program can be managed without cooperative learning groups.

This chapter is a summary of the book, **Meaningful and Manageable Assessment through Cooperative Learning** (Johnson & Johnson, 1996). Readers interested in more detail and a wide variety of practice procedures are referred to that book. Assessment begins with setting learning goals.

Assessment Procedures

Assessment begins with setting learning goals. Once students have formulated and agreed to their learning goals, a variety of assessment procedures can be used. The assessment procedures include tests, compositions, presentations, projects, portfolios, observations, interviews, questionnaires, and learning logs and journals.

Johnson, D. W., Johnson, R., & Smith, K. (1998). **Active Learning: Cooperation in the Collge Classroom.** Edina, MN: Interaction Book Company. (612) 831-9500, FAX (612) 831-9332

Setting And Managing Learning Goals

Without clear learning and instructional goals, assessment cannot take place (Johnson & Johnson, 1996). The goals are created and re-emphasized in three types of conferences with each student: A **goal-setting conference** is conducted to establish a contract containing the student's learning goals, **progress-assessment conferences** are conducted to review the student's progress in achieving his or her goals, and a **post-evaluation conference** is conducted in which the student's accomplishments are explained to interested parties.

Each student must commit to achieve learning goal that specify what he or she needs to accomplish in the immediate future and his or her responsibilities for helping other students learn. These goals are established in a **goal-setting conference**. The goal setting conference may be between the instructor and the student (I/S), the instructor and the cooperative learning group (I/G), the cooperative learning group and the student (G/S), and a cooperative learning group and another group (G/G). In all cases, the emphasis is on helping students set and take ownership for learning goals that meet the START criteria (specific, trackable, achievable, relevant, transferable). The goal-setting conference contains four steps:

1. Diagnosis of current level of expertise (what does the student now know?).

2. Setting START goals focusing on student's (a) academic achievement, reasoning, social skills, attitudes, and work habits and (b) responsibilities for helping groupmates learn.

3. Organizing support systems and resources to help each student achieve his or her goals successfully.

START Goals
S = Specific
M = Measurable, Trackable
A = Challenging But Achieveable
R = Relevant
T = Transfer

4. Constructing a plan for utilizing the resources to achieve the goals and formalizing the plan into a learning contract.

The hard truth is that most instructors do not have the time to conference with each individual student, whether it is a goal-setting conference, a progress-assessment conference, or a post-evaluation conference. This does not mean that such conferences cannot happen. Instructors can engineer and supervise such conferences through appropriate use of cooperative learning groups. Groups can regularly have progress-assessment conferences with each member while the instructor listens in or pulls aside one individual students for conferences.

Johnson, D. W., Johnson, R., & Smith, K. (1998). **Active Learning: Cooperation in the Collge Classroom.** Edina, MN: Interaction Book Company. (612) 831-9500, FAX (612) 831-9332

My Learning Contract

Learning Goals

My Academic Goals	My Responsibilities For Helping Others' Learn	My Group's Goals
1.		
2.		
3.		
4.		

THE PLAN FOR ACHIEVING MY LEARNING GOALS, MEETING MY RESPONSIBILITIES, AND HELPING MY GROUP IS:

THE TIME LINE FOR ACHIEVING MY GOALS IS:

Beginning Date:

First Road-Mark:

Second Road-Mark:

Third Road-Mark:

Final Date:

Signatures:

_____   _____

_____   _____

Johnson, D. W., Johnson, R., & Smith, K. (1998). **Active Learning: Cooperation in the Collge Classroom.** Edina, MN: Interaction Book Company. (612) 831-9500, FAX (612) 831-9332

Types Of Conferences

Conference	Individual Student	Cooperative Learning Group
Goal-Setting Conference	Each class period, day, week, or instructional unit each student sets personal learning goals and publicly commits him- or herself to achieve them in a learning contract.	Each class period, day, week, or instructional unit each cooperative group sets group learning goals and members publicly commit themselves to achieve them in a learning contract.
Progress-Assessment Conferences	The student's progress in achieving his or her learning goals is assessed, what the student has accomplished so far and what is yet to be done is reviewed, and the student's next steps are detailed.	The group's progress in achieving its learning goals is assessed, what the group has accomplished so far and what is yet to be done is reviewed, and the group's next steps are detailed.
Post-Evaluation Conference	The student explains his or her level of achievement (what the student learned and failed to learn during the instructional unit) to interested parties (student's cooperative learning group, instructor(s), and parents), which naturally leads to the next goal-setting conference.	The group explains its level of achievement (what the group has accomplished and failed to accomplish during the instructional unit) to interested parties (members, instructor(s), and parents), which naturally leads to the next goal-setting conference.

Tests And Examinations

Both standardized and instructor-made tests may be used to assess student learning (Johnson & Johnson, 1996). Standardized tests are often high-stake events for which students need to be carefully prepared. Instructor-made tests are often a routine part of an instructional program to assess quickly and efficiently a broad sampling of students' knowledge. They may be multiple-choice, true-false, matching, short answers, interpretative, or essay. Although there are many effective assessment procedures, testing remains a mainstay in what instructors do. Cooperative learning groups may be used with tests through the GIG (group preparation, individual test, group test), group discussion, and Teams-Games-Tournament procedures.

8 : 9

Johnson, D. W., Johnson, R., & Smith, K. (1998). **Active Learning: Cooperation in the Collge Classroom.** Edina, MN: Interaction Book Company. (612) 831-9500, FAX (612) 831-9332

The GIG Procedure For Giving Tests

You should frequently give tests and quizzes to assess (a) how much each student knows and (b) what students still need to learn. Whenever you give a test, cooperative learning groups can serve as bookends by preparing members to take the test and providing a setting in which students review the test. Using the following procedure will result in (a) optimizing each student's preparation for the test, (b) making each student accountable to peers for his or her performance on the test, (c) assessing how much each student knows, (d) assessing what students still need to learn, (e) providing students with immediate clarification of what they did not understand or learn, (f) providing students with immediate remediation of what they did not learn, (g) preventing arguments between you and your students over which answer are correct and why. The procedure is.

1. **Group:** Students prepare for, and review for, a test in cooperative learning groups.

2. **Individual:** Each student takes the test individually, making two copies of his or her answers. Students submit one set of answer to you to grade and keep one set for the group discussion.

3. **Group:** Students retake the test in their cooperative learning groups.

Preparing For A Test In Cooperative Groups

Students meet in their cooperative learning groups and are given (a) study questions and (b) class time to prepare for the examination. The task is for students to discuss each study question and come to consensus about its answer. The cooperative goal is to ensure that all group members understand how to answer the study questions correctly. If students disagree on the answer to any study questions, they must find the page number and paragraph in the resource material explaining the relevant information or procedures. When the study/review time is up, the students give each other encouragement for doing well on the upcoming test.

Taking The Test Individually

Each student takes the test individually, making two copies of his or her answers. The task (and individual goal) is to answer each test question correctly. Students submit one copy of the answers to you (the instructor). You score the answers and evaluate student performance against a preset

Johnson, D. W., Johnson, R., & Smith, K. (1998). **Active Learning: Cooperation in the Collge Classroom.** Edina, MN: Interaction Book Company. (612) 831-9500, FAX (612) 831-9332

criterion of excellence. Students keep one copy for the group discussion. After all group members have finished the test, the group meets to take the test again.

Retaking The Test In Cooperative Groups

Students meet in their cooperative learning groups and retake the test. The **task** is to answer each question correctly. The **cooperative goal** is to ensure that all group members understand the material and procedures covered by the test. Members do so by (a) reaching consensus on the answer for each question and the rationale or procedure underlying the answer and (b) ensuring that all members can explain the answer and the rationale or procedure. The procedure is for members to:

1. Compare their answers on the first question.

2. If there is agreement, one member explains the rationale or procedure underlying the question and the group moves on to question two.

3. If there is disagreement, members find the page number and paragraph in the resource materials explaining the relevant information or procedures. The group is responsible for ensuring that all members understand the material they missed on the test. If necessary, group members assign review homework to each other. When all members agree on the answer and believe other members comprehend the material, the group moves on to question two.

4. The learning groups repeat this procedure until they have covered all test questions.

5. The group members celebrate how hard members have worked in learning the material and how successful they were on the test.

Compositions And Presentations

Every educated person should be able to present what they know in written and oral form. These are difficult competencies and to become skilled writers and presenters, students need to write and present every day. This presents an assessment problem, as someone has to read each composition and listen to each presentation and provide helpful feedback. Using cooperative learning groups to assess members' performances accomplishes four goals at the same time. It allows students to engage in the

Johnson, D. W., Johnson, R., & Smith, K. (1998). **Active Learning: Cooperation in the Collge Classroom.** Edina, MN: Interaction Book Company. (612) 831-9500, FAX (612) 831-9332

performance frequently, receive immediate and detailed feedback on their efforts, observe closely the performances of others and see what is good or lacking in others' performances, and provide the labor needed to allow students to engage in a performance frequently. Two of the most common performances assessed are compositions and presentations. In composition pairs, students are assigned to pairs, discuss and outline each other's composition in their pairs, research their topic alone, in pairs write the first paragraph of each composition, write the composition alone, edit each other's composition, rewrite the composition alone, re-edit each other's compositions, sign-off on partner's composition verifying that it is ready to be handed in, and then process the quality of the partnership. The procedure for presentations is very similar.

Persuasive Argument Composition Rubric

Name: _____ Date: _____ Grade: _____

Title Of Composition: _____

Scoring Scale: Low 1–2–3–4–5 High

Criteria	Score	Weight	Total
Organization: Thesis Statement And Introduction Rationale Presented To Support Thesis Conclusion Logically Drawn From Rationale Effective Transitions		6	(30)
Content: Topic Addressed Reasoning Clear With Valid Logic Evidence Presented To Support Key Points Creativity Evident		8	(40)
Usage: Topic Sentence Beginning Every Paragraph Correct Subject-Verb Agreement Correct Verb Tense Complete Sentences (No Run-Ons, Fragments) Mix Of Simple And Complex Sentences.		4	(20)
Mechanics: Correct Use Of Punctuation Correct Use Of Capitalization Few Or No Misspellings		2	(10)
Scale: 93-100=A, 87 - 85-92=B, 77-84=C		20	(100)

Johnson, D. W., Johnson, R., & Smith, K. (1998). **Active Learning: Cooperation in the Collge Classroom.** Edina, MN: Interaction Book Company. (612) 831-9500, FAX (612) 831-9332

Individual And Group Projects

A standard part of most every course is allowing students to be creative and inventive in integrating diverse knowledge and skills. This is especially important in assessing multiple intelligences and the ability to engage in complex procedures such as scientific investigation. Projects allow students to use multiple modes of learning. The use of cooperative learning groups allows projects to be considerable more complex and elaborate than projects completed by any one student.

Examples Of Projects

Mythological Rap Song: Write and present a rap song about the gods and goddesses in Greek mythology	**Pamphlet: Select and research a disease and prepare an instructional pamphlet to present to the class.**
Select a famous writer, artist, politician, or philosopher from the Renaissance period and become that person on a panel of experts.	Research an international conflict in the world today (for each country a student researchers a different aspect of the country related to the war--history, resolutions, maps, and so forth)
Teaching cycles through gardening (different students are in charge of seeds, fertilizing, and so forth)	**Paint a mural of the history of the earth and humankind (each group takes a section--Greek, Roman, middle ages art)**
Videotape of a community project	Time-line (personal, history, literature, art, geology)
Writing plays, skits, role plays	**College or class newspaper**
Running a college post-office	Mock court
International festival with multi-cultural activity	**Mural based on reading**
Groups write alternative endings with dramatizations	Create a new invention using the computer
Turn a short story or event in history into a movie	**Design an ideal college and have class enact it**
Newscast	Science fair projects

Portfolios

Students become far more sophisticated and educated when they can organize their work into a portfolio that represents the quality of their learning in a course or college year. There is no substitute for having students collect and organize their work samples and write a rationale connecting the work samples into a complete and holistic picture of the student's achievements, growth, and development. The resulting portfolio may feature the student's "best works" or the "process" the student is using to learn. Like all other

Johnson, D. W., Johnson, R., & Smith, K. (1998). **Active Learning: Cooperation in the Collge Classroom.** Edina, MN: Interaction Book Company. (612) 831-9500, FAX (612) 831-9332

complex and challenging tasks, students need considerable help in constructing their portfolios and in presenting them to instructors, advisor, and other interested stakeholders. Portfolios, therefore, may be more manageable when they are constructed within cooperative learning groups. The group can help each member select appropriate work samples and write a coherent and clear rationale. The portfolio may also include the group's assessment of the student's learning and growth.

An extension of portfolios is to have the student, instructor, and student's cooperative learning group all independently decide on what represents the student's best work and why. They have a conference to compare their assessments and resolve any differences.

Contents Of Portfolios

1. **Cover sheet** that creatively reflects the nature of the student's (or group's) work.

2. **Table of contents** that includes the title of each work sample and its page number.

3. The **rationale** explaining what work samples are included, why each one is significant, and how they all fit together in a holistic view of the student's (or group's) work.

4. The **work samples**.

5. A **self-assessment** written by the student or the group members.

6. **Future goals** based on the student's (or group's) current achievements, interests, and progress.

7. **Other's comments and assessments** from the instructor, cooperative learning groups, advisor, and other interested parties.

Johnson, D. W., Johnson, R., & Smith, K. (1998). **Active Learning: Cooperation in the Collge Classroom.** Edina, MN: Interaction Book Company. (612) 831-9500, FAX (612) 831-9332

Cooperative Group Portfolio

What is a cooperative base group?	A **cooperative base group** is a long-term, heterogeneous cooperative learning group with stable membership. It may last for one course, one year, or for several years. Its purposes are to give the support, help, encouragement, and assistance each member needs to make good academic progress and develop cognitively and socially in healthy ways.
What is a group portfolio?	A **group portfolio** is an organized collection of group work samples accumulated over time and individual work samples of each member.
What are its contents?	Cover that creativity reflects group's personality Table of contents Description of the group and its members Introduction to portfolio and rationale for the work samples included. Group work samples (products by the group that any one member could not have produced alone) Observation data of group members interacting as they worked on group projects. Self-assessment of the group by its members. Individual members' work samples that were revised on the basis of group feedback (compositions, presentations, and so forth). Self-assessment of members including their strengths and weaknesses in facilitating group effectiveness and other members' learning. List of future learning and social skills goals for the group and each of its members. Comments and feedback from faculty and other groups

Johnson, D. W., Johnson, R., & Smith, K. (1998). **Active Learning: Cooperation in the Collge Classroom.** Edina, MN: Interaction Book Company. (612) 831-9500, FAX (612) 831-9332

Preparing To Use Portfolios

1. Who will construct the portfolios:

   ____ Individual students with instructor input and help.

   ____ Individual students with the input and help of cooperative learning groups.

   ____ Cooperative base groups (whole group work and individual members' work) with instructor input and help.

2. What type of portfolio do you want to use?
   ____ Best Works Portfolio   ____ Process/Growth Portfolio

3. What are the purposes and objectives of the portfolio?

   a.

   b.

   c.

4. What categories of work samples should go into the portfolio?

   a.

   b.

   c.

5. What criteria will students or groups use to select their entries?

   a.

   b.

   c.

6. Who will develop the rubrics to assess and evaluate the portfolios?
   ____ Faculty   ____ Students

Johnson, D. W., Johnson, R., & Smith, K. (1998). **Active Learning: Cooperation in the Collge Classroom.** Edina, MN: Interaction Book Company. (612) 831-9500, FAX (612) 831-9332

Observing

There is a limit to the information gained by having students turn in completed tests, compositions, projects, and portfolios. Answers on a test and homework assignments handed in can tell instructors whether students can arrive at a correct answer. They cannot, however, inform instructors as to the quality of the reasoning strategies students are using, students' commitment to classmates' success and well-being, or the extent to which students' can work effectively with others. Instructors must find a way to make students' covert reasoning processes overt, demonstrate behaviorally their attitudes and work habits, and show how skillfully they can work with others. Observing students in action thus becomes one of the most important assessment procedures. Observing students has three stages:

1. **Preparing for observing**. Deciding what actions to observe, who will observe, what the sampling plan will be, constructing an observation form, and training observers to use the form.

2. **Observing**. Observations may be formal or informal, structured or unstructured.

3. **Summarizing the data for use by students and other stake-holders**. In summarizing observations, the data may be displayed in bar or run charts. Feedback is then given to the students or other interested parties. The recipients reflect on the feedback and set improvement goals.

One of the primary uses of observation procedures is to assess the use of social skills. **First**, you teach students the targeted social skill. You show the need for the skill, define it with a t-chart, set up practice situations in which students can use the skill, ensure that students receive feedback on their use of the skill and reflect on how to improve, and ensure that students persevere in practicing the skill until it becomes automatic. **Second**, you structure cooperative learning situations so students can use the social skills and you can observe their doing so. **Third**, you intervene in the cooperative learning groups to ensure that members are using the social skills appropriately and to recognize them for doing so. **Fourth**, you have students complete checklists or questionnaires to self-diagnose their mastery of the targeted social skills. **Fifth**, you assign students in setting improvement goals to increase their social competence. **Sixth**, you assess students' knowledge of social skills. **Finally**, you report on the level of students' social skills to interested stakeholders, such as the students, advisors, and potential employers.

Interviewing

Closely related to observing students in action is interviewing students. Like observing, interviews can make the covert overt through asking students more and more detailed questions about their reasoning processes and strategies. The strengths of the interview is

Johnson, D. W., Johnson, R., & Smith, K. (1998). **Active Learning: Cooperation in the Collge Classroom.** Edina, MN: Interaction Book Company. (612) 831-9500, FAX (612) 831-9332

that it is personal and flexible. The personal nature of interviews allows you to build a more positive, supportive, and trusting relationships with each student. The flexibility of interviews allows you to interview either one or a small group of students before, during, and after a lesson and to use the interview for both assessment and teaching purposes. Socrates is an example of using interviewing as an instructional strategy.

Being A Socrates

1. Choose a topic being studied.

2. Develop two or three general questions on what the student knows about the topic to begin an interview.

3. After asking the opening questions, probe what the student knows while looking for inconsistencies, contradictions, or conflicts in what the student is saying.

4. Ask follow-up questions that highlight the conflicts within the student's reasoning and makes the contradictions focal points for the student's attention.

5. Continue the interview until the student has resolved the conflicts by moving towards deeper-level analysis of what he or she knows and arriving at greater and greater insights into the material being studied.

6. Conclude the interview with pointing the student toward further resources to read and study.

Attitude Questionnaires

All learning has affective components and in many ways the attitudes students develop may be more important than their level of academic learning. Getting an "A" in math class, for example, does a student little good if he or she has learned to hate math and never wants to take a math class again. Obviously, loving math and wanting to take math courses throughout one's educational career is far more important than the level of achievement in any one math class. Attitudes largely determine whether students continue to study the subject area, become uninterested, or wish to avoid it in the future. In assessing student attitudes, you (a) decide which attitudes to measure, (b) construct a questionnaire, (c) select a standardized measure if it is appropriate, (d) give the measures near the beginning and end of each instructional unit, semester, or year, (e) analyze and organize the data for feedback to interested stakeholders, (f) give the feedback in a timely and orderly way, and (g) use the results to make decisions about improving the instructional program. In constructing a questionnaire, each question needs to be well-worded and require either an open-ended (fill-in-the-blank or free response) or closed-ended (dichotomous, multiple choice, ranking, or scale) response. The questions are then arranged in an appropriate sequence and given an attractive format. A standardized questionnaire, such as the Classroom Life instrument may be used to measure a broader range of student attitudes.

My View Of This Class Is

Answer each question below with your best opinion. Do not leave any questions blank.

1. My general opinion about history is _____.

2. History is my _____ subject.

3. If someone suggested I take up history as my life's work, I would reply

   _____.

4. History is my favorite college subject. ___ True ___ False

5. Do you intend to take another course in history?
   _____ Yes _____ No _____ I'm not sure

6. How interested are you in learning more about history?
   Very interested 1:2:3:4:5:6:7 Very uninterested

7.   **History**
   Ugly 1:2:3:4:5:6:7 Beautiful
   Bad 1:2:3:4:5:6:7 Good
   Worthless 1:2:3:4:5:6:7 Valuable
   Negative 1:2:3:4:5:6:7 Positive

Learning Logs And Journals

Students often do not spend enough time reflecting on what they are learning and how it relates in a personal way to their lives. Learning logs and journals help students document and reflect on their learning experiences. **Logs** tend to emphasize short entries concerning the subject matter being studied. Logs are especially useful in conjunction with informal cooperative learning. **Journals** tend to emphasize more narrative entries concerning personal observations, feelings, and opinions in response to readings, events, and experiences. These entries often connect what is being studied in one class with

Johnson, D. W., Johnson, R., & Smith, K. (1998). **Active Learning: Cooperation in the Collge Classroom.** Edina, MN: Interaction Book Company. (612) 831-9500, FAX (612) 831-9332

other classes or with life outside of the classroom. Journals are especially useful in having students apply what they are learning to their "action theories."

ASSIGNING POINT VALUES TO ENTRIES

Points	Criteria
20	Completeness Of Entries
10	Entries Recorded On Time
15	Originality Of Entries
15	Higher-Level Reasoning Demonstrated
15	Connections Made With Other Subject Areas
25	Personal Reflection
100	Total

Total Quality Learning

Total quality learning begins with assigning students to teams and assigning them the task of continuously improving the quality of the processes of learning and assessment. **Continuous improvement** is the ongoing search for changes that will increase the quality of the processes of learning, instructing, and assessing. Each time students write a composition, for example, they should find at least one way to improve their writing skills. The changes do not have to be dramatic. Small, incremental changes are fine.

To improve continuously the processes of learning and assessment, students need to engage in eight steps. **First**, they must form teams. Quality learning is difficult without cooperative learning groups. **Second**, team members analyze the assignment and select a learning process for improvement. **Third**, members define the process to improve, usually by drawing a flow chart or cause-and-effect diagram. **Fourth**, team members engage in the process. **Fifth**, students gather data about the process, display the data, and analyze it. Tools to help them do so include observation forms, Pareto charts, run charts, scatter diagrams, and histograms. **Sixth**, on the basis of the analysis, team members make a plan to improve the process. **Seventh**, students implement the plan by engaging in the learning process in a modified and improved way. **Finally**, the team institutionalizes the changes that do in fact improve the quality of the learning process. One way to enhance the use of total quality learning is through the use of student management teams. A **student management team** consists of three or four students plus the instructor who assume responsibility for the success of the class by focusing on

Johnson, D. W., Johnson, R., & Smith, K. (1998). **Active Learning: Cooperation in the Collge Classroom.** Edina, MN: Interaction Book Company. (612) 831-9500, FAX (612) 831-9332

how to improve either the instructor's teaching or the content of the course. The group members monitor the course through their own experience and the comments of classmates. There are four stages of using student management teams: forming the team by recruiting and choosing members, building a cooperative team by structuring the five basic elements, improving the instruction and content of the course, and reaping the long-term gains from the process by carrying on the improvements to the next course.

Teaching Teams And Assessment

The days are gone when a instructor, working in isolation from colleagues, could instruct, assess, and report results by him- or herself. The practices have become so labor intensive and complex that one instructor cannot expect to do them alone. Realistically, colleagial teaching teams are needed to coordinate and continuously improve the instruction, assessment, and reporting process. Instructors need to begin their instruction, assessment, and reporting efforts with forming a colleagial teaching team. This allows them to capitalize on the many ways teams enhance productivity. The team focuses its efforts on continuously improving both student learning and the quality of instruction. The team as a whole conducts the assessment and reporting process by developing rubrics, applying the rubrics effectively, and reporting results to interested audiences. The team then establishes a continuous improvement process focusing on maximizing the quality of instruction of each member. While engaging in the continuous improvement process, the team also engages in continuously retraining aimed at improving the effectiveness of their use of the assessment procedures. The use of colleagial teaching teams provides the framework for developing collegewide criteria and standards to be used in assessment.

Giving Grades   A B C

Instructors need to assess student learning and progress frequently, but they do not need to evaluate or give grades. Assessing involves checking on how students are doing, what they have learned, and what problems or difficulties they have experienced. Grades are symbols that represent a value judgment concerning the relative quality of a student's achievement during a specified period of instruction. Grades are necessary to give students and other interested audiences information about students' level of achievement, evaluate the success of an instructional program, provide students access to certain educational opportunities, and reward students who excel. Grading systems may involve a single grade or multi-grades. It is vital that grades are awarded fairly as they can have considerable influence on students' futures. Being fair includes using a wide variety of assignments to measure achievement. Grades may be supplemented with checklist and narratives to give a more complex and complete summative evaluation of student achievement. Having students work in cooperative groups adds further opportunity to measure aspects of students' learning and assign grades in a variety of ways.

Johnson, D. W., Johnson, R., & Smith, K. (1998). **Active Learning: Cooperation in the Collge Classroom.** Edina, MN: Interaction Book Company. (612) 831-9500, FAX (612) 831-9332

Giving Students Grades in Cooperative Learning

The way grades are given depends on the type of interdependence the instructor wishes to create among students. Norm-referenced grading systems place students in competition with each other. Criterion-referenced grading systems require students to either work individualistically or cooperatively. Here are a number of suggestions for giving grades in cooperative learning situations.

1. **Individual score plus bonus points based on all members reaching criterion:** Group members study together and ensure that all have mastered the assigned material. Each then takes a test individually and is awarded that score. If all group members achieve over a preset criterion of excellence, each receives a bonus. An example is as follows.

Criteria	Bonus	Members	Scores	Bonus	Total
100	15 Points	Bill	100	10	110
90 - 99	10 Points	Juanita	95	10	105
80 - 89	5 Points	Sally	90	10	100

2. **Individual score plus bonus points based on lowest score:** The group members prepare each other to take an exam. Members then receive bonus points on the basis of the lowest individual score in their group. This procedure emphasizes encouraging, supporting, and assisting the low achievers in the group. The criterion for bonus points can be adjusted for each learning group, depending on the past performance of their lowest member. An example is as follows:

Criteria	Bonus	Members	Scores	Bonus	Total
90 - 100	6 Points	Bill	93	2	95
80 - 89	4 Points	Juanita	85	2	87
70 - 79	2 Points	Sally	78	2	80

3. **Individual score plus group average:** Group members prepare each other to take an exam. Each takes the examination and receives his or her individual score. The scores of the group members are then averaged. The average is added to each member's score. An example is given below.

Johnson, D. W., Johnson, R., & Smith, K. (1998). **Active Learning: Cooperation in the Collge Classroom.** Edina, MN: Interaction Book Company. (612) 831-9500, FAX (612) 831-9332

Student	Individual Score	Group Average	Final Score
Bill	66	79	145
Juanita	89	79	168
Sally	75	79	154
Benjamin	86	79	165

4. **Individual score plus bonus based on improvement scores:** Members of a cooperative group prepare each other to take an exam. Each takes the exam individually and receives his or her individual grade. In addition, bonus points are awarded on the basis of whether members percentage on the current test is higher than the average percentage on all past tests (i.e., their usual level of performance). Their percentage correct on past tests serves as their base score that they try to better. Every two tests or scores, the base score is updated. If a student scores within 4 points (above or below) his or her base score, all members of the group receive 1 bonus point. If they score 5 to 9 points above their base score, each group member receives 2 bonus points. Finally, if they score 10 points or above their base score, or score 100 percent correct, each member receives 3 bonus points.

5. **Totaling members' individual scores:** The individual scores of members are added together and all members receive the total. For example, if group members scored 90, 85, 95, and 90, each member would receive the score of 360.

6. **Averaging of members' individual scores:** The individual scores of members are added together and divided by the number of group members. Each member then receives the group average as their mark. For example, if the scores of members were 90, 95, 85, and 90, each group member would receive the score of 90.

7. **Group score on a single product:** The group works to produce a single report, essay, presentation, worksheet, or exam. The product is evaluated and all members receive the score awarded. When this method is used with worksheets, sets of problems, and examinations, group members are required to reach consensus on each question and be able to explain it to others. The discussion within the group enhances the learning considerably.

8. **Randomly selecting one member's paper to score:** Group members all complete the work individually and then check each other's papers and certify that they are perfectly correct. Since each paper is certified by the whole group to be correct, it makes little difference which paper is graded. The instructor picks one at random, grades it, and all group members receive the score.

Johnson, D. W., Johnson, R., & Smith, K. (1998). **Active Learning: Cooperation in the Collge Classroom.** Edina, MN: Interaction Book Company. (612) 831-9500, FAX (612) 831-9332

9. **Randomly selecting one member's exam to score:** Group members prepare for an examination and certify that each member has mastered the assigned material. All members then take the examination individually. Since all members have certified that each has mastered the material being studied, it makes little difference which exam is scored. The instructor randomly picks one, scores it, and all group members receive that score.

10. **All members receive lowest member score:** Group members prepare each other to take the exam. Each takes the examination individually. All group members then receive the lowest score in the group. For example, if group members score 89, 88, 82, and 79, all members would receive 79 as their score. This procedure emphasizes encouraging, supporting and assisting the low-achieving members of the group and often produces dramatic increases in performance by low-achieving students.

11. **Average of academic scores plus collaborative skills performance score:** Group members work together to master the assigned material. They take an examination individually and their scores are averaged. Concurrently, their work is observed and the frequency of performance of specified collaborative skills (such as leadership or trust-building actions) is recorded. The group is given a collaborative skills performance score, which is added to their academic average to determine their overall mark.

12. **Dual academic and nonacademic rewards:** Group members prepare each other for a test, take it individually, and receive an individual grade. On the basis of their group average they are awarded some other valued reward.

Summary

Traditionally, assessment procedures have been quite limited. Instructors often notice the light in a student's eye, changes in voice inflections, the "aha" of discovery, the creative insight resulting from collaborating with others, the persistence and struggle of a student determined to understand complex material, the serendipitous use of skills and concepts beyond the context in which they were learned, and reports from other instructors on the changes in a student resulting from a course of study. What has been lacking is a systematic way of collecting and reporting such evidence.

Times have changed. The diverse assessment procedures discussed in Johnson and Johnson (1996) and outlined in this book are quite developed and may be used effectively as part of any instructional program. Each has its strengths and its weaknesses. Each can be integrated into ongoing instructional program and managed when they are used as part of cooperative learning. Together, they allow cooperative learning groups to engage in total quality learning and provide a comprehensive and fair means of giving grades.

Johnson, D. W., Johnson, R., & Smith, K. (1998). **Active Learning: Cooperation in the Collge Classroom.** Edina, MN: Interaction Book Company. (612) 831-9500, FAX (612) 831-9332

Creating Rubrics To Assess Student Learning

Step One: Review lesson and type of student performance.

a. Lesson: _____

b. Type Of Student Performance: _____

Step Two: Define the assessment procedure. Indicate on the checklist below the procedures that will be used to assess students' learning.

_____ Goal Setting Conferences   _____ Portfolios

_____ Standardized Tests   _____ Observations

_____ Instructor-Made Tests   _____ Questionnaires

_____ Written Compositions   _____ Interviews

_____ Oral Presentations   _____ Learning Logs & Journals

_____ Homework, Extra-Credit   _____ Student Management Teams

_____ Projects, Experiments, Surveys, Historical Research

Step Three: Develop a set of criteria to use in assessing students performances. The steps for doing so are:

_____ a. Brainstorm a potential list of criteria

_____ b. Rank order the criteria from most important to least important.

Step Four: Develop rubrics. Rubrics are needed to assess the quality and quantity of each student's performance for each criterion.

_____ a. Begin with the criterion ranked most important.

_____ b. Find exemplary and terrible student performances and analyze them to help develop indicators that accurately measure their strengths and weaknesses.

_____ c. List indicators of very poor, poor, middle, good, and very good levels of performance. Define very good and very poor performance and then fill in the middle categories.

_____ d. Communicate rubrics to friends so they can help students with homework.

Johnson, D. W., Johnson, R., & Smith, K. (1998). **Active Learning: Cooperation in the Collge Classroom.** Edina, MN: Interaction Book Company. (612) 831-9500, FAX (612) 831-9332

Step Five: Train the students in using the rubric so that they are co-oriented, consistent, and reliable in their use of the rubric. Students have to be able to apply the same rubric in the same way at different times. Different students have to be able to apply the same rubric in the same way. One procedure for training is:

———   a. Students score models of exemplary and substandard work.

———   b. Students score a student performance together as a group, discussing how the performance should be assessed on each criterion.

———   c. Team members score several student performances separately. They compare scoring to see if they are using the rubrics in the same way.

———   d. Compare students' scoring with the instructor's scoring. Discuss any differences until everyone in the class is co-oriented and reliably scores a performance in the same way.

Step Six: Conduct Lesson And Assess Student Performances.

———   a. **Self-Assessment**: Each student assesses his or her own work.

———   b. **Peer Assessment**: Students assess their groupmates' work. At least two team members score each performance. Any differences in the scoring are then discussed until two or more team members agree on the way each student performance is scored.

———   c. **Instructor Assessment**: Instructor assesses each student performance if time allows or assesses samples of students' work if time is short.

Step Seven: On the basis of the assessment, plan how to improve student performances and instructional program.

Step Eight: Continually improve the criteria, the rubrics, and the students' skills in assessing the quality and quantity of their learning. Beware of scoring criteria drift. Periodically recalibrate the instructors and students' use of the scoring rubrics. Search for exemplary criteria, rubrics, and scoring procedures and use them as benchmarks to improve assessment practices.

Johnson, D. W., Johnson, R., & Smith, K. (1998). **Active Learning: Cooperation in the Collge Classroom.** Edina, MN: Interaction Book Company. (612) 831-9500, FAX (612) 831-9332

Assessment Rubric

Student: _____ Date: _____ Class: _____

Type Of Performance: _____

Write the indicators for each of the five levels of performance for each criterion.

VERY POOR	POOR	MIDDLE	GOOD	VERY GOOD
Criterion Example: Topic Addressed				
◆ Paper does not address topic.	◆ Opening sentence does not identify the purpose	◆ Opening sentence partially identifies the purpose.	◆ Opening sentence identifies the purpose.	◆ Opening sentence identifies the purpose.
◆	◆ Few aspects of topic are discussed in disorganized ways.	◆ Several aspects are discussed, but not in separate paragraphs.	◆ All aspects of topic are discussed but not in separate paragraphs.	◆ Each paragraph addresses one aspect of the topic.
◆	◆	◆	◆	◆ All aspects of topic are thoroughly discussed.
Criterion One				
◆	◆	◆	◆	◆
◆	◆	◆	◆	◆
◆	◆	◆	◆	◆
Criterion Two				
◆	◆	◆	◆	◆
◆	◆	◆	◆	◆
◆	◆	◆	◆	◆
Criterion Three				
◆	◆	◆	◆	◆
◆	◆	◆	◆	◆
◆	◆	◆	◆	◆

8 : 27

Johnson, D. W., Johnson, R., & Smith, K. (1998). **Active Learning: Cooperation in the Collge Classroom.** Edina, MN: Interaction Book Company. (612) 831-9500, FAX (612) 831-9332

Assessment Rubric

Student: _____ Date: _____ Class: _____

Type Of Performance: _____

Write indicators for each of the three levels of performance for each criterion.

INADEQUATE	MIDDLE	EXCELLENT
Criterion Example: Clear Reasoning		
♦ Gives conclusion with	♦ Gives some examples	♦ Consistently gives for
♦ no examples or reasons.	♦ and reasons for each	♦ examples and reasons
♦	♦ conclusion.	♦ each conclusion.
Criterion One		
♦	♦	♦
♦	♦	♦
♦	♦	♦
Criterion Two		
♦	♦	♦
♦	♦	♦
♦	♦	♦
Criterion Three		
♦	♦	♦
♦	♦	♦
♦	♦	♦
Criterion Four		
♦	♦	♦
♦	♦	♦
♦	♦	♦

Comments:

8 : 28

Johnson, D. W., Johnson, R., & Smith, K. (1998). **Active Learning: Cooperation in the Collge Classroom.** Edina, MN: Interaction Book Company. (612) 831-9500, FAX (612) 831-9332

Creating Rubrics To Assess Student Learning

Step One: Define the assessment procedure. Indicate on the checklist below the procedures the team will use to assess students' learning.

_____ Quizzes, Tests, Examinations _____ Homework, Extra-Credit

_____ Compositions   _____ Other:

_____ Presentations   _____ Other:

_____ Projects, Experiments, Surveys, Historical Research

Step Two: Develop a set of criteria to use in evaluating the performance produced by students. The steps for doing so are:

 a. Brainstorm a potential list of criteria

 b. Rank order the criteria from most important to least important.

 c. Construct a rubric for each criterion. Begin with the criterion ranked most important by listing indicators of very poor, poor, middle, good, and very good levels of performance.

 d. Find some exemplary and very poor student performances and analyze them to help develop a set of indicators that accurately measures their strengths and weaknesses.

 e. Apply the rubrics to a set of sample performances.

Step Three: Construct rubrics. Rubrics are needed to assess the quality and quantity of each student's performance for each criterion.

_____ a. Begin with the criterion ranked most important.

_____ b. List indicators of very poor, poor, middle, good, and very good levels of performance.

_____ c. Find some exemplary and very poor student performances and analyze them to help develop a set of indicators that accurately measures their strengths and weaknesses.

Johnson, D. W., Johnson, R., & Smith, K. (1998). **Active Learning: Cooperation in the Collge Classroom.** Edina, MN: Interaction Book Company. (612) 831-9500, FAX (612) 831-9332

Step Four: Train the instructors in using the rubric so that they are co-oriented, consistent, and reliable in their use of the rubric. Instructors have to be able to apply the same rubric in the same way at different times. Different instructors have to be able to apply the same rubric in the same way. One procedure for training is:

—— a. Score a student performance together as a group, discussing how the performance should be assessed on each criterion.

—— b. Score a set of student performances separately, with each team member scoring the performances on his or her own. Then compare the scoring to see if team members are using the rubrics in the same way.

—— c. Score all student performances with at least two team members scoring each performance. Any differences in the scoring are then discussed until two or more team members agree on the scoring of each student performance.

Step Five: On the basis of the assessment, plan how to improve the instructional program. Suggestions are:

1.

2.

3.

Step Six: Continually improve the criteria, the indicators for each criterion, and the team members' skills in using the rubrics to assess the quality and quality of student learning. Beware of scoring criteria drift. Remember the need to periodically recalibrate team members' use of the scoring rubrics. Search for exemplary rubrics and scoring procedures in other teams and colleges and use them as benchmarks to improve your team's assessment practices.

8 : 30

Johnson, D. W., Johnson, R., & Smith, K. (1998). **Active Learning: Cooperation in the Collge Classroom.** Edina, MN: Interaction Book Company. (612) 831-9500, FAX (612) 831-9332

Chapter Nine:

The Cooperative College

Introduction

Nothing new that is really interesting comes without collaboration.

James Watson, Nobel Prize Winner (codiscoverer of double helix)

Ford Motor Company knew it had to do something different, dramatically different, to gain back market share from imports. A new mid-sized car was conceived to be Ford's best chance to do so. For years Ford had operated within a mass-manufacturing structure whose motto was "any color as long as it is black." Designers etched out sketches and gave them to manufacturing with the order, "build it!" Sales inherited the car and had to figure out how to sell it. That was the way Ford had always built cars. But not this time. An interdisciplinary team was created made up of designers, engineers, manufacturing and financial executives, and sales and marketing people. Together they created the Taurus, a car whose sales neared one million units in its first four production years and which has consistently won praise from both auto experts and consumers.

Ford is not the only company to switch to cooperative teams. Whereas there is an American myth of progress being spurred on by Lone Rangers, in today's corporations that image is about as current as bustles and spats. From Motorola to AT&T Credit Corporation, self-managing, multi-disciplinary teams are in charge of keeping the company profitable. Teams get things done.

Team development is at the core of the changes necessary to alter the way faculty and students work. It is the way to educate students the right way the first time. Reorganizing students and faculty into teams, however, may not be easy.

Active Learning: Cooperation In The College Classroom, Interaction Book Company, 7208 Cornelia Drive, Edina, MN 55435, (612) 831-9500, FAX (612) 831-9332

Figure 9.1 The Cooperative College

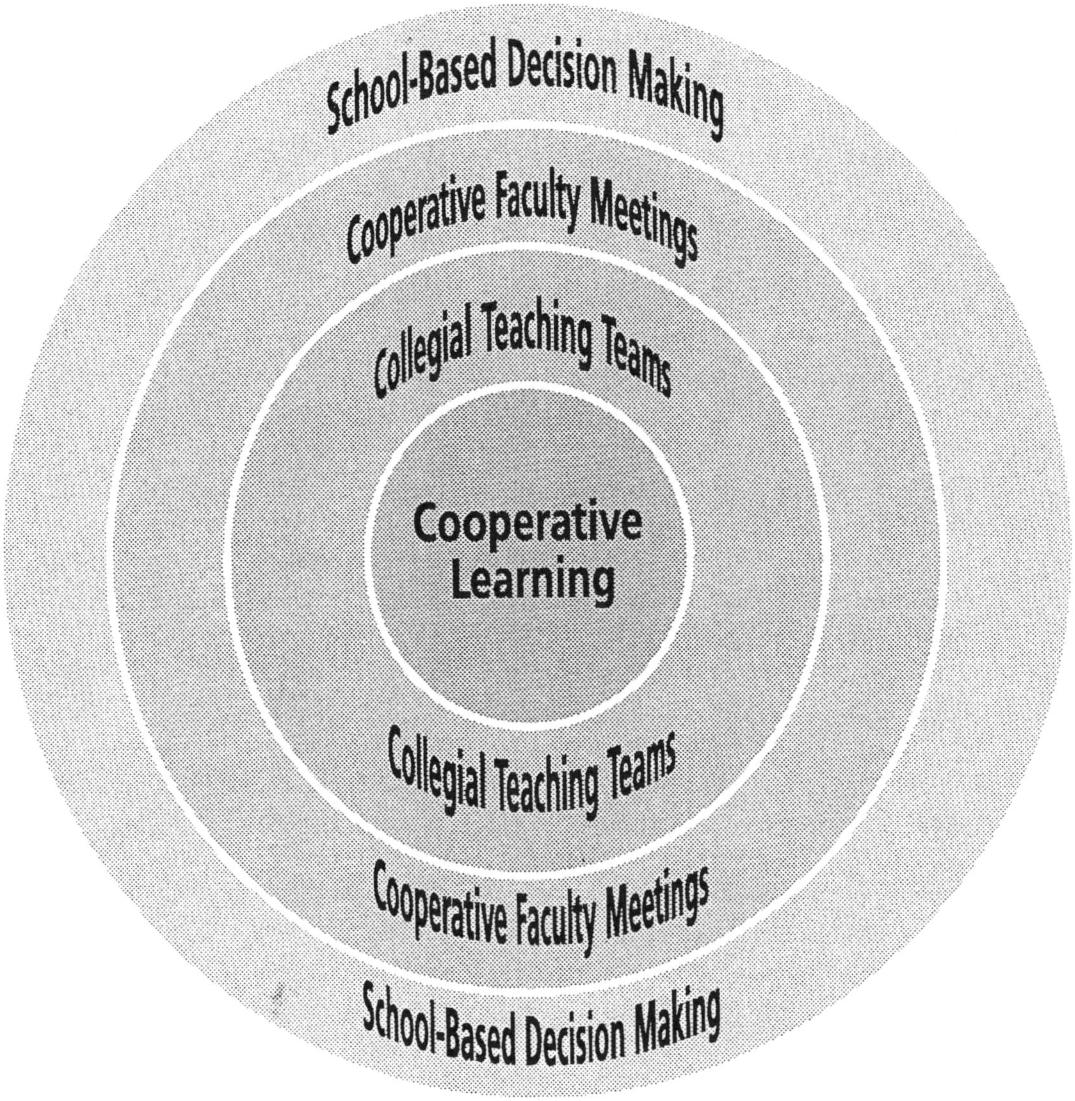

School-Based Decision Making

Cooperative Faculty Meetings

Collegial Teaching Teams

Cooperative Learning

Collegial Teaching Teams

Cooperative Faculty Meetings

School-Based Decision Making

Active Learning: Cooperation In The College Classroom, Interaction Book Company, 7208 Cornelia Drive, Edina, MN 55435, (612) 831-9500, FAX (612) 831-9332

The Cooperative College

The worst poverty is the feeling of loneliness and of being unwanted.

Mother Teresa

For nearly a century, colleges have functioned as "mass production" organizations that divided work into small component parts performed by individuals who worked separately from and, in many cases, in competition with peers. Instructors have worked alone, in their own room, with their own set of students, and with their own set of curriculum materials. Both faculty and students have been considered to be interchangeable parts in the organizational machine. Students can be assigned to any instructor because faculty are all equivalent and, conversely, faculty can be given any student to teach because all students are considered to be the same.

W. Edwards Deming and others have suggested that more than 85 percent of all the things that go wrong in any organization are directly attributable to the organization's structure, not the nature of the individuals involved. Retraining faculty to use cooperative learning while organizing faculty to mass produce educated students is self-defeating. Changing methods of teaching is much easier when the changes are congruent with (not in opposition to) the organizational structure of the college. In order for colleges to focus on the quality of instruction, they need to change from a mass-production, competitive/individualistic organizational structure to a high-performance, cooperative team-based organizational structure known as "the cooperative college." In this structure, work at all levels is organized into whole processes performed by teams focused on joint productivity and continuous improvement (see Johnson & Johnson, 1994).

The **cooperative college** is a team-based, high-performance organizational structure in which teams are used at all levels to increase the productivity and effectiveness of administrators, faculty and staff, and students. In a cooperative college, students work primarily in cooperative learning groups, faculty and college staff work in cooperative teams, and district administrators work in cooperative teams (Johnson & Johnson, 1994). The organizational structure of the classroom, college, and district are then congruent. Each level of cooperative teams supports and enhances the other levels. Structuring cooperative teams is the heart of improving colleges and must precede all other improvement initiatives. Effective teamwork is the very center of improving the quality of instruction and education. It forms the hub around which all other elements of college improvement revolves. The primary units of performance in colleges need to be teams. Teams are, beyond all doubt, the most direct sources of continuous improvement of instruction and education.

A cooperative college structure begins in the classroom with the use of cooperative learning the majority of the time (Johnson & Johnson, 1994). Work teams are the

Active Learning: Cooperation In The College Classroom, Interaction Book Company, 7208 Cornelia Drive, Edina, MN 55435, (612) 831-9500, FAX (612) 831-9332

heart of the team-based organizational structure and cooperative learning groups are the primary work team. Students spend the majority of the day in **formal cooperative learning groups** (students work together for one or several class sessions to achieve shared learning goals and complete specific tasks and assignments) and **informal cooperative learning groups** (students work together in temporary, ad hoc groups that last only for one discussion or class period to achieve joint learning goals) and **cooperative base groups** (students work in long-term groups (lasting for one semester or year) with stable membership whose primary responsibility is to give each member the support, encouragement, and assistance he or she needs to progress academically and develop cognitively and socially in healthy ways). The health of cooperative efforts, however, largely depends on how constructively conflicts among collaborators are managed. In addition, students are taught how to manage conflicts constructively by learning how to engage in **academic controversies** (one student's ideas, information, conclusions, theories, and opinions are incompatible with those of another, and the two seek to reach an agreement) and the peacemaker procedures for **problem-solving negotiations** (procedure by which persons with shared and opposing interests reach an agreement that maximizes joint outcomes and improves their working relationship) and **peer mediation** (a fellow student serves as a neutral person who helps two or more disputants resolve their conflict). Finally, students are taught the **civic values** needed to be part of a learning community.

Quality learning does not take place in isolation, it results from a team effort to challenge each other's reasoning and maximize each other's learning. Cooperative learning is used to increase student achievement, create more positive relationships among students, and generally improve students' psychological well-being. Cooperative learning is also the prerequisite and foundation for most other instructional innovations, including thematic curriculum, whole language, critical thinking, active reading, process writing, materials-based (problem-solving) mathematics, and learning communities. A secondary effect of using cooperative learning is that it affects faculty' attitudes and competencies toward working collaboratively with colleagues. What is promoted in instructional situations tends to dominate relationships among staff members.

The second level in creating a cooperative college is to form colleagial teaching teams, task forces, and ad hoc decision-making groups within the college (Johnson & Johnson, 1994). The use of cooperation to structure faculty and staff work involves (a) **colleagial teaching teams** (two to five faculty members meet to increase their instructional expertise and success in using cooperative learning) and **colleagial study groups** (two to five faculty members meet to read and discuss materials on instructional and assessment procedures that will increase their effectiveness and enhance their use of cooperative learning), (b) faculty meetings in which cooperative procedures are modeled, (c) faculty committees formed to monitor and continuously improve procedures dealing with college life, and (d) college-based decision making . College based decision making begins with the formation of a **instructor task force** which considers a college problem, gather data about the causes and extent of the problem, consider a variety of alternative

Active Learning: Cooperation In The College Classroom, Interaction Book Company, 7208 Cornelia Drive, Edina, MN 55435, (612) 831-9500, FAX (612) 831-9332

solutions, make conclusions, and present a recommendation to the faculty as a whole. **Ad hoc decision-making teams** are formed to (a) listen to the report of a task force, (b) discuss the report and consider whether to accept or modify the task forces' recommendation and (c) inform the entire faculty of their decision. **The whole-faculty decides** on the actions to be taken to solve the problem. The reports of the ad-hoc decision-making teams are combined and the three or four most recommended plans are presented to the faculty. The faculty votes on which plan to adopt. The faculty then implements the plan and the **task force monitors the implementation of the decision** and assesses whether or not the problem is solved.

Faculty meetings represent a microcosm of what administrators think the college should be. The clearest modeling of cooperative procedures in the college may be in faculty meetings. Formal and informal cooperative groups, cooperative base groups, and repetitive structures can be used in faculty meetings just as they can be used in the classroom. In this way, faculty meetings become staff development sessions.

The third level in creating a cooperative college is to implement administrative cooperative teams within the district (Johnson & Johnson, 1994). Administrators are organized into colleagial teams (to increase their expertise and success in leading a cooperative college), task forces, and ad-hoc triads are used as part of the shared decision-making process. In administrative meetings, cooperative procedures dominate to model what the college district should be like. Administrators **support and coach faculty using cooperative learning** to ensure that cooperative learning is used with fidelity, is flexibly adapted to the faculty' students and specific circumstances, and is continuously improved. Finally, administrators **extend cooperation to the community** so that the college, parents, and community are working together to achieve mutual goals.

Team efforts are paramount at every rung of the ladder in modern organizations. Colleges are no exception. Lone wolves who do not pull with their peers will increasingly find themselves the odd person out.

Colleagial Teaching Teams

In mass-production colleges, faculty are isolated from each other and may feel harried, overloaded, and overwhelmed. The isolation and alienation are reduced when faculty form colleagial teaching teams aimed at increasing the quality of instruction. **Faculty generally teach better when they are part of a colleagial teaching team with the purpose of jointly supporting member's efforts to increase their instructional expertise.** Doing so gives faculty ownership of the professional agenda, breaks down the barriers to colleagial interaction, and reduces program fragmentation. The three key activities of a teaching team are (Johnson & Johnson, 1994).

Active Learning: Cooperation In The College Classroom, Interaction Book Company, 7208 Cornelia Drive, Edina, MN 55435, (612) 831-9500, FAX (612) 831-9332

Organizational Structure Of Colleges

Old Paradigm	New Paradigm
Mass-Production College	**Team-Based, High-Performance College**
Faculty Work Alone, Barriers Separate Instructors From Each Other	Faculty Work In Colleagial Teaching Teams
Authority Hierarchy	Flat Organizational Structure
Following Procedures Emphasized	Continuous Improvement Of Quality Emphasized
Work Is Segmented Into Small Parts (Subject Areas, Academic Levels)	Team Is Given Responsibility For Whole Process
Teaching Is Standardized	Increased Responsibility And Autonomy Given To Teaching Teams
Faculty, Staff, Students Seen As Interchangeable, Replaceable Parts	Supportive, Committed, Caring Relationships
Certain Percentage Of Failures And Dropouts Accepted	No Student Failures Or Dropouts Accepted
Loosely Coupled College	**Tightly Coupled College**
Goal Ambiguity	Clear, Positively Interdependent Goals
Low Individual Accountability	Individual And Team Accountability
Independent Work	Promotive Interaction
Social Skills Deemphasized	Teamwork Skills Emphasized
No Structured Reflection On Processes Of Teaching And Learning	Frequent Reflection On Processes Of Teaching And Learning
Underlying Competition	**Underlying Cooperation**
Amorphous Competition Pervades Interactions	Cooperation Pervades Interactions

1. **Frequent professional discussions of cooperative learning** in which a common vocabulary is developed, information is shared, successes are celebrated, and problems connected with implementation are solved. Interaction among colleagues is essential for building collaborative cultures in colleges (Hargreaves, 1991; Little, 1990). Social support is critical for the ongoing professional development of faculty

Active Learning: Cooperation In The College Classroom, Interaction Book Company, 7208 Cornelia Drive, Edina, MN 55435, (612) 831-9500, FAX (612) 831-9332

(Nias, 1984). Expertise in using cooperative learning begins with conceptual understanding of (a) the nature of cooperative learning, (b) how to implement cooperative learning, and (c) what results can be expected from using cooperative learning. Faculty must also think critically about the strategy and adapt it to their specific students and subject areas. In team discussions faculty consolidate and strengthen their knowledge about cooperative learning and provide each other with relevant feedback about the degree to which mastery and understanding have been achieved.

2. **Coplanning, codesigning, copreparing, and coassessing cooperative learning lessons and instructional units.** Once cooperative learning is understood conceptually, it must be implemented. Members of teaching team plan, design, prepare, and assess lesson plans together to share the work of developing the materials and expertise for implementing cooperative learning. Integrated curriculum and thematic teaching depend on coplanning and codesigning. **The cycle of coplanning, parallel teaching, and coprocessing may be followed by one of coplanning, coteaching, and coprocessing.**

3. **Coteaching cooperative lessons.** If faculty are to progress through the initial awkward and mechanical stages to a routine-use, automatic level of mastery, they must (a) receive feedback on the quality of their implementation and (b) be encouraged to persevere in their implementation attempts long enough to integrate cooperative learning into their ongoing instructional practice. The more colleagues are involved in your teaching, the more valuable the help and assistance they can provide. Frequently coteaching cooperative lessons and providing each other with useful feedback provides members with shared experiences to discuss and refer to.

Colleagial teams ideally meet daily. At a minimum, teams should meet weekly. During a typical meeting team members review how they have used cooperative learning since the previous meeting, share a success in doing so, complete a quality chart on their implementation of cooperative learning, set three to five goals to accomplish before the next meeting, establish how each will help the others achieve their goals, learn something new about cooperative learning, and celebrate how hard all members are working (Johnson & Johnson, 1994). Following this agenda ensures that (a) faculty meet with supportive peers who encourage them to learn and grow, (b) continuous training of faculty in how to use cooperative learning is provided, (c) pride of workmanship and self-improvement can be encouraged, recognized, and celebrated, and (d) poor workmanship and negativism can be discouraged.

Active Learning: Cooperation In The College Classroom, Interaction Book Company, 7208 Cornelia Drive, Edina, MN 55435, (612) 831-9500, FAX (612) 831-9332

Form a pair. Rank order the three major activities of colleagial teaching teams from most beneficial ("1") to least beneficial to instructors ("3").

Rank	Colleagial Teaching Team Activities
_____	Frequent professional discussions of cooperative learning
_____	Coplanning, codesigning, copreparing, and coevaluating cooperative learning lessons and instructional units.
_____	Coteaching cooperative lessons.

Continuous Improvement Of Expertise

To have joy one must share it. Happiness was born a twin.

Indian Proverb

For colleges to be successful, everyone in the college must be dedicated to continuous improvement in using cooperative learning. In Japan, this mutual dedication is called **kaizen** (a societywide covenant of mutual help in the process of getting better and better, day by day). **Expertise** is reflected in a person's proficiency, adroitness, competence, and skill in structuring cooperative efforts. Cooperation takes more expertise than do competitive or individualistic efforts, because it involves dealing with other people as well as dealing with the demands of the task (i.e., simultaneously engaging in taskwork and teamwork). Expertise is usually gained in an incremental step-by-step manner, using the progressive refinement process over a period of years in a team.

Faculty progressively refine their competence in using cooperative learning through five steps (Johnson & Johnson, 1994). **First, faculty must understand conceptually what cooperative learning is and how it may be implemented in their classrooms.** Faculty must understand the five basic elements of effective cooperation and the instructor's role in using formal and informal cooperative learning and cooperative base groups. They must be able to adapt and refine cooperative learning to fit their unique, idiosyncratic instructional situation. **Second, faculty try out cooperative learning in their classrooms with their students.** Faculty must be willing to take risks by experimenting with new instructional and managing strategies and procedures. **Third, faculty assess how well cooperative learning lessons went and obtain feedback on their teaching from others.** From the progressive refinement point of view, failure and total success never occur. There are simply approximations of what one wants. Faculty refine and fine-tune procedures to get successively closer and closer to the ideal. **Fourth, faculty reflect on what they did and how it may be improved.** The discrepancy between the real and the ideal is considered and plans are made to alter one's behavior in order to get a better match in the future. Quality charts help this reflection process. **Fifth, faculty**

Active Learning: Cooperation In The College Classroom, Interaction Book Company, 7208 Cornelia Drive, Edina, MN 55435, (612) 831-9500, FAX (612) 831-9332

try out cooperative learning again in a modified and improved way. Perseverance in using cooperative learning again and again and again is required until the instructor can teach a cooperative lesson routinely and without conscious planning or thought. It is through this progressive refinement process that expertise in using cooperative learning is fine-tuned.

Providing Leadership

Knowing is not enough; we must apply. Willing is not enough; we must do.

Goethe

For the cooperative college to flourish the college has to have leadership. In general, leadership is provided by five sets of actions (Johnson & Johnson, 1994).

1. **Challenging The Status Quo:** The status quo is the competitive-individualistic mass-production structure that dominates colleges and classrooms. In the classroom it is represented by lecturing, whole class discussion, individual worksheets, and a test on Friday. In the college it is one instructor to one classroom with one set of students, as well as separating faculty and students into academic levels and academic departments. Leaders challenge the efficacy of the status quo.

2. **Inspiring A Mutual Vision Of What The College Could Be:** Leaders enthusiastically and frequently communicate the dreams of establishing the cooperative college. The leader is the keeper of the dream who inspires commitment to joint goals of creating a team-based, cooperative college.

3. **Empowering Through Cooperative Teams:** This is the most important leadership activities. When faculty or students feel helpless and discouraged, providing them with a team creates hope and opportunity. It is social support from and accountability to valued peers that motivates committed efforts to achieve and succeed. Students are empowered by cooperative learning groups. Faculty members are empowered through colleagial support groups and involvement in site based decision making.

4. **Leading By Example:** Leaders model the use of cooperative strategies and procedures and take risks to increase their professional competence. Actions must be congruent with words. What is advocated must be demonstrated publicly.

5. **Encouraging The Heart To Persist:** Long-term, committed efforts to continuously improve one's competencies come from the heart, not the head. It takes courage and hope to strive for increased knowledge and expertise. It is the social support and concrete assistance from teammates that provides the strength to persist and excel.

Active Learning: Cooperation In The College Classroom, Interaction Book Company, 7208 Cornelia Drive, Edina, MN 55435, (612) 831-9500, FAX (612) 831-9332

To implement the cooperative college, leadership that helps faculty do a better job must be provided (Johnson & Johnson, 1994). Leaders do not spend their time in an office talking on the phone, writing memos, and putting out fires. Leaders spend their time "where the action is" (in Japan this is called **genba**). In colleges, the action is in classrooms. Thus, leaders have to challenge the status quo of the mass-production organization, inspire a mutual vision of the cooperative college, empower faculty through organizing them in teams, lead by example by using cooperative procedures continually, and encourage faculty's heart to persist by being in the classroom recognizing and celebrating their efforts to teach a perfect lesson every time.

Summary

Through the use of teams a congruent organizational structure is created that promotes quality education by creating a constancy of purpose, being committed to educating every student, focusing on improving the quality of instruction, eliminating competition at all levels, building strong personal relationships, reducing waste, and paying careful attention to implementing the five basic elements on a college and learning group level. Teaching teams provide the setting in which a process of continuous improvement in expertise can take place. Faculty and administrators progressively refine their expertise through a procedure involving action, feedback, reflection, and modified action. Faculty help each other learn an expert system of how to implement cooperative learning that they use to create a unique adaptation to their specific circumstances, students, and needs.

Active Learning: Cooperation In The College Classroom, Interaction Book Company, 7208 Cornelia Drive, Edina, MN 55435, (612) 831-9500, FAX (612) 831-9332

Colleagial Support Group Meeting

1. **Membership Grid:** Begin each session with a discussion of a personal (not professional) topic, such as favorite book, movie, restaurant, or renewal place, a vivid childhood memory, or most fun free-time activity. Record in the membership grid what is shared by each group member.

Members					
Frank					
Helen					
Roger					
David					

2. **Share A Success:** Think through what cooperative learning lessons and social skills you have taught during the past week. Share a success in using cooperative learning. Take one good idea from the successes shared by your colleagues and try it in your classroom. Then celebrate as a group.

3. **Goal Setting:** In order to continuously improve your professional expertise and competencies (and to help your colleagues do likewise) set five goals to accomplish this week. One goal should deal with using cooperative learning. One goal should deal with teaching students social skills. One goal should deal with promoting the success of a colleague (another instructor). Two goals should reflect current issues in your classroom.

Goal	Who	How	When/Where
Coop Learning			
Social Skills			
Helped Colleague			

Active Learning: Cooperation In The College Classroom, Interaction Book Company, 7208 Cornelia Drive, Edina, MN 55435, (612) 831-9500, FAX (612) 831-9332

4. **Joint Planning / Contracting:** Each member shares his or her goals for the week. For each goal, another member volunteers to help. How the help will be given and when and where it will take place are noted. The help may range from providing relevant materials to coteaching a lesson. Be specific about the help you will give and when and where you will do so. Make sure that the work is divided so that everyone saves time and energy by being part of the team. Sign the joint planning form of your colleagues to indicate that you understand what they are going to do and you are willing to assist them.

5. **New Content:** Share something new you have learned about the cooperative learning in the last week. This could be summarizing an article you have read, an insight gained from observing a colleague, a summary of a chapter of **Nuts And Bolts Of Cooperative Learning**, or a new way to structure positive interdependence. Guests (such as an innovative instructor, a local businessperson committed to team-based organizations, or the superintendent) may be invited to speak during this part of the meeting. A barrier to creating the cooperative college may be identified and a series of strategies to solving it may be generated.

6. **Celebrate:** Congratulate each member on a good week and send each other off happy, optimistic, and enthusiastic.

Role Of Convener: The role of convener is vital to effective meetings. Rotate this role among members. The convener is in charge of providing the meeting place, gourmet food, any materials required, a procedure for sharing new content, and keeping time so all agenda items are covered in the meeting.

Current Fires: If there is a current crisis in the college or district, save the discussion of it until after all other agenda items have been covered.

Scripting: Take each step of the above agenda and script what you would say to the group to assign the task and structure it cooperatively.

Guided Practice: Role play that you are meeting with a colleagial support group consisting of four of your faculty. Give your statement for structuring each of the meeting's agenda items. Listen to your partner present his or her script. Then work together to create an even better statement.

Active Learning: Cooperation In The College Classroom, Interaction Book Company, 7208 Cornelia Drive, Edina, MN 55435, (612) 831-9500, FAX (612) 831-9332

Using Cooperative Decision-Making Groups In A Meeting

Select A Meeting

Meeting: _____ Date: _____

Members: _____

Time: _____ Place: _____

Objectives

	Task Objectives	Social Skills Objectives
1		
2		

Agenda: Procedure For Decision Making

1. _____   4. _____

2. _____   5. _____

3. _____   6. _____

Pre-Meeting Decisions

1. Group Size: _____

    Advice: Think small. Two to four people in each group.

2. Method Of Assigning Members To Groups: _____

    Advice: Heterogeneous groups are often the most powerful. Over time, each staff member should work with all other members.

3. Roles Assigned:

    1. _____   3. _____

    2. _____   4. _____

Active Learning: Cooperation In The College Classroom, Interaction Book Company, 7208 Cornelia Drive, Edina, MN 55435, (612) 831-9500, FAX (612) 831-9332

4. Room Arrangement: _____

_____

Advice: Members should be close together in a circle so that each can see the others' eyes, preferably without tables or other obstructions in between.

5. Materials: _____

◊ One Copy Per Group   ◊ One Copy Per Person

◊ Jigsaw   ◊ Tournament

◊ Other: _____

Advice: One set of materials per group gives the message, "You are in this together." Alternatively, each group member can be given different materials that need to be shared and synthesized to complete the task.

Explaining Recommendation And Cooperative Goal Structure

1. Decision-Making Task: _____

_____

2. Criteria For Success: _____

_____

3. Positive Interdependence: _____

_____

4. Individual Accountability: _____

_____

5. Intergroup Cooperation: _____

_____

6. Expected Behaviors: _____

_____

Active Learning: Cooperation In The College Classroom, Interaction Book Company, 7208 Cornelia Drive, Edina, MN 55435, (612) 831-9500, FAX (612) 831-9332

Monitoring And Intervening In Decision-Making Groups

1. Observation Procedure: _____ Formal _____ Informal

2. Actions To Be Observed:

	Task Actions	Maintenance Actions
1		
2		
3		
4		

2. Sampling Plan:

   a. How Many Minutes Each Group Is Observed: _____

   b. Order In Which Groups Will Be Observed: _____

        _____

3. How Data Will Be Presented To:

   a. Each Group: _____

   b. Faculty As Whole: _____

4. Intervening To Improve Taskwork And Teamwork:

	Possible Problems	Possible Interventions
1		
2		
3		
4		

Advice: *You should always be an observer and gather data. Make a point of joining each group at least once (offering comments if you wish, but not too many). It is useful to have an observation sheet so that actual*

Active Learning: Cooperation In The College Classroom, Interaction Book Company, 7208 Cornelia Drive, Edina, MN 55435, (612) 831-9500, FAX (612) 831-9332

data on specific behaviors is collected. Each group could have a process observer who collects data on the observation sheet for their group. The data has to be presented without evaluation. Give groups one or two specific questions for the processing.

Making And Implementing Decision

1. Procedure For Reporting Small Group Decisions:

   _____ Each group of three makes decision, combines with another group and remakes the decision in the group of six, combines with another group and makes the decision in the group of twelve, and so forth until the entire faculty has reached consensus.

   _____ Each group of three makes decision and submits it to chair, the chair summarizes the various decisions and presents them to the faculty in the next meeting, the faculty vote to determine the top three alternatives, and then vote again to determine what the decision will be.

   _____ Other: _____

   _____

   _____

   _____ Other: _____

   _____

   _____

2. Procedure For Implementing Decision:

   _____

   _____

   _____

   _____

Active Learning: Cooperation In The College Classroom, Interaction Book Company, 7208 Cornelia Drive, Edina, MN 55435, (612) 831-9500, FAX (612) 831-9332

Evaluating And Processing

1. Procedure For Monitoring And Evaluating Effectiveness Of Decision:

   _____

   _____

   _____

   _____

2. Processing Task For Small Groups: _____

   _____

3. Processing Task For Whole Faculty: _____

   _____

4. Charts And Graphs Used: _____

   _____

5. Procedure For Ensuring All Members Receive Some Positive Feedback:

   _____

7. Procedure For Members Setting A Goal For Improvement: _____

   _____

8. Celebration: _____

   _____

9. Other: _____

Criteria For Assessing Effectiveness Of Decision

_____ The resources of members are fully utilized.

_____ Time is well used.

_____ The decision is of high quality.

_____ The decision is implemented fully by all relevant members.

_____ The problem-solving ability of faculty is enhanced.

Active Learning: Cooperation In The College Classroom, Interaction Book Company, 7208 Cornelia Drive, Edina, MN 55435, (612) 831-9500, FAX (612) 831-9332

Faculty Meeting Worksheet

Tasks:

1. Specify six reasonable and effective courses of action the faculty could take.

2. Circle the three you like best. Include rationale as to why each will work.

	Course Of Action	Rationale
1		
2		
3		
4		
5		
6		

Cooperative:

1. One list from the three of you, everyone must agree, and everyone must be able to explain the rationale under lying your plan.

2. Use the assigned roles of recorder, encourager, and checker.

Individual Accountability: One member of your group will be selected randomly to present your group's plan.

Expected Behaviors: Active participating, encouraging, summarizing, synthesizing.

Signatures

1. _____   3. _____

2. _____   4. _____

Intergroup Cooperation: Whenever it is helpful, check procedures, answers, and strategies with another group. When you are finished, compare your answers with those of another group and discuss.

Active Learning: Cooperation In The College Classroom, Interaction Book Company, 7208 Cornelia Drive, Edina, MN 55435, (612) 831-9500, FAX (612) 831-9332

Chapter Ten:

Reflections

Old Vs. New Paradigm

Whether one believes in a religion or not, and whether one believes in rebirth or not, there isn't anyone who doesn't appreciate kindness and compassion...We must build closer relationships of mutual trust, understanding, respect, and help, irrespective of differences of culture, philosophy, religion, or faith.

The Dalai Lama, 1989 Nobel Peace Prize

Frank Koch, in **Proceedings**, the magazine of the Naval Institute, reported the following: Two battleships assigned to the training squadron had been at sea on maneuvers in heavy weather for several days. I was serving on the lead battleship and was on watch on the bridge as night fell. The visibility was poor with patchy fog, so the captain remained on the bridge keeping an eye on all activities. Shortly after dark, the lookout on the wing of the bridge reported, "*Light, bearing on the starboard bow." "Is it steady or moving astern?*" the captain called out. Lookout replied, "*Steady, captain,*" which meant we were on a dangerous collision course with that ship. The captain then called to the signalman, "*Signal that ship: We are on a collision course, advise you change course 20 degrees.*" Back came a signal, "*Advisable for you to change course 20 degrees.*" The captain said, "*Send, I'm a captain, change course 20 degrees." "I'm a seaman, second class,*" came the reply, "*You had better change course 20 degrees.*" By that time the captain was furious. He spat out, "*Send, I'm a battleship. Change course 20 degrees.*" Back came the flashing light, "*I'm a lighthouse.*" We changed course.

A faculty member may feel like a captain of a battleship too powerful to be challenged cruising through the seas. When faced with the realities of the modern world, however, it is the faculty member who may find that he or she has to change course to stay afloat.

A **paradigm** is a theory, perspective, or frame of reference that determines how you perceive, interpret, and understand the world. The **old paradigm** of college education views teaching as the transfer of faculty's knowledge to passive students while faculty classify and sort students in a norm-referenced, competitive way. It is based on John Locke's assumption that the untrained mind is like a blank sheet of paper on which faculty write. Quality is assured by (a) selecting only the most intelligent and hard-working students for admission and (b) inspecting them continually to weed out those

Active Learning: Cooperation In The College Classroom, Interaction Book Company, 7208 Cornelia Drive, Edina, MN 55435, (612) 831-9500, FAX (612) 831-9332

who prove to be defective. Whether or not colleges "add value" or just serve as a holding ground for students as they mature is unclear.

In college teaching a paradigm shift is taking place. Minor modifications of current teaching practices based on the old paradigm of teaching will not solve the problems with college instruction. A new approach is needed. The **new paradigm** views teaching as helping students construct their knowledge in an active way while working cooperatively with classmates in ways that develop each member's talents and competencies. Quality is assured as students motivate each other to exert extraordinary effort to learn, grow, and develop. Faculty teaching teams help members add value by continuously improving their teaching. Faculty strive to know each student personally and faculty commit themselves to increase each student's intellectual growth and general well-being.

The heart of the new paradigm is cooperative learning and faculty teaching teams. **Cooperative learning** is the instructional use of small groups so students work together to maximize their own and each other's learning. **Colleagial teaching teams** are small groups of faculty working together to maximize the quality of their own and each other's instruction. There is considerable research demonstrating that cooperative efforts produce higher achievement, more positive relationships among students, and healthier psychological adjustment than do competitive or individualistic efforts. These outcomes, however, do not automatically appear when individuals are placed in groups. Cooperative efforts must be carefully structured to include five basic elements: positive interdependence to ensure members believe they "sink or swim together," individual accountability to ensure that everyone does his or her fair share of the work, face-to-face promotive interaction to ensure members help and assist each other, social skills to work effectively with others, and group processing to reflect on and improve the quality of group work.

Types Of Cooperative Learning

There are a number of steps you might consider to increase your expertise. **The first step is to expand your use of cooperative learning to include three types of cooperative learning** (Johnson, Johnson, & Holubec, 1988b): formal cooperative learning groups, informal cooperative learning groups, and cooperative base groups.

Formal Cooperative Learning Groups

Formal cooperative learning groups may last for several minutes to several class sessions to complete a specific task or assignment (such as solving a set of problems, completing a unit, writing a report or theme, conducting an experiment, and reading and comprehending a story, play, chapter, or book). This book has focused on formal cooperative learning groups. Any course requirement or assignment may be reformulated to be cooperative rather than competitive or individualistic through the use

Active Learning: Cooperation In The College Classroom, Interaction Book Company, 7208 Cornelia Drive, Edina, MN 55435, (612) 831-9500, FAX (612) 831-9332

of formal cooperative learning groups. **Gaining expertise in using formal cooperative learning groups provides the foundation for gaining expertise in using informal and base groups.**

Informal Cooperative Learning Groups

Informal cooperative learning groups are temporary, ad hoc groups that last for only one discussion or one class period. Their **purposes** are to focus student attention on the material to be learned, create an expectation set and mood conducive to learning, help organize in advance the material to be covered in a class session, ensure that students cognitively process the material being taught, and provide closure to an instructional session. They may be used at any time, but are especially useful during a lecture or direct teaching. The length of time students can attend to a lecture before their minds drift away is estimated to be from 12 to 15 minutes.

During direct teaching the instructional challenge for the instructor is to ensure that students do the intellectual work of organizing material, explaining it, summarizing it, and integrating it into existing conceptual networks. This may be achieved by having students do the advance organizing, cognitive process what they are learning, and provide closure to the lesson. Breaking up lectures with short cooperative processing times will give you less lecture time, but will enhance what is learned and build relationships among the students in your class. It will help counter what is proclaimed as the main problem of lectures: "The information passes from the notes of the instructor to the notes of the student without passing through the mind of either one."

The following procedure may help to plan a lecture that keeps students actively engaged intellectually. It entails having **focused discussions** before and after a lecture (bookends) and interspersing **turn-to-your-partner** discussions throughout the lecture.

1. **Focused Discussion 1**: Plan your lecture around a series of questions that the lecture answers. Prepare the questions on an overhead transparency or write them on the board so that students can see them. Students will discuss the questions in pairs. The discussion task is aimed at promoting **advance organizing** of what the students know about the topic to be presented and creates an **expectation set** and a learning mood conductive to learning.

2. **Turn-To-Your-Partner Discussions**: Divide the lecture into 10 to 15 minute segments. Plan a short discussion task to be given to pairs of students after each segment. The task needs to be short enough that students can complete it within three or four minutes. Its purpose is to ensure that students are actively thinking about the material being presented. **It is important that students are randomly called on to share their answers after each discussion task.** Such **individual accountability** ensures that the pairs take the tasks seriously and check each other to ensure that both are prepared to answer. Each discussion task should have four components: **formulate** an

10 : 3

Active Learning: Cooperation In The College Classroom, Interaction Book Company, 7208 Cornelia Drive, Edina, MN 55435, (612) 831-9500, FAX (612) 831-9332

© Johnson, Johnson, & Smith

answer to the question being asked, **share** your answer with your partner, **listen** carefully to his or her answer, and to **create** a new answer that is superior to each member's initial formulation through the processes of association, building on each other's thoughts, and synthesizing. Students will need to gain some experience with this procedure to become skilled in doing it within a short period of time.

3. **Focused Discussion 2**: Give students an ending discussion task to provide closure to the lecture. Usually students are given five or six minutes to summarize and discuss the material covered in the lecture. The discussion should result in students integrating what they have just learned into existing conceptual frameworks. The task may also point students toward what the homework will cover or what will be presented in the next class session. Until students become familiar and experienced with the procedure, **process** it regularly to help them increase their skill and speed in completing short discussion tasks.

Informal cooperative learning gets students actively involved in processing what they are learning. It also provides time for you to gather your wits, reorganize your notes, take a deep breath, and move around the class listening to what students are saying. Listening to student discussions provides you with direction and insight into (a) students' levels of reasoning and (b) how the concepts you are teaching are being grasped by your students.

Base Groups

Base groups are long-term, heterogeneous cooperative learning groups with stable membership. **The primary responsibility of members is to provide each other with the support, encouragement, and assistance they need to make academic progress.** The base group verifies that each member is completing the assignments and progressing satisfactorily through the academic program. Base groups may be given the task of letting absent group members know what went on in the class when they miss a session and bring them up to date. The use of base groups tends to improve attendance, personalize the work required and the college experience, and improve the quality and quantity of learning. The base group provides permanent and caring peer relationships in which students are committed to and support each other's educational success.

Base groups last for at least a semester or year and preferably for several years. The larger the class and the more complex the subject matter, the more important it is to have base groups. Learning for your groupmates is a powerful motivator. Receiving social support and being held accountable for appropriate behavior by peers who care about you and have a long-term commitment to your success and well-being is an important aspect of growing up and progressing through college.

It is important that some of the relationships built within cooperative learning groups are permanent. College has to be more than a series of "ship-board romances" that last for only a semester or year. Students should be assigned to permanent base groups. The base groups should then be assigned to most classes so that members spend

10 : 4

Active Learning: Cooperation In The College Classroom, Interaction Book Company, 7208 Cornelia Drive, Edina, MN 55435, (612) 831-9500, FAX (612) 831-9332

much of the day together and regularly complete cooperative learning tasks. Doing so can create permanent caring and committed relationships that will provide students with the support, help, encouragement, and assistance they need to make academic progress and develop cognitively and socially in healthy ways.

When used in combination, these formal, informal, and base cooperative learning groups provide an overall structure to classroom life.

Teaching Students' Social Skills

The second step in increasing your expertise in using cooperative learning is to teach students additional social skills. Sources of social skills that may be taught include **Advanced Cooperative Learning** (Johnson, Johnson, & Holubec, 1992), **Learning to Lead Teams** (Johnson & Johnson, 1997), **Reaching Out** (Johnson, 1997), and **Joining Together** (Johnson & F. Johnson, 1997).

Integrated Use Of All Three Goal Structures

The third step in increasing your expertise in using cooperative learning is to use all three goal structures in an integrated way. While the dominant goal structure within any classroom should be cooperation (which ideally would be used about 60 - 70 percent of the time), competitive and individualistic efforts are useful supplements. Competition may be used as a fun change-of-pace during an instructional unit that is predominantly structured cooperatively and individualistic learning is often productive when the information learned is subsequently used in a cooperative activity. The integrated use of cooperative, competitive, and individualistic learning is described in depth with in Johnson and Johnson (1994) and Johnson, Johnson, and Holubec (1992).

Utilizing Creative Conflict

The fourth step is to promote the creative use of conflict. Cooperation and conflict go hand-in-hand. The more group members care about achieving the group's goals, and the more they care about each other, the more likely they are to have conflicts with each other. How conflict is managed largely determines how successful cooperative efforts tend to be. In order to ensure that conflicts are managed constructively, students must be taught two procedures and sets of skills:

1. **Use Academic Controversies To Facilitate Achievement And Cognitive and Social Development** (Johnson & Johnson, 1995b): In order to maximize academic learning and higher-level reasoning, engage students in intellectual conflicts. Organize students into cooperative learning groups of four. Divide

Active Learning: Cooperation In The College Classroom, Interaction Book Company, 7208 Cornelia Drive, Edina, MN 55435, (612) 831-9500, FAX (612) 831-9332

them into two pairs. Give one pair the pro position and the other the con position on the issue being studied. Students research and prepare positions, make a persuasive presentation of their position, refute the opposing position while rebutting attacks on their own position, view the issue from both perspectives, and create a synthesis or integration of the best reasoning on both sides.

2. **Implement The Peacemaker Program** (Johnson & Johnson, 1995a): First, teach students what is and is not a conflict. Second, teach students how to engage in problem-solving negotiations. Students are taught to state what they want and how they feel, explain the reasons why they want and feel as they do, accurately understand the opposing perspective, create a number of optional agreements that maximize joint outcomes, and reach an agreement as to which option to adopt. Third, teach students how to mediate. When students cannot successfully negotiate a constructive resolution to their conflicts, mediators are available to end hostilities, ensure commitment to the mediation process, facilitate negotiations, and formalize the agreement.

The combination of knowing how to manage intellectual disagreements and how to negotiate/mediate conflicts among students' wants, needs, and goals ensures that the power of cooperative efforts will be maximized. The productivity of learning groups increases dramatically when members are skilled in how to manage conflicts constructively.

Empowering Staff Through Cooperative Teams

The fifth step is to create a cooperative college. What is good for students is even better for faculty. A cooperative college is one in which cooperative learning dominates the classroom and cooperative teams dominate faculty efforts (Johnson & Johnson, 1994). It is social support from and accountability to valued peers that motivates committed efforts to succeed. Empowering individuals through cooperative teamwork is done in three ways: (1) **colleagial support groups** (to increase instructors' instructional expertise and success), (2) **task forces** (to plan and implement solutions to college-wide issues and problems), and (3) **ad hoc decision-making groups** (to use during faculty meetings to involve all staff members in important college decisions). How to structure and use these three types of cooperative teams may be found in **Leading the Cooperative School** (Johnson & Johnson, 1994).

10 : 6

Active Learning: Cooperation In The College Classroom, Interaction Book Company, 7208 Cornelia Drive, Edina, MN 55435, (612) 831-9500, FAX (612) 831-9332

Creating A Learning Community

Frances Hodgson Burnett, in her book, The Secret Garden, stated, *Where you tend a rose, a thistle cannot grow.* Colleges should tend roses. They do so by creating a learning community characterized by cooperative efforts to achieve meaningful goals. In a recent review of the research (**Within Our Reach: Breaking the Cycle of Disadvantage**) Lisbeth Schorr concludes that the most important attribute of effective colleges is caring. Educational historians David Tyack and Elizabeth Hansot (1982) concluded that the theme that runs through all successful schools is that students, faculty, administrators, and parents share a sense of community and a "socially integrating sense of purpose."

A **community** is a limited number of people who share common goals and a common culture (Johnson, Johnson, Stevahn, & Hodne, 1997). The smaller the size of the community, the more personal the relationships, and the greater the personal accountability. Everyone knows everyone else. Relationships are long-term and have a future rather than being temporary brief encounters. Instruction becomes personalized. The students are thought of as citizens, and the faculty are thought of as the community leaders. A sense of belonging tends to boost the desire to learn. The learning community becomes an extended family where mutual achievement and caring for one another are important. With citizenship in the community comes an ethical code that includes such rules as (a) be prepared for classes each day, (b) pay attention in class, (c) be your personal best, and (d) respect other people and their property. In order to create a learning community, students (and instructors) need to be organized into cooperative teams.

Expertise is difficult to attain without the help of a colleagial teaching team. Long-term, persistent efforts to improve continuously come from the heart, not the head. A colleagial teaching team will provide you with the support and joint commitment essential to maintaining a love affair with teaching. Through implementing cooperative learning in your classes and being a contributing member of a teaching team, a true learning community of scholars may be created for both your students and yourself.

Class / School Management: The Three Cs

It is time for class management systems to move beyond behaviorism (with its emphasis on self-interest and behaving in order to achieve extrinsic rewards and avoid punishments) to positive learning environment (with its emphasis on intrinsic motivation to contribute to own and other's well being and success and to the overall common good) (Johnson & Johnson, 1998; Johnson, Johnson, Stevahn, & Hodne, 1997). The latter is built on three interrelated programs: **cooperative community, constructive conflict resolution, and civic values**. To establish a learning community, cooperation must be carefully structured at all levels in the college. To maintain the learning community, constructive conflict resolution procedures must be taught to all members of the college.

Active Learning: Cooperation In The College Classroom, Interaction Book Company, 7208 Cornelia Drive, Edina, MN 55435, (612) 831-9500, FAX (612) 831-9332

To guide and direct the cooperation and constructive conflict resolution, civic values must be inculcated in all college members. While each of the Cs may be discussed and implemented separately, together they represent a gestalt in which each enhances and promotes the others.

Cooperation creates a structure within which faculty, students, and administrators work together to educate the students. The more cooperative the structure, the more committed and dedicated faculty, students, and parents are to providing quality education. The greater the commitment to the college's goals, the more frequent and intense the **conflicts** around how best to achieve the goals and coordinate behavior. When the controversy and problem-solving negotiation procedures are used skillfully, the conflicts lead to higher-level reasoning, the utilization of diverse perspectives, creative insights, synthesis of different positions, high quality and novel solutions, and trusting, supportive, and caring relationships. **Civic values**, that highlight the need to work together toward the common good and maximize joint (not individual) benefits, are the glue that holds the college together and defines how members should act towards each other.

The Three Cs result in students being more autonomous individuals who can regulate and control their own actions by monitoring, modifying, refining, and changing how they behave in order to act appropriately and competently. Students who work effectively with others and resolve conflicts with skill and grace and who have internalized civic values have a developmental advantage that increases their future academic and career success, improves the quality of their relationships with friends, colleagues, and family, and generally enhances their life-long happiness.

Together the three Cs are a complete management program for creating effective and nurturing colleges where few management problems occur and the well-being of students and other members of the learning community is promoted.

Mission, Product, Customers

The community stagnates without the impulse of the individual; the impulse dies away without the sympathy of the community.

William James, **Great Men and Their Environment**

To determine whether colleges are adding value by giving students a high-quality education, the mission of the college has to be determined. The mission has to specify who the college's customers are and what the product is. There are at least two complementary ways to describe the mission of colleges. **First**, the college may be viewed as an industry that produces and sells knowledge. The college's product is validated theory and its customers are those who need it. The **mission** of the college is to

10 : 8

Active Learning: Cooperation In The College Classroom, Interaction Book Company, 7208 Cornelia Drive, Edina, MN 55435, (612) 831-9500, FAX (612) 831-9332

create and test theory through systematic programs of research. Concerns about **quality** focus on how well faculty develop sound theory, conduct systematic programs of reliable research to test the theory, operationalize the results into procedures consumers may use, and convince consumers to implement the procedures.

Second, the college may be viewed as a service organization that functions as a broker between (a) students and (b) employers and graduate schools. While colleges serve both students and the people who hire its graduates, the more important of the two is the student, as the success of a college's graduates will determine the level of demand for future graduates. The "product" of a college is the education it provides and students are its primary consumers. The **mission** of a college, therefore, is to provide quality education to students in order that they will be hired by desirable or prestigious companies or enter prestigious graduate schools. This requires more than intellectual development. Students should also be moral, decent, loving, and loveable people. Concerns about **quality** focus on how well students are educated and trained. The harder it is to get a job or be admitted to graduate school, the more pressure there is on colleges to provide a quality education. In determining the quality of a college's educational program there are at least three factors to consider:

1. Do all instructors provide high-quality teaching? High-quality teaching may be defined as the skillful and effective use of the new (rather than the old) paradigm. Faculty cannot grow by mimicking the past. Cooperative learning must dominate the classroom. Other new instructional methods, processes, procedures, and practices have to be adopted.

2. What is the time it takes to develop and implement improvements in teaching? This may be the most critical factor in a college being successful. In general, cycle time must be continuously reduced.

3. Has a process of continuous improvement in instruction been institutionalized to keep teaching in general and the use of cooperative learning in particular at the state-of-the-art level?

In order to improve faculty's teaching, reduce cycle time, and ensure a process of continuous improvement in instruction, colleges may wish to promote commitment to the new paradigm of teaching, use a benchmarking process to set goals, and adopt a cooperative-team organizational structure.

Benchmarking And Goal Setting

*Almost every evening, either I went to Braque's studio or Braque came to mine. Each of us **had** to see what the other had done during the day. We criticized each other's work. A canvas wasn't finished unless both of us felt it was.*

Active Learning: Cooperation In The College Classroom, Interaction Book Company, 7208 Cornelia Drive, Edina, MN 55435, (612) 831-9500, FAX (612) 831-9332

Pablo Picasso (in a letter to Francoise Gilot)

The things Picasso and I said to one another during those years will never be said again, and even if they were, no one would understand them anymore. It was like being roped together on a mountain.

Georges Braque

The benchmarking process involves establishing operating targets based on best known practices. There are four steps to using the benchmark process to set organizational goals. **First, identify the "best in class" in the world** (search for the practices that will lead to superior performance of students, faculty, and administrators). **Second, set a goal to achieve that level of performance as a minimum** (establish operating targets based on the best possible practices). A college must benchmark its instructional program against the leading instructional programs in the world to determine where the college is today and what the faculty needs to do to maintain or reach "world-class" instruction. Doing so involves examining quality of instruction, its cost, its flexibility, and its speed of delivery. **Third, develop performance measures to evaluate every function's contribution toward reaching the college's goals**. These measures must go beyond student achievement. Ways to measure effort to achieve, team skills, ability to enhance team problem solving, commitment to quality work, and commitment to continuous improvement of competencies need to be developed to supplement the traditional focus on achievement tests. **Fourth, continue to move your benchmark higher as initial goals are reached**. Expertise is not a state, it is a process of progressive refinement of one's use of cooperative formal, informal, and base groups. Either faculty are improving their skills in implementing cooperative learning or else their skills are gradually deteriorating. Their expertise in using cooperative learning cannot stand still. Perfection is never reached but should be strived for in realistic steps.

The Japanese use the concept **Dantotsu**--striving to be the "best of the best"--to describe the benchmarking process. The steps of dantotsu are:

1. Know who your competitors are, especially internationally.

2. Benchmark.

3. Do not "mimic the past." New methods, processes, practices have to be uncovered and adopted.

4. Identify the "best of the best" in instructional procedures. The strategies and procedures identified have to fit together logically.

Active Learning: Cooperation In The College Classroom, Interaction Book Company, 7208 Cornelia Drive, Edina, MN 55435, (612) 831-9500, FAX (612) 831-9332

5. Conduct research on instructional methods and either adopt what is proven to be effective or adapt the good features of an instructional procedure to fit into your teaching.

An important aspect of the benchmarking process is having faculty see each other teach. Just as a ball-player needs to see other people play in order to form a frame-of-reference as to how good he or she is and where improvement is needed, faculty need to access their use of cooperative learning within a broad **frame-of- reference** based on observing many other faculty members using cooperative learning.

In order to form a frame-of-reference within which to set goals for improvement in one's use of cooperative learning, faculty members must understand (a) what cooperative learning is and (b) the basic elements of a well-implemented cooperative lesson. Otherwise, the fidelity of the implementation of cooperative learning may suffer. Most instructional innovations fade away because their implementation deteriorates and becomes approximate and sloppy. Cooperative learning will be in danger of deteriorating into traditional classroom grouping unless faculty pay attention to the exactness of its implementation. **Fidelity of use** depends on the inclusion of positive interdependence, face-to-face promotive interaction, individual accountability, interpersonal and small group skills, and group processing. Any cooperative lesson or activity should have these basic elements. They must be operationalized into any cooperative assignment.

Once a benchmarking process is established for setting and continually upgrading goals for world-class quality of instruction, colleges will wish to modernized their organizational structure.

Faculty Development And The State-Of-The-Art Use Of Cooperative Learning

More and more companies, as they move into global competitiveness, see that personnel are the one factor that can make a difference in the world market. Raw material, technology, and systems are available to everybody. The right people can be a unique commodity. To be a world-class college and provide a world-class education, each faculty member must be developed to his or her highest potential as a instructor. To do so requires that faculty maintain a state-of-the-art use of cooperative learning.

The term **state-of-the-art** is an engineering concept that involves the set of heuristics describing best available practice. Like most heuristics it is difficult to define but easy to recognize. Take sound reproduction technology, for example. The current state-of-the-art is digital-audio tape (DAT), the previous "best available practice" and currently commercially available technology is Compact Disk. Before that it was phonograph record. Best available practice usually persists for a limited period of time, and is eventually replaced by a superior approach. The changes that have occurred in the development of cooperative learning represent a progressive refinement in the state-of-the-art. Improvement is expected to continue, since cooperative learning is a dynamic area in education and the research investigating its nature and use is continuing.

Approaches to implementing cooperative learning may be placed on a continuum with direct applications at one end and conceptual applications at the other. **Direct applications** consist of packaged lessons, curricula, and strategies that are used in a lock-step prescribed manner. Direct applications can be divided into three subcategories. Instructors can adopt a strategy (such as groups-of-four in intermediate math) that is aimed at using cooperative learning in a specific subject area for a certain age student (**the script or strategy approach**), they can adopt a curriculum package that is aimed at a specific subject area and grade level (**the curriculum package approach**), or they can replicate a lesson they observed another teach (**the lesson approach**). In essence, faculty are trained to use a specific cooperative activity, lesson, strategy, or curriculum package in a Step 1, Step 2, Step 3 manner without any real understanding of cooperation. Some of the more powerful strategies include the jigsaw method developed by Elliot Aronson and his colleagues (Aronson, 1978), the coop/coop strategy developed by Spencer Kagan (Kagan, 1988), the group project method developed by the Sharans (Sharan & Sharan, 1976).

The **conceptual approach** is based on an interaction among theory, research, and practice. The two conceptual approaches to cooperative learning have been developed by Elizabeth Cohen (1986) and the authors of this book (Johnson & Johnson, 1975/1999; Johnson, Johnson, & Holubec, 1984/1998). Cohen bases her conceptual principles on expectation-states theory while we base our conceptual principles on the theory of cooperation and competition Morton Deutsch derived from Kurt Lewin's field theory. Instructors are taught a general conceptual model of cooperative learning (based on the essential elements of positive interdependence, face-to-face interaction, individual accountability, social skills, and group processing--**the essential elements approach**) that they use to tailor cooperative learning specifically for their circumstances, students, and needs. Faculty are taught to apply a conceptual system to build cooperative activities, lessons, strategies, and curricula. Using the five basic elements of cooperation, faculty can (a) analyze their current curricula, students, and instructional goals and (b) design cooperative learning experiences specifically adapted for their instructional goals and the ages, abilities, and backgrounds of their students. Becoming competent in implementing the basic elements is a requirement for building real expertise in cooperative learning. In essence, faculty are taught an **expert system** of how to implement cooperative learning that they use to create a unique adaptation to their specific circumstances, students, and needs. The resulting expertise is based on a metacognitive understanding of cooperative learning.

At the Cooperative Learning Center of the University of Minnesota we have focused on five interrelated activities: reviewing and synthesizing the research, developing theory,

Active Learning: Cooperation In The College Classroom, Interaction Book Company, 7208 Cornelia Drive, Edina, MN 55435, (612) 831-9500, FAX (612) 831-9332

conducting systematic research to validate or disconfirm the theory, operationalizing the research into "state-of-the-art" cooperation procedures, and implementing cooperative learning and faculty teams in a network of colleges and school districts throughout the United States and other parts of the world. Our training consists of learning the fundamentals of cooperative learning the first year, training in more integrated, refined, and advanced use of cooperative learning in the second year, and training in the use of structured academic controversies the third year. For administrators there is an additional year of training (Johnson & Johnson, 1994). And since the theory and research are continually progressing, refresher training is recommended every few years.

In Retrospect

I couldn't have done it without the boys.

Casey Stengel (after winning his ninth American League pennant in ten years)

There is an old story about 12 men in a lifeboat. One of the men announced that he had decided to bore a series of holes in the bottom of the boat. *"You can't do that,"* the other eleven men cried. *"Why not?"* the man answered. *"I've divided the boat into twelve equal parts. Each of us has part of the boat. We can do anything to our part of the boat we want to. I've decided to drill holes in the bottom of my part. You do anything you want with your part. It's your right!"* Many people see the world in these terms. They are unaware of their interdependence with others and the ways that their actions spread out like ripples in a pond to touch others.

Cooperation is the *"air"* of society that we constantly breathe--it is completely necessary but relatively unnoticed. We notice changes in the air, a whiff of perfume or a blanket of smog, but these are the rare instances. Like the perfume, the time we are locked (or licked) in competition and the things we achieve "on our own" stand out and are remembered because they are different from the majority of our efforts, which are cooperative. Just as the parochial myth that *"smog is what most air is like, and we need to learn to live with it"* can grow in the minds of those who live in a large city, so egocentric myths like *"it's a survival-of-the-fittest society"* have grown and have nourished by those who ignore the many cooperative aspects of their lives, while concentrating on those aspects that are competitive. In American society (and colleges) we share a common language, we drive on the appropriate side of the street, we take turns going through doors, we raise families, we seek friendship, we share the maintenance of life through an intricate division of labor. This is not to say that the skills of competitive and individualistic efforts are unimportant. They are important, but only within the larger context of cooperation with others. A person needs to know when it is appropriate to cooperate, compete, or work individualistically. Unfortunately, instruction in colleges at present stresses competitive and individualistic efforts without much attention to the skills needed to facilitate effective cooperation. To encourage a positive

Active Learning: Cooperation In The College Classroom, Interaction Book Company, 7208 Cornelia Drive, Edina, MN 55435, (612) 831-9500, FAX (612) 831-9332

learning environment and to promote the outcomes of colleges, we must realize that cooperation is the forest--competitive and individualistic efforts are but trees.

As the authors look back on the aspects of our growing up together, we realize that we may have misled you. The competition between us was a rather small part of the time we spent together. What made the instances of competition bearable was our partnership and the constant supportive cooperation within our family, and later with our friends and our families. Without cooperation and the skills that it requires, life in a society or a college would not be possible.

Active Learning: Cooperation In The College Classroom, Interaction Book Company, 7208 Cornelia Drive, Edina, MN 55435, (612) 831-9500, FAX (612) 831-9332

Review and Celebration

The greatest rewards come only from the greatest commitment.

Arlene Blum, Mountain Climber and Leader, American Women's Himalayan Expedition

Task 1: Review of Progress

Meet in your base groups. Every member should have his or her:

1. Journal.
2. Case studies.
3. Log sheet.
4. Lesson plans of lessons and units taught.
5. Completed implementation assignments.

Task: Group members have ten minutes to summarize their implementation of cooperative learning. The summary should include personal learnings as recorded in their journals, the impact of the cooperative lessons on the students being followed for case studies, the number and type of lessons they have conducted, and their overall experiences in teaching cooperative skills to students. Once all members have summarized their implementation of cooperative learning, the group makes at least three conclusions about their experiences to share with the entire class. This is a **cooperative** activity, everyone should participate, listen carefully to groupmates, provide support and encouragement, and celebrate the group's effort in implementing cooperative learning into their classrooms and colleges.

Task 2: Sharing Successes

Stay in your base groups. Your **task** is to share your successes in implementing cooperative learning and help each groupmates do the same. Work **cooperatively** in answering the following questions:

1. How have your students benefited from cooperative learning?

2. What cooperative lesson was most successful?

3. Which student benefited most from working cooperatively?

Active Learning: Cooperation In The College Classroom, Interaction Book Company, 7208 Cornelia Drive, Edina, MN 55435, (612) 831-9500, FAX (612) 831-9332

4. What cooperative lesson was most important to you personally?

Task 3: Cooperative Learning Review Quiz

Divide your base group into pairs. Your **task** is to answer each question in the Review Quiz correctly. Work **cooperatively**. Each pair takes the quiz together, one answer for the pair, with both members in agreement and able to explain each answer. When finished, reform as a base group and take the Review Quiz again. If there is any disagreement as to the answer to a question, find the page number in the book the answer appears on and clarify until all members are in agreement and can explain the answer.

Task 4: Basic Concepts Review

Divide your base group into pairs. Starting with Chapter One, identify the basic concepts in each chapter and ensure both pair members can correctly define each one. When finished, reform as a base group and compare the concepts identified for each chapter and their definitions. If there is disagreement as to the definitions, identify what page the definition is on and clarify the definition until all members of the group agree and are able to explain it. Make sure all base group members can define each concept.

Task 5: Planning Your Cooperative Learning Future

Your **tasks** are to (1) diagnose your current level of expertise in using cooperative learning and (2) make a plan for increasing your expertise. The diagnosis and plan must be in writing and signed by all base group members.

Work **cooperatively** Meet in your base group and ensure all members (a) have completed the above two tasks and (b) agree with each member's diagnosis and plan (noted by the signatures on each member's plan).

In diagnosing where you stand in gaining expertise in cooperative learning consider:

1. The long-term goals of being able to:

   a. Take any lesson in any subject area and teach it cooperatively.

   b. Use cooperative learning at the routine-use level.

Active Learning: Cooperation In The College Classroom, Interaction Book Company, 7208 Cornelia Drive, Edina, MN 55435, (612) 831-9500, FAX (612) 831-9332

    c. Use cooperative learning at least 60 percent of the time.

    d. Be a member of an ongoing colleagial support groups.

2. The amount of training you have received.

3. The amount of experience you have in using cooperative learning.

4. The effectiveness of your colleagial support group in encouraging and assisting members' implementation efforts.

5. Your ability to experiment, take risks, and generally stay on the edge of your comfort zone in order to increase your expertise.

6. The quality and quantity of the feedback you are receiving on your implementation efforts.

7. The quality and quantity of your reflections and problem solving on the feedback received.

8. Your persistence in using cooperative learning again and again.

9. Your experience in encouraging and assisting your colleagues' efforts to implement cooperative learning.

What are your next steps in increasing your expertise in cooperative learning? Your plan should include a:

1. List of units coming up in which cooperative learning should be used.

2. List of cooperative skills you plan to teach to your students.

3. Plan for:

    a. Forming and maintaining a colleagial support group in your college to focus on cooperative learning.

    b. Your own skill development in working cooperatively with colleagues.

    c. A **time schedule** as to when cooperative skills will be taught and perfected by your students while you provide opportunities for the use of the skills, feedback on how well each student is performing the skill, and encouragement for each student to continue practicing the skill.

Active Learning: Cooperation In The College Classroom, Interaction Book Company, 7208 Cornelia Drive, Edina, MN 55435, (612) 831-9500, FAX (612) 831-9332

d. The phone numbers of your base group members and the time you will call each one and give him or her a report on your progress.

Task 6: Whole Class Review By Drawing Names

The purpose of this activity is to provide a fun review of the course. The instructor will ask a question and then draw a participant's name from a hat. The participant named must give an interesting and truthful answer.

Task 7: Thanking Your Learning Partners

Seek out the people who have helped you learn how to implement cooperative learning. **Thank them.**

Action Plan

1. **Your Next Steps:**	
a.	c.
b.	d.
2. **Support From Whom**	**In What Ways**
a.	
b.	
c.	
d.	
3. **Realities To Be Faced:**	
a.	c.
b.	d.

4. Your Vision Of The Cooperative Class And College:

10 : 18

Active Learning: Cooperation In The College Classroom, Interaction Book Company, 7208 Cornelia Drive, Edina, MN 55435, (612) 831-9500, FAX (612) 831-9332

Appendix A:

History And Research: Cooperative, Competitive, Individualistic Efforts

Introduction

No logic nor wisdom nor will-power could prevail to stop the sailors. Buffeted by the hardships of life at sea, the voices came out of the mist to the ancient Greek sailors like a mystical, ethereal love song with tempting and seductive promises of ecstasy and delight. The voices and the song were irresistible. The mariners helplessly turned their ships to follow the Sirens' call with scarcely a second thought. Lured to their destruction, the sailors crashed their ships on the waiting rocks and drowned in the tossing waves, struggling with their last breath to reach the source of that beckoning song.

Centuries later, the Sirens still call. Educators seem drawn to competitive and individualistic learning, crashing their teaching on the rocks due to the seductive and tempting attractions of explicating knowledge to an adoring audience and teaching as they were taught. Yet if you ask individuals who have made remarkable achievements during their lifetimes, they typically say their success came from cooperative efforts (Kouses & Posner, 1967). Not only is cooperation connected with success, competitiveness has been found to be detrimental to career success (Kohn, 1992). The more competitive a person is, the less chance they have of being successful. Perhaps the most definitive research on this issue has been conducted by Robert L. Helmreich and his colleagues (Helmreich, 1982; Helmreich, Beane, Lucker, & Spence, 1978; Helmreich, Sawin, & Carsrud, 1986; Helmreich Spence, et al., 1980). They first determined that high achievers, such as scientists, MBA's, and pilots tend **not** to be very competitive individuals. Then Helmreich and his associates examined the relationship between the competitive drive within individuals and career success. They conceptualized the desire to achieve consisting of competitiveness (desire to win in interpersonal situations, where one tends to see that success depends on another's failure), mastery (desire to take on challenging tasks), and work (positive attitudes toward hard work). A sample of 103 male Ph.D. scientists was rated on the three factors based on a questionnaire. Achievement was defined as the number of times their work was cited by colleagues. The result was that the most citations were obtained by those high on the Work and Mastery but low on the Competitiveness Scale. Startled by these results, Helmreich and his associates conducted follow-up studies with academic psychologists, businessmen working in "cut-throat" big business (measuring achievement by their salaries), undergraduate male and female students (using grade-point average as the achievement

Active Learning: Cooperation In The College Classroom. Edina, MN: Interaction Book Company, 7208 Cornelia Drive, Edina, Minnesota 55435, (612) 831-9500; FAX (612) 831-9332.

measure), fifth- and sixth-grade students (measuring achievement by performance on standardized achievement tests), airline pilots (measuring achievement by performance ratings), airline reservation agents (measuring achievement by performance ratings), and super-tanker crews. In all cases they found a negative correlation between achievement and competitiveness. With regard to the faculty members, the researchers proposed that competitive individuals focus so heavily on outshining others and putting themselves forward that they lose track of the scientific issues and produce research that is more superficial and less sustained in direction. As yet Hemreich and his colleagues have not been able to identify a single professional arena where highly competitive individuals tended to be more successful.

Given that competitiveness seems to be detrimental to career success, why has it been so prevalent in classrooms? One answer may be that the above evidence is not enough. Interesting, but not conclusive. In this chapter, therefore, the research directly comparing the relative effects of competitive, individualistic, and cooperative efforts is reviewed.

> *"Let us put our minds together...and see what life we can make for our children."*
>
> Sitting Bull

History Of Cooperative Learning

Two are better than one, because they have a good reward for toil. For if they fall, one will lift up his fellow; but woe to him who is alone when he falls and has not another to lift him up...And though a man might prevail against one who is alone, two will withstand him. A threefold cord is not quickly broken.

Ecclesiastics 4:9-12

Cooperative learning has been around a long time. It will probably never go away. Its rich history of theory, research, and actual use in the classroom makes it one of the most distinguished of all instructional practices. Theory, research, and practice all interact and enhance each other. Theory both guides and summarizes research. Research validates or disconfirms theory, thereby leading to its refinement and modification. Practice is guided by validated theory, and applications of the theory reveal inadequacies that lead to refining of the theory, conducting new research studies, and modifying the application. The history of cooperative learning is reviewed with the emphasis being on the theories that have guided the development of cooperative learning and the research they have generated.

A : 2

Active Learning: Cooperation In The College Classroom. Edina, MN: Interaction Book Company, 7208 Cornelia Drive, Edina, Minnesota 55435, (612) 831-9500; FAX (612) 831-9332.

Time-Line: History Of Cooperative Learning

Given below is a partial time-line on the history of cooperative learning. In limited space it is not possible to list all the people and events important to the history of cooperative learning. The absence of anyone or any event that should be listed is unintended.

Date	Event
BC	Talmud
First Century	Quintillion, Seneca (*Qui Docet Discet*)
1600s	Johann Amos Comenius of Moravia
1700s	Joseph Lancaster, Andrew Bell
1806	Lancaster School Established In United States
Early 1800s	Common School Movement In United States
Late 1800s	Colonel Frances Parker
Early 1900s	John Dewey, Kurt Lewin, Jean Piaget, Lev Vygotsky
1929 - 1930s	Books on Cooperation & Competition by Maller, Mead, May & Dobb Liberty League & Nat. Ass. Manufacturers promoted competition
1940s	
1940s	WWII, Office of Strategic Services, Military Related Research
1949	Morton Deutsch, Theory & Research On Cooperation & Competition
1950s	
1950s	Applied Group Dynamics Movement, National Training Laboratories Deutsch Research On Trust, Individualistic Situations Naturalistic Studies
1960s	
1960s	Stuart Cook (1969) Research On Cooperation Madsen (Kagan) Research On Cooperation & Competition in Children Inquiry (Discovery) Learning Movement: Bruner, Suchman B. F. Skinner, Programmed Learning, Behavior Modification
1962	Morton Deutsch Nebraska Symposium, Cooperation & Trust, Conflict Robert Blake & Jane Mouton, Research On Intergroup Competition

Active Learning: Cooperation In The College Classroom. Edina, MN: Interaction Book Company, 7208 Cornelia Drive, Edina, Minnesota 55435, (612) 831-9500; FAX (612) 831-9332.

© Johnson, Johnson, & Smith

1966	David Johnson, U of MN, Began Training Teachers In Coop. Learning
1969	Roger Johnson Joined David At University of Minnesota
1970s	
1970	David W. Johnson, **Social Psychology of Education**
1971	Robert Hamblin: Behavioral Research On Cooperation/Competition
1973	David DeVries & Keith Edwards, Combined Instructional Games Approach With Intergroup Competition, Teams-Games-Tournament
1974 - 1975	David & Roger Johnson Research Review On Cooperation/Competition, David & Roger Johnson, **Learning Together And Alone**
Mid 1970s	Annual Symposium At APA Began (David DeVries & Keith Edwards, David & Roger Johnson, Stuart Cook, Elliot Aronson, Elizabeth Cohen, Others) Robert Slavin Began Development Of Cooperative Curricula Spencer Kagan Continued Research On Cooperation Among Children
1976	Shlomo & Yael Sharan, **Small Group Teaching** (Group Investigation)
1978	Elliot Aronson, **Jigsaw Classroom** **Journal of Research & Development In Education**, Cooperation Issue Jeanne Gibbs, **Tribes**
1979	First IASCE Conference in Tel Aviv, Israel
1980s	
1981, 1983	David & Roger Johnson, Meta-Analyses Of Research On Cooperation
1985	Elizabeth Cohen, **Designing Groupwork**
	Spencer Kagan Developed Structures Approach To Cooperative Learning
	AERA and ASCD Special Interest Groups Founded
1989	David & Roger Johnson, **Cooperation & Competition: Theory & Research**
1990s	
Early 1990s	Cooperative Learning Gains Popularity Among Educators
1996	First Annual Cooperative Learning Leadership Conference, Minneapolis

A : 4

Active Learning: Cooperation In The College Classroom. Edina, MN: Interaction Book Company, 7208 Cornelia Drive, Edina, Minnesota 55435, (612) 831-9500; FAX (612) 831-9332.

Where We Have Been: Theoretical Roots

Theories are causal explanations of how things work. Theory guides and improves practice. Theory is to practice what the soil is to plants. If the soil is appropriate, the plant will grow and flourish. If the theory is appropriate, the practice will grow and continuously improve. Without an appropriate theory, practice is static and stagnant. There are at least three general theoretical perspectives that have guided research on and practice of cooperative learning—social interdependence, cognitive-developmental, and behavioral learning theories.

Social Interdependence Theory

The most influential theorizing on cooperative learning focused on **social interdependence**. In the early 1900s, one of the founders of the Gestalt School of Psychology, Kurt Koffka, proposed that groups were dynamic wholes in which the interdependence among members could vary. One of his colleagues, Kurt Lewin (1935) refined this notion in the 1920s and 1930s while stating that (a) the essence of a group is the interdependence among members (created by common goals) which results in the group being a "dynamic whole" so that a change in the state of any member or subgroup changes the state of any other member or subgroup, and (b) an intrinsic state of tension within group members motivates movement toward the accomplishment of the desired common goals. One of Lewin's graduate students, Morton Deutsch, refined Lewin's notions and formulated a theory of cooperation and competition in the late 1940s (Deutsch, 1949a, 1962), noting that interdependence can be positive (cooperation) or negative (competition). One of Deutsch's graduate students, David Johnson (working with his brother Roger Johnson), extended Deutsch's work into social interdependence theory (Johnson & Johnson, 1974, 1989).

Social interdependence theory posits that the way social interdependence is structured determines how individuals interact which, in turn, determines outcomes. Positive interdependence (cooperation) results in **promotive interaction** as individuals encourage and facilitate each other's efforts to learn. Negative interdependence (competition) typically results in **oppositional interaction** as individuals discourage and obstruct each other's efforts to achieve. In the absence of interdependence (individualistic efforts) there is **no interaction** as individuals work independently without any interchange with each other. Promotive interaction leads to increased efforts to achieve, positive interpersonal relationships, and psychological health. Oppositional and no interaction leads to decreased efforts to achieve, negative interpersonal relationships, and psychological maladjustment.

Cognitive-Developmental Theory

The **cognitive developmental perspective** is largely based on the theories of Piaget (1950), Vygotsky (1978), cognitive science, and academic controversy (Johnson &

Active Learning: Cooperation In The College Classroom. Edina, MN: Interaction Book Company, 7208 Cornelia Drive, Edina, Minnesota 55435, (612) 831-9500; FAX (612) 831-9332.

Johnson, 1979, 1995). To Jean Piaget, **cooperation** is the striving to attain common goals while coordinating one's own feelings and perspective with a consciousness of others' feelings and perspective. From Piaget and related theories comes the premise that when individuals co-operate on the environment, socio-cognitive conflict occurs that creates cognitive disequilibrium, which in turn stimulates perspective-taking ability and cognitive development. Cooperative learning in the Piagetian tradition is aimed at accelerating a student's intellectual development by forcing him or her to reach consensus with other students who hold opposing points of view about the answer to the school task.

Lev Semenovich Vygotsky and related theorists claim that our distinctively human mental functions and accomplishments have their origins in our social relationships. Mental functioning is the internalized and transformed version of the accomplishments of a group. Knowledge is social, constructed from cooperative efforts to learn, understand, and solve problems. A central concept is the **zone of proximal development**, which is the zone between what a student can do on his or her own and what the student can achieve while working under the guidance of instructors or in collaboration with more capable peers. Unless students work cooperatively, they will not grow intellectually and, therefore, the time students work alone on school tasks should be minimized.

From the cognitive science viewpoint, cooperative learning involves modeling, coaching, and scaffolding (conceptual frameworks provided for understanding what is being learned). The learner must cognitively rehearse and restructure information for it to be retained in memory and incorporated into existing cognitive structures (Wittrock, 1978). An effective way of doing so is explaining the material being learned to a collaborator. Tutoring, therefore, is a form of cooperative learning.

Controversy theory (Johnson & Johnson, 1979, 1995c) posits that being confronted with opposing points of view creates uncertainty or conceptual conflict, which creates a reconceptualization and an information search, which results in a more refined and thoughtful conclusion. The key steps are organizing what is known into a position, advocating that position to someone who is advocating the opposing position, attempting to refute the opposing position while rebutting the attacks on one's own position, reversing perspectives so that the issue may be seen from both points of view simultaneously, and creating a synthesis to which all sides can agree.

Behavioral-Learning Theory

The **behavioral learning perspective** assumes that students will work hard on those tasks for which they secure a reward of some sort and will fail to work on tasks that yield no reward or yield punishment (Bandura, 1977; Skinner, 1968). Cooperative learning is designed to provide incentives for the members of the group to participate in a group effort since it is assumed that students will not intrinsically help their classmates or work toward a common goal. Skinner focused on group contingencies, Bandura focused on imitation, and Homans as well as Thibaut and Kelley focused on the balance of rewards and costs in social exchange among interdependent individuals.

Active Learning: Cooperation In The College Classroom. Edina, MN: Interaction Book Company, 7208 Cornelia Drive, Edina, Minnesota 55435, (612) 831-9500; FAX (612) 831-9332.

Figure A.1 A General Theoretical Framework

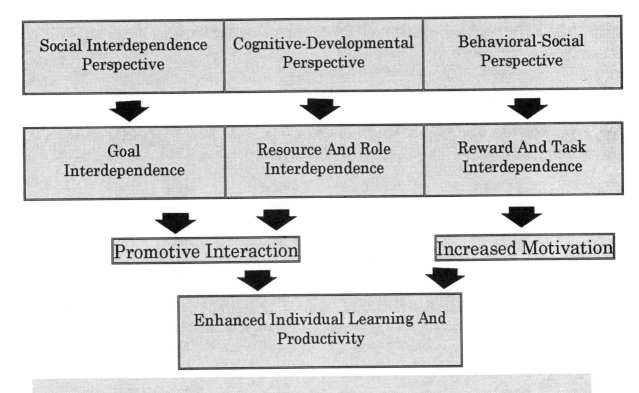

Differences Among Theories

These three theories provide a classic triangulation of validation for cooperative learning. Social interdependence theory, behavioral-learning theory, and cognitive-developmental theory all predict that cooperative learning would promote higher achievement than would competitive or individualistic learning. Each theory has generated considerable research, which is reviewed below. There are, however, basic differences among the theoretical perspectives. Social interdependence theory assumes that cooperative efforts are based on intrinsic motivation generated by interpersonal factors in working together and joint aspirations to achieve a significant goal. Behavioral-learning theory assumes that cooperative efforts are powered by extrinsic motivation to achieve rewards. Social interdependence theory is made up of relational concepts dealing with what happens among individuals (e.g., cooperation is something that exists only among individuals, not within them), while the cognitive-developmental perspective is focused on what happens within a single person (e.g., disequilibrium, cognitive reorganization). The differences in basic assumptions among the theoretical perspectives have yet to be fully explored or resolved.

Usefulness Of Theories

While all three theories have inspired research on cooperation, the most fully developed, the most clearly related to practice, and the greatest inspiration of research, is social

Active Learning: Cooperation In The College Classroom. Edina, MN: Interaction Book Company, 7208 Cornelia Drive, Edina, Minnesota 55435, (612) 831-9500; FAX (612) 831-9332.

interdependence theory. Besides giving the clearest and most precise definitions of cooperative, competitive, and individualistic efforts, social interdependence theory specifies (a) the conditions under which cooperation is most effective, (b) the outcomes most effected by cooperation, and (c) the procedures teachers should use in implementing cooperative learning (Deutsch, 1949, 1962; Johnson, 1970; Johnson & Johnson, 1974, 1989; Johnson, Johnson, & Holubec, 1998).

Where We Have Been: Research

We know a lot about cooperation and we have known it for some time. In the late 1800's Triplett (1898) in the United States, Turner (1889) in England, and Mayer (1903) in Germany conducted a series of studies on the factors associated with competitive performance. Since then we have found out a lot about cooperation. In 1929 Maller wrote a book about it (Cooperation and Competition: An Experimental Study in Motivation). In 1936 Margaret Mead (Cooperation and Competition Among Primitive Peoples) and in 1937 May and Doob (Competition and Cooperation) wrote research reviews on it. In 1949 Deutsch published a research study and a theory on it. In the 1950s Muzafer Sherif (Sherif & Hovland, 1961) conducted his famous studies on three summer camps in which he engineered intense intergroup competition and studied its resolution. Stuart Cook (1969), in collaboration with Shirley and Larry Wrightsman, conducted a study on the impact of cooperative interaction on relationships between black and white college students. James Coleman (1961) published an observational study of American schools in which a pervasive competitiveness was documented. In 1963 Miller and Hamblin reviewed 24 studies on cooperation and competition. From an anthropological perspective, Millard C. Madsen (1967) and his associates developed a series of dyadic games that allowed comparison of children's preferences for competitive and cooperative interaction, across ages and various cultures. One of Madsen's students, Spencer Kagan, began a series of studies on cooperation and competition in children. The research of Madsen and Kagan presents a consistent picture of rural children collaborating more than urban children, and middle-class urban American children being most strongly motivated to compete.

In 1970 (**The Social Psychology of Education**), 1974, and 1975 (**Learning Together and Alone**, first edition) the authors of this book published comprehensive research reviews on cooperation and competition. From then on the research review articles are too many to mention. Since 1898 over 550 experimental and 100 correlational research studies have been conducted on cooperative, competitive, and individualistic efforts (see Johnson & Johnson, 1989 for a complete review of these studies).

The effectiveness of cooperative learning has been confirmed by both theoretical and demonstration research. There is a "scientific" literature and a "professional" literature on cooperative learning. The scientific literature is made up of carefully controlled research studies conducted to validate or disconfirm theory. Most of the studies are either laboratory or field experimental studies. The vast majority of the research on cooperative learning was conducted to validate or disconfirm theory. The

A : 8

Active Learning: Cooperation In The College Classroom. Edina, MN: Interaction Book Company, 7208 Cornelia Drive, Edina, Minnesota 55435, (612) 831-9500; FAX (612) 831-9332.

theoretical studies typically are carefully controlled and have high internal validity, randomly assigning subjects to conditions, carefully operationalizing the independent variable, ensuring that the measures of the dependent variables were both reliable and valid. The theoretical studies have focused on a wide variety of dependent variables from achievement to higher-level reasoning to friendships between majority and minority individuals to accuracy of perspective taking to self-esteem to psychological health. The results of these theoretical studies are highly consistent in supporting the use of cooperative over competitive and individualistic learning. It is this combination of hundreds of studies producing validated theory that could be operationalized into practice that has created such interest in cooperative learning.

There are problems with theoretical studies. They lack credibility with many practitioners. Most of the theoretical studies on cooperative learning were conducted in social psychology laboratories using college students as subjects. Although they clarified the power of cooperative efforts, they did not in fact demonstrate that cooperative learning could work in the "real world."

The professional literature is made up of field quasi-experimental or correlational studies demonstrating that cooperative learning works in real classrooms for a prolonged period of time. Demonstration studies have tended to focus on external validity. The demonstration studies may be grouped into four categories:

1. **Summative Evaluations:** By far the largest category of demonstration studies is straightforward summative evaluation in which the central question is whether a particular cooperative learning program produces beneficial results. The comparison is typically between a cooperative learning method and "traditional" classroom learning. The Johns Hopkins research on specific cooperative learning programs (Teams-Games-Tournaments, Student Team Achievement Divisions, Team-Assisted Individualization) are examples that focused primarily achievement on lower-level learning tasks. The reviews of these studies (Slavin, 1983, 1991) are organized around a particular method, not a particular skill or knowledge to be learned. This serves the advocates of the method, but users of cooperative learning may not be so concerned with whether STAD works or does not work, but instead would like to know the best procedures for maximizing learning or higher-level reasoning. While these evaluation studies are of interest, the information value of their conclusions is limited for designing effective instructional programs.

2. **Comparative Summative Evaluations:** Less research attention has been devoted to the comparative question of which cooperative learning methods produce the most beneficial effects when compared on the same criterion measures. The jigsaw method, for example, might be compared with Team Assisted-Individualization. There is an inherent problem with such studies, as it is difficult if not impossible to tell if both methods have been implemented at the same strength. The results can be easily biased through carefully implementing one method at full strength and implementing the other method at partial strength.

Active Learning: Cooperation In The College Classroom. Edina, MN: Interaction Book Company, 7208 Cornelia Drive, Edina, Minnesota 55435, (612) 831-9500; FAX (612) 831-9332.

3. **Formative Evaluations:** Very little research focused on where a cooperative learning program went wrong and how it could be improved makes its way into the literature. Formative evaluations are aimed at improving ongoing implementations of cooperation learning. The critical incident method seems well suited to the diagnosis of training deficiencies or unintended consequences, as does a combination of surveys with follow-up interviews of a representative subsample of respondents.

4. **Survey Studies:** A few studies have conducted large scale surveys of the impact of cooperation on students (Johnson & Johnson, 1991d). These studies have (a) correlated attitudes toward cooperative, competitive, and individualistic learning with such variables as perceived social support, self-esteem, and attitudes learning and (b) compared the responses of students in high-use classrooms (where cooperative learning was frequently used) with the responses of students in low-use classrooms (where cooperative learning was never or rarely used) on a number of learning climate variables (e.g., Johnson, Johnson, & Anderson, 1983; Johnson & Johnson, 1983; Johnson, Johnson, Buckman, & Richards, 1986). While these studies are not direct evaluations of cooperative learning procedures, they do provide interesting data about the long-term impact of cooperative learning on a variety of attitudinal and learning climate outcomes.

Demonstration studies have both weaknesses and strengths. **First**, like all case studies, demonstration studies simply indicate that a certain method worked at that time in those circumstances. **Second**, demonstration studies are always in danger of being biased because the researcher is typically evaluating programs they have developed themselves and have a professional and sometimes a financial stake in their success. By definition, such researchers favor cooperative learning. Reviews of demonstration studies, furthermore, suffer the same limitation as they are most often conducted by the researchers who invented the cooperative learning programs. The **third** problem with demonstration studies is that what is labeled as cooperative learning is not always cooperation. In many cases, the "cooperative learning method" being evaluated was only one element of a broader educational package and, therefore, cooperative learning was confounded with other variables. The original jigsaw procedure (Aronson, 1978), for example, is a combination of resource interdependence (cooperative) and individual reward structure (individualistic). Teams-Games-Tournaments (DeVries & Edwards, 1974) and Student-Teams-Achievement-Divisions (Slavin, 1980) are mixtures of cooperation and intergroup competition. Team-Assisted-Instruction (Slavin, Leavey, & Madden, 1982) is a mixture of individualistic and cooperative learning. It is difficult to interpret the results of studies evaluating the effectiveness of such mixtures as it is impossible to know which elements contributed which part of the found effects.

Fourth, demonstration studies often lack methodological rigor, focusing far more on external validity (such as length of study) than on internal validity (such as experimental control). In many demonstration studies, the comparison has been with an ambiguous and unknown "traditional classroom learning." When differences are found, it is not

A : 10

Active Learning: Cooperation In The College Classroom. Edina, MN: Interaction Book Company, 7208 Cornelia Drive, Edina, Minnesota 55435, (612) 831-9500; FAX (612) 831-9332.

clear what has been compared with what. The lack of methodological quality to most demonstration studies add further doubts as to how seriously their results can be taken. **Finally**, most demonstration studies have been conducted in elementary schools. Very few have been conducted at the secondary and college levels. This reduces their relevance.

> *A human being is a part of the whole, called by us "Universe," a part limited in time and space. He experiences himself, his thoughts and feelings as something separated from the rest--a kind of optical delusion of consciousness. This delusion is a kind of prison for us, restricting us to our personal desires and to affection for a few persons nearest to us. Our task must be to free ourselves from this prison by widening our circle of compassion to embrace all living creatures, and the whole nature in its beauty.*
>
> Albert Einstein

There are at least two strengths to demonstration studies. **First**, there is a clear value to demonstration studies when their results are viewed in combination with more controlled and more theoretical studies. When the results of the demonstration studies agree with and support the results of the theoretical studies, the demonstration studies strengthen the validity of the theory and make it more credible. **Second**, demonstration studies provide a model for teachers who wish to implement identical programs.

Cooperative learning can be used with some confidence at any grade level, in every subject area, and with any task. Research participants have varied as to economic class, age, sex, nationality, and cultural background. A wide variety of research tasks, ways of structuring cooperation, and measures of the dependent variables have been used. The research has been conducted by many different researchers with markedly different orientations working in different settings, countries, and decades. The research on cooperative learning has a validity and a generalizability rarely found in the educational literature.

Cooperation is a generic human endeavor that affects many different instructional outcomes simultaneously. Over the past 90 years researchers have focused on such diverse outcomes as achievement, higher-level reasoning, retention, achievement motivation, intrinsic motivation, transfer of learning, interpersonal attraction, social support, friendships, prejudice, valuing differences, social support, self-esteem, social competencies, psychological health, moral reasoning, and many others. These numerous outcomes may be subsumed within three broad categories (Johnson & Johnson, 1989): effort to achieve, positive interpersonal relationships, and psychological health (see Figure A.2 and Table A.1).

A : 11

Active Learning: Cooperation In The College Classroom. Edina, MN: Interaction Book Company, 7208 Cornelia Drive, Edina, Minnesota 55435, (612) 831-9500; FAX (612) 831-9332.

Figure A.2 Outcomes Of Social Interdependence

Table A.1 Mean Effect Sizes for Social Interdependence

Conditions	Achievement	Interpersonal Attraction	Social Support	Self-Esteem
Total Studies				
Coop vs. Comp	0.67	0.67	0.62	0.58
Coop vs. Ind	0.64	0.60	0.70	0.44
Comp vs. Ind	0.30	0.08	-0.13	-0.23
High Quality Studies				
Coop vs. Comp	0.88	0.82	0.83	0.67
Coop vs. Ind	0.61	0.62	0.72	0.45
Comp vs. Ind	0.07	0.27	-0.13	-0.25
Mixed Operationalizations				
Coop vs. Comp	0.40	0.46	0.45	0.33
Coop vs. Ind	0.42	0.36	0.02	0.22
Pure Operationalizations				
Coop vs. Comp	0.71	0.79	0.73	0.74
Coop vs. Ind	0.65	0.66	0.77	0.51

Note: Coop = Cooperation, Comp = Competition, Ind = Individualistic
(Source: D. W. Johnson & R. Johnson, **Cooperation and competition: Theory and research**. Edina, MN: Interaction Book Company. Reprinted with permission.)

A : 12

Active Learning: Cooperation In The College Classroom. Edina, MN: Interaction Book Company, 7208 Cornelia Drive, Edina, Minnesota 55435, (612) 831-9500; FAX (612) 831-9332.

Research In Different Cultures

Part of the generalizability of the research on cooperation is the diversity of settings in which the research has been conducted. Research on cooperation has been conducted in numerous countries and cultures. In North America (United States, Canada, Mexico), for example, research has been conducted with Caucasian, Black-American, Native-American, Hispanics subject populations. In addition, cooperation has been researched in Asia (Japan), Southeast Asia (Australia, New Zealand), the Middle East (Israel), Africa (Nigeria, South Africa), Europe (Greece, Norway, Sweden, Finland, Germany, France, Netherlands, England), and many other countries. Essentially, the findings have been consistent. Higher productivity, more positive relationships, and increased social adjustment and competencies are found in cooperative than in competitive or individualistic situations. The robustness of the research in a wide variety of cultures adds to the validity and generalizability of the theory. The critical research, however, has yet to be conducted. It seems reasonable that different cultures have different definitions of (a) what is cooperative and competitive and (b) where each is appropriate. Within the United States, for example, different Native American tribes have quite different views of cooperation and competition and different ways of expressing them. Given the hundreds of studies that have established the basic theory of cooperation and competition, there is a need for considerable more research to establish the cultural nuances of how cooperative efforts are conducted.

History Of Practical Use Of Cooperative Learning

There is a rich and long history of practical use of cooperative learning. Thousands of years ago the **Talmud** stated that in order to understand the Talmud, one must have a learning partner. As early as the first century, **Quintillion** argued that students could benefit from teaching one another. The Roman philosopher, **Seneca** advocated cooperative learning through such statements as, "*Qui Docet Discet*" (when you teach, you learn twice). **Johann Amos Comenius** (1592-1679) believed that students would benefit both by teaching and being taught by other students. In the late 1700's **Joseph Lancaster** and **Andrew Bell** made extensive use of cooperative learning groups in England, and the idea was brought to America when a Lancastrian school was opened in New York City in 1806. Within the **Common School Movement** in the United States in the early 1800s there was a strong emphasis on cooperative learning. Certainly, the use of cooperative learning is not new to American education. There have been periods in which cooperative learning had strong advocates and was widely used to promote the educational goals of that time.

One of the most successful advocates of cooperative learning in America was **Colonel Francis Parker**. In the last three decades of the 19th Century, Colonel Parker brought to his advocacy of cooperative learning enthusiasm, idealism, practicality, and an intense devotion to freedom, democracy, and individuality in the public schools. His fame and success rested on the vivid and regenerating spirit that he brought into the schoolroom

A : 13

Active Learning: Cooperation In The College Classroom. Edina, MN: Interaction Book Company, 7208 Cornelia Drive, Edina, Minnesota 55435, (612) 831-9500; FAX (612) 831-9332.

and on his power to create a classroom atmosphere that was truly cooperative and democratic. When he was superintendent of the public schools at Quincy, Massachusetts (1875-1880), he averaged more than 30,000 visitors a year to examine his use of cooperative learning procedures (Campbell, 1965). Parker's instructional methods of structuring cooperation among students dominated American education through the turn of the century. Following Parker, ^John Dewey^ promoted the use of cooperative learning groups as part of his famous project method in instruction (Dewey, 1924). In the late 1930's, however, interpersonal competition began to be emphasized in public schools (Pepitone, 1980).

In the mid 1960s, the authors began training teachers how to use cooperative learning at the University of Minnesota. **The Cooperative Learning Center** resulted from our efforts to (a) synthesize existing knowledge concerning cooperative, competitive, and individualistic efforts (Johnson, 1970; Johnson & Johnson, 1974, 1978, 1983, 1989), (b) formulate theoretical models concerning the nature of cooperation and its essential components, (c) conduct a systematic program of research to test our theorizing, (d) translate the validated theory into a set of concrete strategies and procedures for using cooperation in classrooms, schools, and school districts (Johnson, Johnson, & Holubec, 1984/1993, 1989b, 1992a, 1992b), and (e) build and maintain a network of schools and colleges implementing cooperative strategies and procedures throughout North America and a variety of other countries. Related to cooperative learning was the development of academic controversy (Johnson & Johnson, 1995b) and conflict resolution and peer mediation programs (Johnson & Johnson, 1995a).

In the 1970's David DeVries and Keith Edwards at Johns Hopkins University developed Teams-Games-Tournaments (TGT) and Sholmo and Yael Sharan in Israel developed the group investigation procedure for cooperative learning groups. Robert Slavin extended Devries and Edward's work at Johns Hopkins University by modifying TGT into Student-Team-Achievement-Divisions (STAD) and modifying computer-assisted instruction into Team-Assisted Instruction (TAI). Concurrently, Spencer Kagan developed the Co-op Co-op procedure. In the 1980s, Donald Dansereau developed a number of cooperative scripts and many other individuals worked out further cooperative procedures. In the 1990s, cooperative learning was extended into conflict resolution and peer mediation programs (Johnson & Johnson, 1995a, 1995b).

Research On Social Interdependence

Building on the theorizing of Kurt Lewin and Morton Deutsch, the premise may be made that the type of interdependence structured among individuals determines how they interact with each other which, in turn largely determines outcomes. Structuring situations cooperatively results in promotive interaction, structuring situations competitively results in oppositional interaction, and structuring situations individualistically results in no interaction among students. These interaction patterns affect numerous variables, which may be subsumed within the three broad and interrelated outcomes of effort exerted to achieve, quality of relationships among

Active Learning: Cooperation In The College Classroom. Edina, MN: Interaction Book Company, 7208 Cornelia Drive, Edina, Minnesota 55435, (612) 831-9500; FAX (612) 831-9332.

participants, and participants' psychological adjustment and social competence (see Figure A.1) (Johnson & Johnson, 1989). Between 1898 and 1989, over 575 experimental and 100 correlational studies were conducted by a wide variety of researchers in different decades with different age subjects, in different subject areas, and in different settings (see Johnson & Johnson, 1989 for a complete listing of these studies). In most cases, references to individual studies are not included in this chapter. Rather, the reader is referred to the reviews that contain the references to the specific studies that corroborate the point being made.

Interaction Patterns

Positive interdependence creates promotive interaction. **Promotive interaction** occurs as individuals encourage and facilitate each other's efforts to reach the group's goals (such as maximizing each member's learning). Group members promote each other's success by (Johnson & Johnson, 1989):

1. Giving and receiving help and assistance (both task-related and personal).

2. Exchanging resources and information. Group members seek information and other resources from each other, comprehend information accurately and without bias, and make optimal use of the information provided. There are a number of beneficial results from (a) orally explaining, elaborating, and summarizing information and (b) teaching one's knowledge to others. Explaining and teaching increase the degree to which group members cognitively process and organize information, engage in higher-level reasoning, attain insights, and become personally committed to achieving. Listening critically to the explanations of groupmates provides the opportunity to utilize other's resources.

3. Giving and receiving feedback on taskwork and teamwork behaviors. In cooperative groups, members monitor each other's efforts, give immediate feedback on performance, and, when needed, give each other help and assistance.

4. Challenging each other's reasoning. Intellectual controversy promotes curiosity, motivation to learn, reconceptualization of what one's knows, higher quality decision making, greater insight into the problem being considered, and many other important benefits (Johnson & Johnson, 1979, 1995b).

5. Advocating increased efforts to achieve. Encouraging others to achieve increases one's own commitment to do so.

6. Mutually influencing each other's reasoning and behavior. Group members actively seek to influence and be influenced by each other. If a member has a better way to complete the task, groupmates usually quickly adopt it.

A : 15

Active Learning: Cooperation In The College Classroom. Edina, MN: Interaction Book Company, 7208 Cornelia Drive, Edina, Minnesota 55435, (612) 831-9500; FAX (612) 831-9332.

7. Engaging in the interpersonal and small group skills needed for effective teamwork.

8. Processing how effectively group members are working together and how the group's effectiveness can be continuously improved.

Negative interdependence typically results in oppositional interaction. **Oppositional interaction** occurs as individuals discourage and obstruct each other's efforts to achieve. Individuals focus both on increasing their own success and on preventing any one else from being more successful than they are. **No interaction** exists when individuals work independently without any interaction or interchange with each other. Individuals focus only on increasing their own success and ignore as irrelevant the efforts of others. Each of these interaction patterns creates different outcomes.

Outcomes Of Social Interdependence

Social interdependence is a generic human phenomenon that has impact on many different outcomes simultaneously. Over the past 95 years, researchers have focused on such diverse dependent variables as individual achievement and retention, group and organizational productivity, higher-level reasoning, moral reasoning, achievement motivation, intrinsic motivation, transfer of training and learning, job satisfaction, interpersonal attraction, social support, interpersonal affection and love, attitudes toward diversity, prejudice, self-esteem, personal causation and locus of control, attributions concerning success and failure, psychological health, social competencies, and many others. These numerous outcomes may be subsumed within three broad categories (Johnson & Johnson, 1989): (1) effort to achieve, (2) positive relationships, and (3) psychological health (see Figure A.1).

If research is to have impact on theory and practice, it must be summarized and communicated in a complete, objective, impartial, and unbiased way. In an age of information explosion, there is considerable danger that theories will be formulated on small and nonrepresentative samples of available knowledge, thereby resulting in fallacious conclusions that in turn lead to mistaken practices. A quantitative reviewing procedure, such as meta-analysis, allows for more definitive and robust conclusions. A **meta-analysis** is a method of statistically combining the results of a set of independent studies that test the same hypothesis and using inferential statistics to draw conclusions about the overall result of the studies. The essential purpose of a meta-analysis is to summarize a set of related research studies, so that the size of the effect of the independent variable on the dependent variable is known.

Effort to Achieve

The investigation of the relative impact of cooperative, competitive, and individualistic efforts on achievement is the longest standing research tradition within American social

Active Learning: Cooperation In The College Classroom. Edina, MN: Interaction Book Company, 7208 Cornelia Drive, Edina, Minnesota 55435, (612) 831-9500; FAX (612) 831-9332.

psychology. Between 1898 and 1989, researchers conducted over 375 experimental studies with over 1,700 findings on social interdependence and productivity and achievement (Johnson & Johnson, 1989). And that does not count the research on social facilitation and other related areas where implicit competition may be found. Since research participants have varied widely as to sex, economic class, age, and cultural background, since a wide variety of research tasks and measures of the dependent variables have been used, and since the research has been conducted by many different researchers with markedly different orientations working in different settings and in different decades, the overall body of research on social interdependence has considerable generalizability.

A meta-analysis of all studies (Johnson & Johnson, 1989) found that the average person cooperating performed at about 2/3 a standard deviation above the average person learning within a competitive (effect size = 0.67) or individualistic situation (effect size = 0.64) (see Table A.1). Not all the research, however, has been carefully conducted. The methodological shortcomings found within many research studies may significantly reduce the certainty of the conclusion that cooperative efforts produce higher achievement than do competitive or individualistic efforts. When only studies with high internal validity were included in the analysis, the effect sizes were 0.88 and 0.61, respectively. Further analyses revealed that the results held constant when group measures of productivity were included as well as individual measures, for short-term as well as long-term studies, and when symbolic as well as tangible rewards were used.

A number of the studies conducted operationally defined cooperation in a way that included elements of competition and individualistic work. The original jigsaw studies, for example, operationalized cooperative learning as a combination of positive resource interdependence and an individualistic reward structure (Aronson, 1978). Teams-Games-Tournaments (TGT; DeVries & Edwards, 1974) and Student-Team-Achievement-Divisions (STAD; Slavin, 1986) operationalized cooperative learning as a combination of ingroup cooperation and intergroup competition, and Team-Assisted-Individualization (TAI; Slavin, 1986) is a mixture of cooperative and individualistic learning. When such "mixed" operationalizations were compared with "pure" operationalizations, the effect-sizes for the cooperative vs. competitive comparison were 0.45 and 0.74 respectively, $t(37) = 1.60$, $p < 0.06$ (Johnson & Johnson, 1989). The effect-sizes for the cooperative vs. individualistic comparisons were 0.13 and 0.61 respectively, $t(10) = 1.64$, $p < 0.07$.

Achievement in cooperative learning groups involves more than the level of learning of its members. It is also important to understand (a) the extent to which members of cooperative learning groups influence each other's achievement and (b) the direction of the influence (students could uniformly achieve higher or lower within a learning group). If group members do influence each other's achievement, their test scores should be quite similar. If little influence occurs, the level of achievement among group members could be dissimilar due to some members doing all the work while other members loaf. Few studies have examined this issue. The current evidence implies that even when students are quite diverse with one member of each group being academically gifted and at least one member of each group being academic handicapped, (a) academic ability is a better

Active Learning: Cooperation In The College Classroom. Edina, MN: Interaction Book Company, 7208 Cornelia Drive, Edina, Minnesota 55435, (612) 831-9500; FAX (612) 831-9332.

predictor of achievement in individualistic than in cooperative learning situations, (b) within cooperative learning groups members influence each other's learning to such an extent that initial differences in achievement level (whether a student is a low, medium, or high achiever) do not determine what the student learns, and (c) since achievement was significantly higher in the cooperative than in the individualistic condition, it may be assumed that members influence each other in ways that raise achievement (Archer-Kath, Johnson, & Johnson, 1994; Smith, Johnson, & Johnson, 1981).

Besides higher achievement and greater retention, cooperation, compared with competitive or individualistic efforts, tends to result in more (Johnson & Johnson, 1989):

1. Willingness to take on difficult tasks and persist, despite difficulties, in working toward goal accomplishment. There is intrinsic motivation, high expectations for success, high incentive to achieve based on mutual benefit, high epistemic curiosity and continuing interest in learning, and high commitment to achieve.

2. Long-term retention of what is learned.

3. Higher-level reasoning, critical thinking, and meta-cognitive thought. The aims of education includes developing individuals "*who can sort sense from nonsense*," or who have the critical thinking abilities of grasping information, examining it, evaluating it for soundness, and applying it appropriately. Cooperative learning promotes a greater use of higher level reasoning strategies and critical thinking than do competitive or individualistic learning strategies. Cooperative learning experiences promote more frequent insight into and use of higher-level cognitive and moral reasoning strategies than do competitive or individualistic learning experiences (effect sizes = 0.93 and 0.97 respectively). Even on writing assignments, students working cooperatively show more higher-level thought.

4. Creative thinking (process gain). **Process gain** occurs when new ideas, solutions, or efforts are generated through group interaction that are not generated when persons work individually. In cooperative groups, members more frequently generate new ideas, strategies, and solutions that they would think of on their own.

5. Transfer of learning from one situation to another (group to individual transfer). **Group-to-individual transfer** occurs when individuals who learned within a cooperative group demonstrate mastery on a subsequent test taken individually. What individuals learn in a group today, they are able to do alone tomorrow.

6. Positive attitudes toward the tasks being completed. Cooperative efforts result in more positive attitudes toward the tasks being completed and greater continuing motivation to complete them. The positive attitudes extend to the work experience and the organization as a whole.

Active Learning: Cooperation In The College Classroom. Edina, MN: Interaction Book Company, 7208 Cornelia Drive, Edina, Minnesota 55435, (612) 831-9500; FAX (612) 831-9332.

7. Time on task. Over 30 studies did in fact measure time on task. They found that cooperators spent more time on task than did competitors (effect size = 0.76) or students working individualistically (effect size = 1.17). Competitors spent more time on task than did students working individualistically (effect size = 0.64). These effect sizes are quite large, indicating that members of cooperative learning groups do seem to spend considerable more time on task than do students working competitively or individualistically.

Since the most credible studies (due to their high-quality methodologically) and the "pure" operationalizations of cooperative learning produced stronger effects, considerable confidence can be placed in the conclusion that cooperative efforts promote more positive cross-ethnic relationships than do competitive or individualistic efforts.

Kurt Lewin often stated, *"I always found myself unable to think as a single person."* Most efforts to achieve are a personal but social process that requires individuals to cooperate and to construct shared understandings and knowledge. Both competitive and individualistic structures, by isolating individuals from each other, tend to depress achievement.

> *The highest and best form of efficiency is the spontaneous cooperation of a free people.*
>
> Woodrow Wilson

Positive Interpersonal Relationships

A faithful friend is a strong defense, and he that hath found him, hath found a treasure.

Ecclesiastics 6:14

Since 1940, over 180 studies have compared the impact of cooperative, competitive, and individualistic efforts on interpersonal attraction (Johnson & Johnson, 1989). Cooperative efforts, compared with competitive and individualistic experiences, promoted considerable more liking among individuals (effect sizes = 0.66 and 0.62 respectively) (see Table 2). The effects sizes were higher for (a) high quality studies and (b) the studies using pure operationalizations of cooperative learning than for studies using mixed operationalizations. The weighted effect sizes for cooperation versus competition and cooperation versus individualistic efforts are 0.65 and 0.64, respectively. When only the methodologically high quality studies are examined, the effect sizes go up to 0.77 and 0.67. "Pure" cooperation results in greater effects than do mixtures of cooperative, competitive, and individualistic efforts (cooperative vs. competitive, pure = 0.75 and mixed = 0.48; cooperative vs. individualistic, pure = 0.67 and mixed = 0.36).

Much of the research on interpersonal relationships has been conducted on relationships between white and minority students and between nonhandicapped and handicapped

Active Learning: Cooperation In The College Classroom. Edina, MN: Interaction Book Company, 7208 Cornelia Drive, Edina, Minnesota 55435, (612) 831-9500; FAX (612) 831-9332.

students (Johnson & Johnson, 1989). There have been over 40 experimental studies comparing some combination of cooperative, competitive, and individualistic experiences on cross-ethnic relationships and over 40 similar studies on mainstreaming of handicapped students (Johnson & Johnson, 1989). Their results are consistent. Working cooperatively creates far more positive relationships among diverse and heterogeneous students than does learning competitively or individualistically.

An extension of social interdependence theory is **social judgment theory** which focuses on relationships among diverse individuals (Johnson & Johnson, 1989). The social judgments individuals make about each other increase or decrease the liking they feel towards each other. Such social judgments are the result of either a process of acceptance or a process of rejection (Johnson & Johnson, 1989). **The process of acceptance** is based on the individuals promoting mutual goal accomplishment as a result of their perceived positive interdependence. The promotive interaction tends to result in frequent, accurate, and open communication; accurate understanding of each other's perspective; inducibility; differentiated, dynamic, and realistic views of each other; high self-esteem; success and productivity; and expectations for positive and productive future interaction. **The process of rejection** results from oppositional or no interaction based on perceptions of negative or no interdependence. Both lead to no or inaccurate communication; egocentrism; resistance to influence; monopolistic, stereotyped, and static views of others; low self-esteem; failure; and expectations of distasteful and unpleasant interaction with others. The processes of acceptance and rejection are self-perpetuating. Any part of the process tends to elicit all the other parts of the process.

The positive relationships among members promoted by cooperative efforts have considerable impact on a wide variety of variables. Generally, the more positive the relationships among group members (i.e., the more cohesive the group), the lower the absenteeism, the fewer the members who drop out of the group, and the more likely students will commit effort to achieve educational goals, feel personally responsibility for learning, take on difficult tasks, be motivated to learn, persist in working toward goal achievement, have high morale, be willing to endure pain and frustration on behalf of learning, listen to and be influenced by classmates and teachers, commit to each other's learning and success, and achieve and produce (Johnson & F. Johnson, 1997).

Positive peer relationships influence the social and cognitive development of students and such attitudes and behaviors as educational aspirations and staying in school (Johnson & Johnson, 1989). Relationships with peers influence what attitudes and values students adopt, whether students become prosocial or antisocial oriented, whether students learn to see situations from a variety of perspectives, the development of autonomy, aspirations for post-secondary education, and whether students learn how to cope with adversity and stress.

Besides liking each other, cooperators give and receive considerable social support, both personally and academically (Johnson & Johnson, 1989). Since the 1940s, over 106 studies comparing the relative impact of cooperative, competitive, and individualistic efforts on social support have been conducted. Social support may be aimed at

Active Learning: Cooperation In The College Classroom. Edina, MN: Interaction Book Company, 7208 Cornelia Drive, Edina, Minnesota 55435, (612) 831-9500; FAX (612) 831-9332.

enhancing another person's success (task-related social support) or at providing support on a more personal level (personal social support). Cooperative experience promoted greater task-oriented and personal social support than did competitive (effect size = 0.62) or individualistic (effect size = 0.70) experiences. Social support tends to promote achievement and productivity, physical health, psychological health, and successful coping with stress and adversity.

Interpersonal relationships are at the heart of communities of practice. Learning communities, for example, are based as much on relationships as they are on intellectual discourse. The more students care about each other and the more committed they are to each other's success, the harder each student will work and the more productive students will be.

Psychological Health

"The reason we were so good, and continued to be so good, was because he (Joe Paterno) forces you to develop an inner love among the players. It is much harder to give up on your buddy, than it is to give up on your coach. I really believe that over the years the teams I played on were almost unbeatable in tight situations. When we needed to get that six inches we got it because of our love for each other. Our camaraderie existed because of the kind of coach and kind of person Joe was."

Dr. David Joyner

Psychological health is the ability to develop, maintain, and appropriately modify interdependent relationships with others to succeed in achieving goals (Johnson & Johnson, 1989). To manage social interdependence, individuals must correctly perceive whether interdependence exists and whether it is positive or negative, be motivated accordingly, and act in ways consistent with normative expectations for appropriate behavior within the situation. Four studies have directly measured the relationship between social interdependence and psychological health. The samples studied included suburban high-school seniors (Johnson & Norem-Heibeisen, 1977), juvenile and adult prisoners (N. James & Johnson, 1983), step-couples (S. James & Johnson, 1988), and Olympic hockey players (Johnson, Johnson, & Krotee, 1986). The results indicated that (a) working cooperatively with peers and valuing cooperation result in greater psychological health than does competing with peers or working independently and (b) cooperative attitudes are highly correlated with a wide variety of indices of psychological health, competitiveness was in some cases positively and in some cases negatively related to psychological health, and individualistic attitudes were negative related to a wide variety of indices of psychological health. Cooperativeness is positively related to a number of indices of psychological health, such as emotional maturity, well-adjusted social relations, strong personal identity, ability to cope with adversity, social competencies, and basic trust in and optimism about people. Personal ego-strength, self-confidence, independence, and autonomy are all promoted by being involved in cooperative efforts. Individualistic attitudes tend to be related to a number of indices of psychological pathology, such as emotional immaturity, social maladjustment,

Active Learning: Cooperation In The College Classroom. Edina, MN: Interaction Book Company, 7208 Cornelia Drive, Edina, Minnesota 55435, (612) 831-9500; FAX (612) 831-9332.

delinquency, self-alienation, and self-rejection. Competitiveness is related to a mixture of healthy and unhealthy characteristics. Whereas inappropriate competitive and individualistic attitudes and efforts have resulted in alienating individuals from others, healthy and therapeutic growth depends on increasing individuals' understanding of how to cooperate more effectively with others. Cooperative experiences are not a luxury. They are absolutely necessary for healthy development.

Social interdependence theory has been extended to self-esteem. A **process of self-acceptance** is posited to be based on (a) internalizing perceptions that one is known, accepted, and liked as one is, (b) internalizing mutual success, and (c) evaluating oneself favorably in comparison with peers. A process of self-rejection may occur from (a) not wanting to be known, (b) low performance, (c) overgeneralization of self-evaluations, and (d) the disapproval of others. Since the 1950s, there have been over 80 studies comparing the relative impact of cooperative, competitive, and individualistic experiences on self-esteem (Johnson & Johnson, 1989). Cooperative experiences promote higher self-esteem than do competitive (effect size = 0.58) or individualistic (effect-size = 0.44) experiences. Our research demonstrated that cooperative experiences tend to be related to beliefs that one is intrinsically worthwhile, others see one in positive ways, one's attributes compare favorably with those of one's peers, and one is a capable, competent, and successful person. In cooperative efforts, students (a) realize that they are accurately known, accepted, and liked by one's peers, (b) know that they have contributed to own, others, and group success, and (c) perceive themselves and others in a differentiated and realistic way that allows for multidimensional comparisons based on complementarity of own and others' abilities. Competitive experiences tend to be related to conditional self-esteem based on whether one wins or loses. Individualistic experiences tend to be related to basic self-rejection.

A number of studies have related cooperative, competitive, and individualistic experiences to perspective-taking ability (the ability to understand how a situation appears to other people) (Johnson & Johnson, 1989). Cooperative experiences tend to increase perspective-taking ability while competitive and individualistic experiences tend to promote egocentrism (being unaware of other perspectives other than your own) (effect sizes of 0.61 and 0.44 respectively). Individuals, furthermore, who are part of a cooperative effort learn more social skills and become more socially competent than do persons competing or working individualistically. Finally, it is through cooperative efforts that many of the attitudes and values essential to psychological health (such as self-efficacy) and learned and adopted.

An important aspect of psychological health is social competence. **Social skills and competencies tend to increase more within cooperative than in competitive or individualistic situations** (Johnson & Johnson, 1989). Working together to get the job done increases students' abilities to provide leadership, build and maintain trust, communicate effectively, and manage conflicts constructively. Employability and career success depend largely on such social skills. Most modern work occurs within teams. Intelligence and technical expertise are of no use if individuals are not skillful group members. The social skills learned within cooperative learning groups, furthermore,

Active Learning: Cooperation In The College Classroom. Edina, MN: Interaction Book Company, 7208 Cornelia Drive, Edina, Minnesota 55435, (612) 831-9500; FAX (612) 831-9332.

provide the basis for building and maintaining life-long friendships, loving and caring families, and cohesive neighborhoods.

Reciprocal Relationships Among The Three Outcomes

"The reason we were so good, and continued to be so good, was because he (Joe Paterno) forces you to develop an inner love among the players. It is much harder to give up on your buddy, than it is to give up on your coach. I really believe that over the years the teams I played on were almost unbeatable in tight situations. When we needed to get that six inches we got it because of our love for each other. Our camaraderie existed because of the kind of coach and kind of person Joe was."

David Joyner

Each of the outcomes of cooperative efforts (effort to achieve, quality of relationships, and psychological health) influences the others and, therefore, they are likely to be found together (Johnson & Johnson, 1989). **First**, caring and committed friendships come from a sense of mutual accomplishment, mutual pride in joint work, and the bonding that results from joint efforts. The more individuals care about each other, on the other hand, the harder they will work to achieve mutual goals. **Second**, joint efforts to achieve mutual goals promote higher self-esteem, self-efficacy, personal control, and confidence in one's competencies. The healthier psychologically individuals are, on the other hand, the better able they are to work with others to achieve mutual goals. **Third**, psychological health is built on the internalization of the caring and respect received from loved-ones. Friendships are developmental advantages that promote self-esteem, self-efficacy, and general psychological adjustment. The healthier people are psychologically (i.e., free of psychological pathology such as depression, paranoia, anxiety, fear of failure, repressed anger, hopelessness, and meaninglessness), on the other hand, the more caring and committed their relationships. Since each outcome can induce the others, you are likely to find them together. They are a package with each outcome a door into all three. Together they induce positive interdependence and promotive interaction.

Competitive And Individualistic Efforts

The basic social psychological query is, "*Under what conditions are cooperative, competitive, and individualistic efforts effective?*" The hundreds of studies that have been conducted to try to answer this question indicated that under most conditions, cooperation has more powerful effects on the variables studied than do competitive or individualistic efforts. Under most conditions, cooperative efforts are more effective than are competitive and individualistic efforts. There is some evidence that on very simple, overlearned, repetitive motor tasks, competition may produce higher achievement than does cooperation (Johnson & Johnson, 1989). It is unclear whether individualistic efforts have any advantage over cooperative efforts. There is considerable more research needed to clarify the conditions under which competitive or individualistic efforts may have more powerful effects than cooperation.

A : 23

Active Learning: Cooperation In The College Classroom. Edina, MN: Interaction Book Company, 7208 Cornelia Drive, Edina, Minnesota 55435, (612) 831-9500; FAX (612) 831-9332.

Mediators: The Basic Elements Of Cooperation

The truly committed cooperative learning group is probably the most productive tool humans have. Creating and maintaining truly committed cooperative groups, however, are far from easy. Not every group is effective. Almost everyone has been part of a group that wasted time, was inefficient, and generally produced poor work. In most situations cooperative groups are rare, perhaps because many individuals (a) are confused about what is (and is not) a cooperative group and (b) lack the discipline required to implement the basics of cooperative efforts in a rigorous way in every lesson.

Individuals fool themselves if they think well-meaning directives *to "work together," "cooperate,"* and *"be a team,"* will be enough to create cooperative efforts among members. **There is a discipline to creating cooperation.** Making teams work is like being on a diet. It does no good to diet one or two days a week. If you wish to lose weight, you have to control what you eat every day. Similarly, it does no good to structure a team carefully every fourth or fifth meeting. The basic elements are a regimen that, if followed rigorously, will produce the conditions for effective cooperation. **The basic components of effective cooperative efforts are** positive interdependence, face-to-face promotive interaction, individual and group accountability, appropriate use of social skills, and group processing.

Positive Interdependence: We Instead Of Me

All for one and one for all.

Alexandre Dumas

Within a football game, the quarterback who throws the pass and the receiver who catches the pass are positively interdependent. The success of one depends on the success of the other. It takes two to complete a pass. One player cannot succeed without the other. Both have to perform competently to assure their mutual success. If one fails, they both fail.

Positive interdependence exists when one perceives that one is linked with others in a way so that one cannot succeed unless they do (and vice versa) and/or that one must coordinate one's efforts with the efforts of others to complete a task (Johnson & Johnson, 1989). The discipline of using cooperative groups begins with structuring positive interdependence. Group members have to know that they "*sink or swim together,*" that is, they have two responsibilities: to maximize their own productivity and to maximize the productivity of all other group members. There are two major categories of interdependence: outcome interdependence and means interdependence (Johnson & Johnson, 1989). When persons are in a cooperative or competitive situation, they are oriented toward a desired outcome, end state, goal, or reward. If there is no outcome interdependence (goal and reward interdependence), there is no cooperation or competition. In addition, the means through which the mutual goals or rewards are to be

Active Learning: Cooperation In The College Classroom. Edina, MN: Interaction Book Company, 7208 Cornelia Drive, Edina, Minnesota 55435, (612) 831-9500; FAX (612) 831-9332.

accomplish specify the actions required on the part of group members. Means interdependence includes resource, role, and task interdependence (which are overlapping and not independent from each other).

Positive interdependence has numerous effects on individuals' motivation and productivity, not the least of which is to highlight the fact that the efforts of all group members are needed for group success. When members of a group see their efforts as dispensable for the group's success, they may reduce their efforts (Kerr, 1983; Kerr & Bruun, 1983; Sweeney, 1973). When group members perceive their potential contribution to the group as being unique, they increase their efforts (Harkins & Petty, 1982). When goal, task, resource, and role interdependence are clearly understood, individuals realize that their efforts are required in order for the group to succeed (i.e., there can be no "free-riders") and that their contributions are often unique. In addition, reward interdependence needs to be structured to ensure that one member's efforts do not make the efforts of other members unnecessary. If the highest score in the group determined the group grade, for example, low-ability members might see their efforts as unnecessary and contribute minimally, and high ability members might feel exploited and become demoralized and, therefore, decrease their efforts so as not to provide undeserved rewards for irresponsible and ungrateful "free-riders" (Kerr, 1983).

A series of research studies was conducted to clarify the impact of positive interdependence on achievement. The results indicated the following:

1. Group membership in and of itself does not seem sufficient to produce higher achievement and productivity--positive interdependence is also required (Hwong, Casswell, Johnson, & Johnson, 1993). Knowing that one's performance affects the success of groupmates seems to create "responsibility forces" that increase one's efforts to achieve.

2. Interpersonal interaction is insufficient to increase productivity--positive interdependence is required (Lew, Mesch, Johnson, & Johnson, 1986a, 1986b; Mesch, Johnson, & Johnson, 1988; Mesch, Lew, Johnson, & Johnson, 1986). Individuals achieved higher under positive goal interdependence than when they worked individualistically but had the opportunity to interact with classmates.

3. Goal and reward interdependence seem to be additive (Lew, Mesch, Johnson, & Johnson, 1986a, 1986b; Mesch, Johnson, & Johnson, 1988; Mesch, Lew, Johnson, & Johnson, 1986). While positive goal interdependence is sufficient to produce higher achievement and productivity than do individualistic efforts, the combination of goal and reward interdependence is even more effective.

4. Both working to achieve a reward and working to avoid the loss of a reward produced higher achievement than did individualistic efforts (Frank, 1984). There is no significant difference between the working to achieve a reward and working to avoid a loss.

Active Learning: Cooperation In The College Classroom. Edina, MN: Interaction Book Company, 7208 Cornelia Drive, Edina, Minnesota 55435, (612) 831-9500; FAX (612) 831-9332.

5. Goal interdependence promotes higher achievement and greater productivity than does resource interdependence (Johnson, Johnson, Ortiz, & Stanne, 1991).

6. Resource interdependence by itself may decrease achievement and productivity compared with individualistic efforts (Johnson, Johnson, Stanne, & Garibaldi, 1990; Ortiz, Johnson, & Johnson, 1995).

7. The combination of goal and resource interdependence increased achievement than goal interdependence alone or individualistic efforts (Johnson, Johnson, Stanne, & Garibaldi, 1990; Ortiz, Johnson, & Johnson, 1995).

8. Positive interdependence does more than simply motivate individuals to try harder, it facilitates the development of new insights and discoveries through promotive interaction (Gabbert, Johnson, & Johnson, 1986; D. Johnson & Johnson, 1981; D. Johnson, Skon, & Johnson, 1980; Skon, Johnson, & Johnson, 1981). Members of cooperative groups use higher level reasoning strategies more frequently than do individuals working individualistically or competitively.

9. The more complex the procedures involved in interdependence, the longer it will take group members to reach their full levels of productivity (Ortiz, Johnson, & Johnson, 1995). The more complex the teamwork procedures, the more members have to attend to teamwork and the less time they have to attend to taskwork. Once the teamwork procedures are mastered, however, members concentrate on taskwork and outperform individuals working alone.

Positive interdependence is the defining nature of cooperation. If there is no positive interdependence, no cooperative exists.

Individual Accountability / Personal Responsibility

After positive interdependence, a key variable mediating the effectiveness of cooperation is a sense of personal responsibility for contributing one's efforts to accomplish the group's goals. This involves being responsible for (1) completing one's share of the work and (2) facilitating the work of other group members and minimally hindering their efforts. Personal responsibility is promoted by individual accountability. Certainly lack of individual accountability reduces feelings of personal responsibility. Members will reduce their contributions to goal achievement when the group works on tasks where it is difficult to identify members' contributions, when there is an increased likelihood of redundant efforts, when there is a lack of group cohesiveness, and when there is lessened responsibility for the final outcome (Harkins & Petty, 1982; Ingham, Levinger, Graves, & Peckham, 1974; Kerr & Bruun, 1981; Latane, Williams & Harkins, 1979; Moede, 1927; Petty, Harkins, Williams, & Lantane, 1977; Williams, 1981; Williams, Harkins, & Latane, 1981). If, however, there is high individual accountability and it is clear how much effort each member is contributing, if redundant efforts are avoided, if every member is responsible for the final outcome, and if the group is cohesive, then the social loafing effect vanishes. The smaller the size of the group, in addition, the greater the individual accountability may be (Messich & Brewer, 1983).

Archer-Kath, Johnson, and Johnson (1994) investigated was whether or not positive interdependence and individual accountability are two separate and independent dimensions. They compared the impact of feedback to the learning group as a whole with the individual feedback to each member on achievement, attitudes, and behavior in cooperative learning groups. Students received either individual or group feedback in written graph/chart form only on how frequently members engaged in the targeted behaviors. If individual accountability and positive interdependence are unrelated, no differences should be found in perceived positive interdependence between conditions. If they are related, students in the individual feedback condition should perceive more positive interdependence than students in the group feedback condition. Individual feedback resulted in greater perceptions of cooperation, goal interdependence, and resource interdependence than did group feedback, indicating that positive interdependence and individual accountability are related and by increasing individual accountability perceived interdependence among group members may also be increased.

The results of these studies indicated that individual accountability does increase the effectiveness of a group by ensuring that all members achieve and contribute to the achievement of their groupmates.

Promotive (Face-To-Face) Interaction

Promotive interaction may be defined as individuals encouraging and facilitating each other's efforts to complete tasks and achieve in order to reach the group's goals. Promotive interaction is characterized by students (a) providing other with efficient and effective help and assistance, (b) exchanging needed resources such as information and materials and processing information more efficiently and effectively, (c) providing each other with feedback in order to improve their subsequent performance on assigned tasks and responsibilities, (d) challenging each other's conclusions and reasoning in order to promote higher quality decision making and greater insight into the problems being considered, (e) advocating exerting efforts to achieve mutual goals, (f) influencing each other's efforts to achieve mutual goals, (g) acting in trusting and trustworthy ways, (h) being motivated to strive for mutual benefit, and (i) feeling less anxiety and stress (Johnson & Johnson, 1989). The amount of research documenting the impact of promotive interaction on achievement is too voluminous to review here. Interested readers are referred to Johnson and Johnson (1989).

Social Skills

Placing socially unskilled students in a learning group and telling them to cooperate will obviously not be successful. Students must be taught the interpersonal and small group skills needed for high quality cooperation, and be motivated to use them. To coordinate efforts to achieve mutual goals students must (1) get to know and trust each other, (2)

A : 27

Active Learning: Cooperation In The College Classroom. Edina, MN: Interaction Book Company, 7208 Cornelia Drive, Edina, Minnesota 55435, (612) 831-9500; FAX (612) 831-9332.

communicate accurately and unambiguously, (3) accept and support each other, and (4) resolve conflicts constructively (Johnson, 1997; Johnson & F. Johnson, 1997). Interpersonal and small group skills form the basic nexus among individuals, and if individuals are to work together productively and cope with the stresses and strains of doing so, they must have a modicum of these skills. Students need to master and use interpersonal and small group skills to capitalize on the opportunities presented by a cooperative learning situation. Especially when learning groups function on a long-term basis and engage in complex, free exploratory activities over a prolonged period, the interpersonal and small group skills of the members may determine the level of members' achievement and productivity.

In their studies on the long-term implementation of cooperation learning, Marvin Lew and Debra Mesch (Lew, Mesch, Johnson, & Johnson, 1986a, 1986b; Mesch, Johnson, & Johnson, 1993; Mesch, Lew, Johnson, & Johnson, 1986) investigated the impact of a reward contingency for using social skills as well as positive interdependence and a contingency for academic achievement on performance within cooperative learning groups. In the cooperative skills conditions students were trained weekly in four social skills and each member of a cooperative group was given two bonus points toward the quiz grade if all group members were observed by the teacher to demonstrate three out of four cooperative skills. The results indicated that the combination of positive goal interdependence, an academic contingency for high performance by all group members, and a social skills contingency, promoted the highest achievement. Archer-Kath, Johnson, and Johnson (1994) trained students in the social skills of praising, supporting, asking for information, giving information, asking for help, and giving help. Students received either individual or group feedback in written graph/chart form on how frequently members engaged in the targeted behaviors. The researchers found that giving students individual feedback on how frequently they engaged in targeted social skills was more effective in increasing students' achievement than was group feedback. The more socially skillful students are, the more attention teachers pay to teaching and rewarding the use of social skills, and the more individual feedback students receive on their use of the skills, the higher the achievement that can be expected within cooperative learning groups.

Not only do social skills promote higher achievement, they contribute to building more positive relationships among group members. Putnam, Rynders, Johnson, and Johnson (1989) demonstrated that, when students were taught social skills, observed by the teacher, and given individual feedback as to how frequently they engaged in the skills, their relationships became more positive.

Group Processing

In order to achieve, students in cooperative learning groups have to work together effectively. Effective group work is influenced by whether or not groups periodically reflect on how well they are functioning and plan how to improve their work processes. A **process** is an identifiable sequence of events taking place over time, and **process goals** refer to the sequence of events instrumental in achieving outcome goals. **Group**

Active Learning: Cooperation In The College Classroom. Edina, MN: Interaction Book Company, 7208 Cornelia Drive, Edina, Minnesota 55435, (612) 831-9500; FAX (612) 831-9332.

processing may be defined as reflecting on a group session to (a) describe what member actions were helpful and unhelpful and (b) make decisions about what actions to continue or change. The purpose of group processing is to clarify and improve the effectiveness of the members in contributing to the joint efforts to achieve the group's goals.

Yager, Johnson, and Johnson (1985) examined the impact on achievement of (a) cooperative learning in which members discussed how well their group was functioning and how they could improve its effectiveness, (b) cooperative learning without any group processing, and (c) individualistic learning. The results indicate that the high-, medium-, and low-achieving students in the cooperation with group processing condition achieved higher on daily achievement, post-instructional achievement, and retention measures than did the students in the other two conditions. Students in the cooperation without group processing condition, furthermore, achieved higher on all three measures than did the students in the individualistic condition.

Putnam, Rynders, Johnson, and Johnson (1989) conducted a study in which there were two conditions: cooperative learning with social skills training and group processing and cooperative learning without social skills training and group processing. Forty-eight fifth-grade students (32 nonhandicapped and 16 students with IQ's ranging from 35 to 52 students) participated in the study. In the cooperative learning with social skills training condition the teacher gave students examples of specific cooperative behaviors to engage in, observed how frequently students engaged in the skills, gave students feedback as to how well they worked together, and had students discuss for five minutes how to use the skills more effectively in the future. In the uninstructed cooperative groups condition students were placed in cooperative groups and worked together for the same period of time with the same amount of teacher intervention (aimed at the academic lesson and unrelated to working together skillfully). Both nonhandicapped and handicapped students were randomly assigned to each condition. They found more positive relationships developed between handicapped and nonhandicapped students in the cooperative skills condition and that these positive relationships carried over to post-instructional free-time situations.

Johnson, Johnson, Stanne, and Garibaldi (1990) conducted a study comparing cooperative learning with no processing, cooperative learning with teacher processing (teacher specified cooperative skills to use, observed, and gave whole class feedback as to how well students were using the skills), cooperative learning with teacher and student processing (the teacher specified cooperative skills to use, observed, gave whole class feedback as to how well students were using the skills, and had learning groups discuss how well they interacted as a group), and individualistic learning. Forty-nine high ability high Black American school seniors and entering college freshmen at Xavier University participated in the study. A complex computer-assisted problem-solving assignment was given to all students. All three cooperative conditions performed higher than did the individualistic condition. The combination of teacher and student processing resulted in greater problem solving success than did the other cooperative conditions.

Active Learning: Cooperation In The College Classroom. Edina, MN: Interaction Book Company, 7208 Cornelia Drive, Edina, Minnesota 55435, (612) 831-9500; FAX (612) 831-9332.

Archer-Kath, Johnson, and Johnson (1994) provided learning groups with either individual or group feedback on how frequently members had engaged in targeted social skills. Each group had five minutes at the beginning of each session to discuss how well the group was functioning and what could be done to improve the group's effectiveness. Group processing with individual feedback was more effective than was group processing with whole group feedback in increasing students' (a) achievement motivation, actual achievement, uniformity of achievement among group members, and influence toward higher achievement within cooperative learning groups, (b) positive relationships among group members and between students and the teacher, and (c) self-esteem and positive attitudes toward the subject area.

The results of these studies indicated that engaging in group processing clarifies and improves the effectiveness of the members in contributing to the joint efforts to achieve the group's goals, especially when specific social skills are targeted and students receive individual feedback as to how frequently and how well they engaged in the skills.

Summary

There is nothing magical about telling individuals to work together as a team. The basic elements must be vigilantly structured into every group session. They (positive interdependence, individual accountability, promotive interaction, appropriate use of social skills, and group processing) are a regimen that, if followed rigorously, will produce the conditions for effective cooperation.

Enhancing Variables: Trust And Conflict

During the 1950s and 1960s, Deutsch (1962, 1973) researched two aspects of the internal dynamics of cooperative groups that potentially enhanced outcomes: trust and conflict. The greater the trust among group members, the more effective their cooperative efforts tend to be (Deutsch, 1962; Johnson, 1997; Johnson & Noonan, 1972).

Conflict within cooperative groups, when managed constructively, enhances the effectiveness of cooperative efforts. There are two types of conflict that occur frequently and regularly within cooperative groups--controversy and conflicts of interests (Johnson & Johnson, 1995a, 1995b). **Controversy** exists when group members have different information, perceptions, opinions, reasoning processes, theories, and conclusions, and they must reach agreement (Johnson & Johnson, 1979, 1995c). Compared with concurrence-seeking, debate, and individualistic efforts, controversy results in greater mastery and retention of the subject matter, higher quality problem solving, greater creativity in thinking, greater motivation to learn more about the topic, more productive exchange of expertise among group members, greater task involvement, more positive relationships among group members, more accurate perspective taking, and higher self-esteem. In addition, students enjoy it more. Controversies tend to be constructive when the situational context is cooperative, group members are heterogeneous, information and

Active Learning: Cooperation In The College Classroom. Edina, MN: Interaction Book Company, 7208 Cornelia Drive, Edina, Minnesota 55435, (612) 831-9500; FAX (612) 831-9332.

expertise is distributed within the group, members have the necessary conflict skills, and the canons of rational argumentation are followed.

A **conflict of interests** occurs when the actions of one person striving to achieve his or her goal interfere with and obstruct the actions of another person striving to achieve his or her goal (Johnson & Johnson, 1995a, 1995b, 1996). Cooperative efforts tend to be more effective when group members (a) negotiate integrative agreements to resolve their conflicts of interests and (b) mediate the conflicts among their groupmates. What results is more constructive resolution of conflicts, fewer discipline problems, less teacher and administrator time spent in arbitrating student conflicts, and higher academic achievement. By teaching students integrative negotiation and peer mediation procedures, colleges may not only enhance the quality and effectiveness of cooperative efforts, they also empower students to regulate their own behavior.

Other Variables Of Interest To College Faculty

Attitudes Toward Subject Area And College Experience

Cooperative learning experiences, compared with competitive and individualistic ones, promote more positive attitudes toward the subject area, more positive attitudes toward the instructional experience, and more continuing motivation to learn more about the subject area being studied (Johnson & Johnson, 1989). Guetzkow, Kelley, and McKeachie (1954) and McKeachie (1951) found in a study comparing group discussion and lecturing that students in discussion sections were significantly more favorable than the other groups in attitude toward psychology and a follow-up of the students three years later revealed that seven men each from the tutorial and discussion groups majored in psychology, whereas none of those in the recitation group did so. Bligh (1972) found that students who had in-class opportunities to interact actively with classmates and the teacher were more satisfied with their learning experience than were students who were taught exclusively by the lecture method. Kulik and Kulik (1979) reported from their comprehensive literature review on college teaching that students who participated in discussion groups in class were more likely to develop positive attitudes toward the course's subject matter. One of the major conclusions of the Harvard Assessment Seminars was that the use of cooperative learning groups resulted in a large increase in satisfaction with the class (Light, 1990). These findings have important implications for influencing female and minority students to enter science and math oriented careers.

Student Retention

> ... instructors should give greater attention to the passive or reticent student...Passivity is an important warning sign that may reflect a lack of involvement that impedes the learning process and leads to unnecessary attrition.
>
> National Institute of Education (1984)

A : 31

Active Learning: Cooperation In The College Classroom. Edina, MN: Interaction Book Company, 7208 Cornelia Drive, Edina, Minnesota 55435, (612) 831-9500; FAX (612) 831-9332.

Tinto (1975, 1987), synthesizing the retention research, concluded that the greater the degree of students' involvement in their learning experience, the more likely they were to persist to graduation. The social-networking processes of social involvement, integration, and bonding with classmates are strongly related with higher rates of student retention. Astin (1985), on the basis of research conducted over 10 years, found that student involvement academically and socially in the school experience was the "cornerstone" of persistence and achievement. Astin and his associates (1972) had earlier concluded that active involvement in the learning experience was especially critical for "withdrawal-prone" students, such as disadvantaged minorities, who have been found to be particularly passive in academic settings.

Cooperative learning experiences tend to lower attrition rates in schools. Students working on open-ended problems in small groups of four to seven members were more likely to display lower rates of attrition and higher rates of academic achievement than those not involved in the group learning approach (Wales & Stager, 1978). Treisman (1985) found that the five-year retention rate for black students majoring in math or science at Berkeley who were involved in cooperative learning was 65 percent (compared to 41 percent for black students not involved). The percentage of black students involved in cooperative learning experiences who graduated in mathematics-based majors was 44 percent (compared to only 10 percent for a control group of black students not participating in cooperative learning groups).

College students report greater satisfaction with courses that allow them to engage in group discussion (Bligh, 1972; Kulik & Kulik, 1979). Students are more likely to stay in school if they are satisfied with their learning experiences (Noel, 1985). Cooperative learning allows for significant amounts of meaningful student discussion that enhances students' satisfaction with the learning experience and, in so doing, promotes student retention.

Reducing The Discrepancy

The research results consistently indicate that cooperative learning will promote higher achievement, more positive interpersonal relationships, and greater psychological health than will competitive or individualistic efforts. With the amount of research evidence available, it is surprising that classroom practice is so oriented toward competitive and individualistic learning and colleges are so dominated by competitive and individualistic organizational structures. **It is time for the discrepancy to be reduced between what the research indicates is effective in teaching and what faculty actually do.**

A : 32

Active Learning: Cooperation In The College Classroom. Edina, MN: Interaction Book Company, 7208 Cornelia Drive, Edina, Minnesota 55435, (612) 831-9500; FAX (612) 831-9332.

Glossary

Ad hoc decision-making groups: Faculty members listen to a recommendation, are assigned to small groups, meet to consider the recommendation, report to the entire faculty their decision, and then participate in a whole-faculty decision as to what the course of action should be.

Additive tasks: Tasks for which group productivity represents the sum of individual member efforts.

Arbitration: The submission of a dispute to a disinterested third person who makes a final judgment as to how the conflict will be resolved. A form of third-party intervention in negotiations in which recommendations of the person intervening are binding on the parties involved.

Authentic assessment: Requiring students to demonstrate the desired procedure or skill in a "real life" context.

Base group: A long-term, heterogeneous cooperative learning group with stable membership whose primary purpose is for members to give each other the support, help, encouragement, and assistance each needs to progress academically.

Benchmarking: Establishing operating targets based on best known practices.

Bumping: A procedure used to ensure that competitors are evenly matched. It involves (a) ranking the competitive triads from the highest (the three highest achievers are members) to the lowest (the three lowest achievers are members), (b) moving the winner in each triad up to the next highest triad, and (c) moving the loser down to the next lowest triad.

Cohesiveness: All the forces (both positive and negative) that cause individuals to maintain their membership in specific groups. These include attraction to other group members and a close match between individuals' needs and the goals and activities of the group. The attractiveness that a group has for its members and that the members have for one another.

Colleagial teaching teams: Small cooperative groups (from two to five faculty members) whose purpose is to increase instructors' instructional expertise and success.

College-based decision-making: Task force considers a college problem and proposes a solution to the faculty as a whole, small ad-hoc decision making groups consider the proposal, the entire faculty decides what to do, the decision is implemented by the faculty, and the task force assesses whether or not the problem is solved.

Communication: A message sent by a person to a receiver(s) with the conscious intent of affecting the receiver's behavior. The exchange of thoughts and feelings through symbols that represent approximately the same conceptual experience for everyone involved.

Communication networks: Representations of the acceptable paths of communication between persons in a group or organization.

Competition: A social situation in which the goals of the separate participants are so linked that there is a negative correlation among their goal attainments; when one student achieves his or her goal, all others with whom he or she is competitively linked fail to achieve their goals.

G : 1

Active Learning: Cooperation In The College Classroom, Interaction Book Company, 7208 Cornelia Drive, Edina, MN 55435, (612) 831-9500, FAX (612) 831-9332

Competitive learning: The focusing of student effort on performing faster and more accurately than classmates.

Compliance: Behavior in accordance with a direct request. Behavioral change without internal acceptance.

Conceptual/adaptive approaches to cooperative learning: Instructors are trained in how to use a general conceptual framework to plan and tailor cooperative learning lessons specifically for their students, circumstances, curricula, and needs.

Conceptual conflict: When incompatible ideas exist simultaneously in a person's mind.

Conflict-of-interests: When the actions of one person attempting to maximize his or her needs and benefits prevent, block, interfere with, injure, or in some way make less effective the actions of another person attempting to maximize his or her needs and benefits.

Conjunctive tasks: Tasks for which group productivity is determined by the effort or ability of the weakest member.

Consensus: A collective opinion arrived at by a group of individuals working together under conditions that permit communications to be sufficiently open and the group climate to be sufficiently supportive for everyone in the group to feel that he or she has had a fair chance to influence the decision.

Continuous improvement: Ongoing search for changes that will increase the quality of the processes of learning, instructing, and assessing.

Controversy: When one person's ideas, information, conclusions, theories, and opinions are incompatible with those of another, and the two seek to reach an agreement.

Cooperation: Working together to accomplish shared goals and maximize own and other's success. Individuals perceiving that they can reach their goals if and only if the other group members also do so.

Cooperation imperative: We desire and seek out opportunities to operate jointly with others to achieve mutual goals.

Cooperative learning: Students working together to accomplish shared learning goals and maximize their own and their groupmates' achievement.

Cooperative learning scripts/structures: Standard content-free cooperative procedures for either conducting generic, repetitive lessons or managing classroom routines that proscribe students actions step-by-step.

Cooperative college: Team-based, high-performance organizational structure specifically applied to colleges, characterized by cooperative learning in the classroom, colleagial teaching teams and college-based decision making.

Decision making: Obtaining some agreement among group members as to which of several courses of action is most desirable for achieving the group's goals. The process through which groups identify problems in achieving the group's goals and attain solutions to them.

Delusion of individualism: Believing that (1) they are separate and apart from all other individuals and, therefore, (2) others' frustration, unhappiness, hunger, despair, and misery have no significant bearing on their own well-being.

Active Learning: Cooperation In The College Classroom, Interaction Book Company, 7208 Cornelia Drive, Edina, MN 55435, (612) 831-9500, FAX (612) 831-9332

Deutsch, Morton: Social psychologist who theorized about cooperative, competitive, and individualistic goal structures.

Direct/prescriptive approach to cooperative learning: Instructors are trained to use prepackaged lessons, curricula, strategies, and activities in a lock-step prescribed manner (step 1, step 2, step 3).

Disjunctive tasks: Tasks for which group performance is determined by the most competent or skilled member.

Distributed-actions theory of leadership: The performance of acts that help the group to complete its task and to maintain effective working relationships among its members.

Divisible task: Can be divided into subtasks that can be assigned to different people.

Effective communication: When the receiver interprets the sender's message in the same way the sender intended it.

Egocentrism: Embeddedness in one's own viewpoint to the extent that one is unaware of other points of view and of the limitations of one's perspectives.

Expert system: An understanding of a conceptual system that is used to engineer effective applications in the real world.

Expertise: A person's proficiency, adroitness, competence, and skill.

Feedback: Information that allows individuals to compare their actual performance with standards of performance.

Fermenting skills: Skills needed to engage in ^academic controversies^ to stimulate reconceptualization of the material being studied, cognitive conflict, the search for more information, and the communication of the rationale behind one's conclusions.

Forming skills: Management skills directed toward organizing the group and establishing minimum norms for appropriate behavior.

Formulating skills: Skills directed toward providing the mental processes needed to build deeper level understanding of the material being studied, to stimulate the use of higher quality reasoning strategies, and to maximize mastery and retention of the assigned material.

Functioning skills: Skills directed toward managing the group's efforts to complete their tasks and maintain effective working relationships among members.

Formal cooperative learning: Cooperative groups that last from one class period to several weeks to complete any academic assignment or course requirement (such as solving a set of problems, completing a unit, writing a theme or report, conducting an experiment, or reading and comprehending a story, play, poem, chapter, or book). It ensures that students are actively involved in the intellectual work of organizing material, explaining it, summarizing it, and integrating it into existing conceptual structures.

Goal: A desired place toward which people are working, a state of affairs that people value.

Goal structure: The type of social interdependence structured among students as they strive to accomplish their learning goals.

Active Learning: Cooperation In The College Classroom, Interaction Book Company, 7208 Cornelia Drive, Edina, MN 55435, (612) 831-9500, FAX (612) 831-9332

Group: Two or more individuals in face-to-face interaction, each aware of his or her membership in the group, each aware of the others who belong to the group, and each aware of their positive interdependence as they strive to achieve mutual goals.

Group accountability: The overall performance of the group is assessed and the results are given back to all group members to compare against a standard of performance.

Group processing: Reflecting on a group session to (a) describe what member actions were helpful and unhelpful and (b) make decisions about what actions to continue or change.

Horizontal teams: A number of instructors from the same grade level or subject area are given responsibility for a number of students for one year or one semester.

Individual accountability: The measurement of whether or not each group member has achieved the group's goal. Assessing the quality and quantity of each member's contributions and giving the results to all group members.

Individualistic goal structure: No correlation among group members' goal attainments; when group members perceive that obtaining their goal is unrelated to the goal achievement of other members. Individuals working by themselves to accomplish goals unrelated to and independent from the goals of others.

Individualistic learning: Individuals working by themselves to ensure their own learning meets a preset criterion independently from the efforts of other students.

Informal cooperative learning: The use of temporary, ad hoc discussion groups that last for only one discussion or one class period, whose purposes are to (a) focus student attention on the material to be learned, (b) create an expectation set and mood conductive to learning, (c) help organize in advance the material to be covered in a class session, (d) ensure that students cognitively process the material being taught, and (e) provide closure to an instructional session.

Jigsaw: The work of a group is divided into separate parts that are completed by different members and taught to their groupmates.

Lewin, Kurt: Father of group dynamics; social psychologist who originated field theory, experimental group dynamics, and applied group dynamics.

Maximizing task: Success is determined by quantity of performance.

Means interdependence: The actions required on the part of group members to achieve their mutual goals and rewards. There are three types of means interdependence: resource, task, and role.

Mediation: When a third person intervenes to help resolve a conflict between two or more people. A form of third-party intervention in negotiations in which a neutral person recommends a nonbinding agreement.

Motivation: A combination of the perceived likelihood of success and the perceived incentive for success. The greater the likelihood of success and the more important it is to succeed, the higher the motivation.

Negotiation: A process by which persons with shared and opposing interests who want to come to an agreement try to work out a settlement by exchanging proposals and counterproposals.

Norms: The rules or expectations that specify appropriate behavior in the group; the standards by which group members regulate their actions.

Active Learning: Cooperation In The College Classroom, Interaction Book Company, 7208 Cornelia Drive, Edina, MN 55435, (612) 831-9500, FAX (612) 831-9332

Optimizing task: Success is determined by quality of performance; a good performance is one that most closely approximates the optimum performance.

Outcome interdependence: When the goals and rewards directing individuals' actions are positively correlated, that is, if one person accomplishes his or her goal or receives a reward, all others with whom the person is cooperatively linked also achieve their goals or receive a reward. Learning goals may be actual, based on involvement in a fantasy situation, or based on overcoming an outside threat.

Performance-based assessment: Requiring students to demonstrate what they can do with what they know by performing a procedure or skill.

Perspective taking: Ability to understand how a situation appears to another person and how that person is reacting cognitively and emotionally to the situation.

Positive environmental interdependence: When group members are bound together by the physical environment in some way.

Positive fantasy interdependence: When students imagine that they are in an emergency situation (such as surviving a ship wreak) or must deal with problems (such as ending air pollution in the world) that are compelling but unreal.

Positive goal interdependence: When students perceive that they can achieve their learning goals if, and only if, all other members of their group also attain their goals.

Positive identity interdependence: When the group establishes a mutual identity through a name, flag, motto, or song.

Positive interdependence: The perception that you are linked with others in a way so that you cannot succeed unless they do (and vice versa), that is, their work benefits you and your work benefits them.

Positive outside enemy interdependence: When groups are placed in competition with each other; group members then feel interdependent as they strive to beat the other groups.

Positive resource interdependence: When each member has only a portion of the information, resources, or materials necessary for the task to be completed and members' resources have to be combined in order for the group to achieve its goal. Thus, the resources of each group member are needed if the task is to be completed.

Positive reward interdependence: When each group member receives the same reward for achieving the goal.

Positive role interdependence: When each member is assigned complementary and interconnected roles that specify responsibilities that the group needs in order to complete a joint task.

Positive task interdependence: When a division of labor is created so that the actions of one group member have to be completed if the next team member is to complete his or her responsibilities. Dividing an overall task into subunits that must be performed ˆin a set orderˆ is an example of task interdependence.

Procedural learning: Learning conceptually what the skill is, when it should be used, how to engage in the skill, practicing the skill while eliminating errors, until an automated level of mastery is attained.

Promotive interaction: Individuals encouraging and facilitating each other's efforts to achieve, complete tasks, and produce in order to reach the group's goals..

Active Learning: Cooperation In The College Classroom, Interaction Book Company, 7208 Cornelia Drive, Edina, MN 55435, (612) 831-9500, FAX (612) 831-9332

Role Interdependence: Interdependence created by assigning complementary and interconnected roles to each group member.

Routine-use level: Automatic use of a skill as a natural part of one's behavioral repertoire.

Self-efficacy: The expectation of successfully obtaining valued outcomes through personal effort; expectation that if one exerts sufficient effort, one will be successful.

Self-regulation: Ability to act in socially approved ways in the absence of external monitors.

Social dependence: When the outcomes of Person A are affected by Person B's actions, but the reverse is not true.

Social facilitation: The enhancement of well-learned responses in the presence of others. Effects on performance resulting from the presence of others.

Social independence: When individuals' outcomes are unaffected by each other's actions.

Social interdependence: When each individuals' outcomes are affected by the actions of others.

Social loafing: A reduction of individual effort when working with others on an additive group task.

Social skills: The interpersonal and small group skills needed to interact effectively with other people.

Social support: Significant others who collaboratively share a person's tasks and goals and provide resources (such as emotional concern, instrumental aid, information, and feedback) that enhance the individual's wellbeing and helps the individual mobilize his or her resources to deal with challenging and stressful situations.

Student management team: Three or four students plus the instructor who assume responsibility for the success of the class by meeting regularly and focusing on how to improve either the instructor's teaching or the content of the course.

Superordinate goals: Goals that cannot be easily ignored by members of two antagonistic groups, but whose attainment is beyond the resources and efforts of either group alone; the two groups, therefore, must join in a cooperative effort in order to attain the goals.

Synthesizing: Integrating a number of different positions containing diverse information and conclusions into a new, single, inclusive position that all group members can agree on and commit themselves to.

Team: A set of interpersonal relationships structured to achieve established goals.

T-chart: Procedure to teach social skills by specifying the nonverbal actions and verbal phrases that operationalize the skill.

Total quality learning: Continuous improvement of the process of students helping teammates learn) can take place.

Transfer: Instructors taking what they learn about cooperative learning in training sessions and using it in their classrooms.

Whole-class processing: Teachers give the class feedback and have students share incidents that occurred in their groups.

Active Learning: Cooperation In The College Classroom, Interaction Book Company, 7208 Cornelia Drive, Edina, MN 55435, (612) 831-9500, FAX (612) 831-9332